The Poetry Reader

The Poetry Reader

An Anthology

Edited by Mark Yakich

BLOOMSBURY ACADEMIC
NEW YORK • LONDON • OXFORD • NEW DELHI • SYDNEY

BLOOMSBURY ACADEMIC
Bloomsbury Publishing Inc
1385 Broadway, New York, NY 10018, USA
50 Bedford Square, London, WC1B 3DP, UK
29 Earlsfort Terrace, Dublin 2, Ireland

BLOOMSBURY, BLOOMSBURY ACADEMIC and the Diana logo are trademarks of Bloomsbury Publishing Plc

First published in the United States of America 2025

Copyright © Mark Yakich, 2025

This English Translation of "Opposition" by Mitsuharu Kaneko © Loren Goodman, 2025

For legal purposes the Acknowledgments on pp. 207–216 constitute an extension of this copyright page.

Cover design: Eleanor Rose
Cover image: Emma Amos, *The Reader*, 1967 © Emma Amos; Courtesy of RYAN LEE Gallery, New York

All rights reserved. No part of this publication may be reproduced or transmitted in any form or by any means, electronic or mechanical, including photocopying, recording, or any information storage or retrieval system, without prior permission in writing from the publishers.

Bloomsbury Publishing Inc does not have any control over, or responsibility for, any third-party websites referred to or in this book. All internet addresses given in this book were correct at the time of going to press. The author and publisher regret any inconvenience caused if addresses have changed or sites have ceased to exist, but can accept no responsibility for any such changes.

Library of Congress Cataloging-in-Publication Data
Names: Yakich, Mark, editor.
Title: The poetry reader: an anthology / edited by Mark Yakich.
Description: New York: Bloomsbury Academic, 2025. | Includes bibliographical references and index.
Identifiers: LCCN 2024024660 (print) | LCCN 2024024661 (ebook) | ISBN 9798765104101 (paperback) | ISBN 9798765104095 (hardback) | ISBN 9798765104118 (ebook) | ISBN 9798765104125 (pdf)
Subjects: LCSH: Poetry–Collections. | LCGFT: Poetry.
Classification: LCC PN6101.P5447 2025 (print) | LCC PN6101 (ebook) | DDC 808.81–dc23/eng/20240607
LC record available at https://lccn.loc.gov/2024024660
LC ebook record available at https://lccn.loc.gov/2024024661

ISBN:	HB:	979-8-7651-0409-5
	PB:	979-8-7651-0410-1
	ePDF:	979-8-7651-0412-5
	eBook:	979-8-7651-0411-8

Typeset by Integra Software Services Pvt. Ltd.
Printed and bound in the United States of America

To find out more about our authors and books visit www.bloomsbury.com and sign up for our newsletters.

Contents

Introduction	1
READING	5
Poetic Aims	7
Ars Poetica *Archibald MacLeish*	7
Ars Poetica #100: I Believe *Elizabeth Alexander*	8
Ars Poetica *José Olivarez*	8
Poetry *Marianne Moore*	9
Biography	9
Memoir *Vijay Seshadri*	9
Diving into the Wreck *Adrienne Rich*	10
the children of immigrants *Lenelle Moïse*	12
Ontology of Chang and Eng, the Original Siamese Twins *Cathy Park Hong*	14
Close Reading	15
Introduction to Poetry *Billy Collins*	16
Vertigo *Anne Stevenson*	16
Viewpoint *Mahmoud Darwish*	16
His Days Go by the Way Her Years *Ye Mimi*	17
Someone I'm Afraid Of *Zaki Ovais*	17
Emotion	18
Western Wind *Anonymous, Sixteenth Century*	18
Blues Haiku [let me be yo wil] *Sonia Sanchez*	18
Not Once *Sharon Olds*	18
Bird-Understander *Craig Arnold*	19
Pattern and Variation	20
from *Macbeth* (Act 5, Scene 5) *William Shakespeare*	21
The Tyger *William Blake*	21
One Art *Elizabeth Bishop*	22
Ecclesiastes *Khaled Mattawa*	22
katherine with the lazy eye. short. and not a good poet. *francine j. harris*	23

Ineffability — 24
Limitations   *Henrietta Cordelia Ray* — 25
from *The Book of Questions*   *Pablo Neruda* — 25
The Snow Man   *Wallace Stevens* — 27
Writer   *Joe Wenderoth* — 27

Sound Work — 28
Love (III)   *George Herbert* — 28
Musée des Beaux Arts   *W.H. Auden* — 29
Altruism   *Molly Peacock* — 29
Widening Income Inequality   *Frederick Seidel* — 30

Rhythm — 31
Shards   *Aline Murray Kilmer* — 31
Dulce et decorum est   *Wilfred Owen* — 32
Any Lit   *Harryette Mullen* — 32
Gyre's Galax   *N.H. Pritchard* — 33

Enjambment — 36
ode to the flute   *Ross Gay* — 36
Advice to Pallbearers   *Benjamin Gucciardi* — 36
what remains two   *Truong Tran* — 37
Pity the Bathtub Its Forced Embrace of the
   Human Form   *Matthea Harvey* — 37

The Line — 39
Facing It   *Yusef Komunyakaa* — 39
The Secret   *Denise Levertov* — 40
In Strength Sweetness   *Elizabeth Willis* — 41
The Boy Calls Twilight   *Shane McCrae* — 42

The Lyric — 43
Fragment 22   *Sappho* — 43
Love Songs (section III)   *Mina Loy* — 44
This Room and Everything in It   *Li-Young Lee* — 44
Having a Coke with You   *Frank O'Hara* — 45
Horizon   *Kim Hyesoon* — 46
How (Not) to Speak of God   *Mary Szybist* — 47

Metaphor — 47
85   from *The Exeter Book of Riddles* — 48
Psalm 23   *The King James Bible* — 48
Now You Need Me   *Virginia Hamilton Adair* — 49
Here I Am, Lord   *Michael Chitwood* — 49
No Metaphor   *Bryan Walpert* — 50

Punctum / Metaphor *Carolina Ebeid*	51
Apocatastasis *G.C. Waldrep*	51
Ambiguity	51
All Your Horses *Kay Ryan*	52
An Argument about Horses *Kedarnath Singh*	52
Language Lesson 1976 *Heather McHugh*	54
Paradoxes and Oxymorons *John Ashbery*	54
Dickinson	55
Tell all the truth but tell it slant *Emily Dickinson*	55
After great pain, a formal feeling comes – *Emily Dickinson*	55
Because I could not stop for Death – *Emily Dickinson*	56
I cannot live with You – *Emily Dickinson*	56
Classics	58
Cantico del Sole *Ezra Pound*	58
Romantic Poetry *Diane Seuss*	59
Myths	61
We Were All Odysseus in Those Days *Amorak Huey*	61
Waiting for Icarus *Muriel Rukeyser*	62
Ganymede *Jericho Brown*	63
Confession *Leila Chatti*	63
Creation Myth *Mathias Svalina*	64
Great Books	65
from *A Pillow Book*: "A Great Book can be read again and again …" *Suzanne Buffam*	66
One Book *Mary Ruefle*	67
Whitman	67
I Saw in Louisiana A Live-Oak Growing *Walt Whitman*	67
A Supermarket in California *Allen Ginsberg*	68
Ode to the Whitman line "When lilacs last in the dooryard bloom'd" *Kimiko Hahn*	68
Imagery	69
Haiku *Jyoin*	69
The Garden by Moonlight *Amy Lowell*	70
Lying in a Hammock at William Duffy's Farm in Pine Island, Minnesota *James Wright*	70
Wild Geese *Mary Oliver*	71
My Voice Will Weigh on You *Irma Pineda*	71
Eight Buffalo *Cecilia Llompart*	71

Roses 72
  [somewhere i have never travelled,gladly beyond] *E.E. Cummings* 73
  One Perfect Rose *Dorothy Parker* 73
  Hothouse *Raymond McDaniel* 74
Prose Poetry 74
  Crate *Francis Ponge* 75
  The Adventures of a Turtle *Russell Edson* 75
  Part of Eve's Discussion *Marie Howe* 75
  Hive Minds *Jennifer L. Knox* 76
  A BOX. *Gertrude Stein* 76
Narrative 77
  Borges and I *Jorge Luis Borges* 77
  The Silence *Timothy Liu* 78
  Hunting Words with My Father [Preface] *Mũkoma wa Ngũgĩ* 79
  38 *Layli Long Soldier* 81
Criticism and Theory 85
  No Theory *David Ignatow* 85
  Platonic Love *Curt Anderson* 86
Pessoa 86
  Autopsychography *Fernando Pessoa* 86
  Others Narrate with Lyres or Harps *Fernando Pessoa* 87
  The Tobacco Shop *Fernando Pessoa* 87
Political Poetry 91
  The Tragic Condition of the Statue of Liberty *Bernadette Mayer* 92
  Ginsberg *Julia Vinograd* 92
  The Last Analysis; or, I Woke Up *Jameson Fitzpatrick* 93
  The War Works Hard *Dunya Mikhail* 94
  from *The Little Book of Unsuspected Subversion* *Edmond Jabès* 95
Aesthetics 97
  Why We Oppose Pockets for Women *Alice Duer Miller* 97
  Opposition *Mitsuharu Kaneko* 98
  Dramaturgy *Jason Schneiderman* 99
Reader Response 100
  Napoleon *Miroslav Holub* 101
  A Rugged Coast *Edward Mullany* 101
  The Politics of Narrative: Why I Am a Poet *Lynn Emanuel* 102
  The Price of a Finger *Wang Ping* 103

Classroom Reading	108
Early Poem *Lucy Ives*	109
Poetry Readings	111
At the Student Poetry Reading *Kim Stafford*	112
Nondisabled Demands *The Cyborg Jillian Weise*	112
Poetry Reading *Anna Swir*	113
Spirituality	113
Preface to a Twenty-Volume Suicide Note *Amiri Baraka*	114
Your Animal *Gerald Stern*	114
Goodtime Jesus *James Tate*	115
Making Applesauce with My Dead Grandmother *Bianca Stone*	116
Down Jacket God *Moon Bo Young*	116
Substance, Shadow, and Spirit *T'ao Ch'ien*	117
Flight	118
Waiting for a Ride *Gary Snyder*	118
Gate A-4 *Naomi Shihab Nye*	119
Reading *Moby-Dick* at 30,000 Feet *Tony Hoagland*	120
WRITING	123
First Principles	124
so you want to be a writer? *Charles Bukowski*	124
no more grandma poems *Yolanda Wisher*	125
Form	126
The Fish *Marianne Moore*	127
from Chapter E of *Eunoia* *Christian Bök*	128
Personals *C.D. Wright*	129
what's not to liken? *Evie Shockley*	129
Sonnet	130
from *Nets* *Jen Bervin*	130
Sonnet 19 *John Milton*	131
Sonnet 132 *Gaspara Stampa*	131
Love is Not All (Sonnet XXX) *Edna St. Vincent Millay*	131
shattered sonnet #3 *Olena Kalytiak Davis*	132
American Sonnet for My Past and Future Assassin *Terrance Hayes*	132
Identity	133
This Be The Verse *Philip Larkin*	133
Where Do You Come From? *Meena Alexander*	133

Poppies in October   *Sylvia Plath*   134
The Red Poppy   *Louise Glück*   135
Self-Expression   135
from *Song of Myself* (1892 version)   *Walt Whitman*   136
Still I Rise   *Maya Angelou*   140
"You Should Write a Poem About That," They Say   *Emilia Phillips*   141
The Self in Poetry: A GNAT (Grossly Non-Academic Talk) with a Weaving Metaphor   *Rachel Zucker*   142
Memory   145
The Road Not Taken   *Robert Frost*   146
Standing by a Shelf   *Brandon D. Johnson*   146
Theories of Time and Space   *Natasha Trethewey*   147
My Father's Mother Asks Him to Forget the War   *John Z. Guzlowski*   148
Digging   *Seamus Heaney*   148
Sublimation   149
When I Am Asked   *Lisel Mueller*   150
the mother   *Gwendolyn Brooks*   150
How to Write the Great American Indian Novel   *Sherman Alexie*   151
Dreams   *Ashley Durant*   152
Imitation   153
from *Jubilate Agno*   *Christopher Smart*   153
Arrival   *Jeffrey Harrison*   155
To His Coy Mistress   *Andrew Marvell*   156
Coy Mistress   *Annie Finch*   157
Variations on a Theme by Elizabeth Bishop   *John Murillo*   158
Avant-Garde   158
To make a dadaist poem   *Tristan Tzara*   159
Revision   159
Revision   *Maya Abu Al-Hayyat*   159
Poet-Teachers   160
Pencil   *Marianne Boruch*   160
Theme for English B   *Langston Hughes*   161
Professionalization   162
With Tenure   *David Lehman*   163
Portrait of an Administrator with Strategic Plan and Office Supplies   *Jehanne Dubrow*   164

Literary Magazines	164
Rejections *Etheridge Knight*	165
Publication	165
Publication Date *Franz Wright*	165
Series, Sequence	166
On Living *Nâzım Hikmet*	166
Children (from *Holocaust*) *Charles Reznikoff*	168
from *My Life* *Lyn Hejinian*	171
Series as Opposed to Sequence *Mary Leader*	174
Collections	178
Dedication *Czesław Miłosz*	178
Poetic Practices	179
You Fixed It *Zeina Hashem Beck*	179
Writing Prompt *Michael Torres*	180
Moods	181
Catullus: Odi et Amo *Frank Bidart*	182
Catullus: Excrucior *Frank Bidart*	182
Catullus: Id faciam *Frank Bidart*	182
from *Please Bury Me in This* *Allison Benis White*	182
Self-Portrait with Profanity *Safia Elhillo*	182
A Brief for the Defense *Jack Gilbert*	183
Happiness *Jane Kenyon*	184
Depression	185
The Love Song of J. Alfred Prufrock *T. S. Eliot*	185
McDonalds Is Impossible *Chelsea Martin*	189
Psychoanalysis: An Elegy *Jack Spicer*	192
Cotton in a Pill Bottle *Dean Young*	194
To Sleep *John Keats*	195
Solitary Observation Brought Back from a Sojourn in Hell *Louise Bogan*	195
Meditation	195
Zazen on Ching-t'ing Mountain *Li Bai*	196
To Be a Good Buddhist Is Ensnarement *Jenny Xie*	196
Meditation at Lagunitas *Robert Hass*	196
Meditation Denying Everything *Katie Peterson*	197

Procrastination ... 199
   The Unwritten   W.S. Merwin ... 199
End Notes ... 200
   Ornithology   *Ron Koertge* ... 200
   All the Generations Before Me   *Yehuda Amichai* ... 201
   Things No One Knows   *Wanda Coleman* ... 202
   from *OBIT*   *Victoria Chang* ... 203
   Mourning   *Carolyn Forché* ... 203
   Under a Certain Little Star   *Wisława Szymborska* ... 204

Notes ... 206
Acknowledgments ... 207
Index of Titles & First Lines ... 217

Introduction

You have picked up this book because you are a poetry reader. Or you are about to be one. Because as soon as you read a poem, that's what you are. And because you are reading a book called *The Poetry Reader*, you are in a very important way the thing you are reading.

In a classroom setting, *The Poetry Reader* might technically be called an anthology: a collection of various poems by various poets. But I associate the word "anthology" with a tome of diaphanous pages, tedious school assignments, and a nightstand groaning under heavy weight. Groaning is a pathetic fallacy which I must have learned in the classroom where I found the hit-and-miss quality of anthologies to be dispiriting. Like others, I grew up with the idea of an anthology as a survey of canonical works whose premise seemed to be "here is the best of the best." Later, I came across anthologies that questioned this premise, focusing on either reworking the canon or establishing their own canons. Yet I still wasn't convinced about all this anthologizing. When I would pick up one of these books, I would discover only a handful of poems I liked or found curious out of what seemed like an absolute hodgepodge.

The book you now hold originated out of such disappointment with nearly all those tomes I was taught from and have tried to use in my twenty-five years of teaching poetry reading and writing. Equally important has been my own struggle with venerating and detesting poetry often in the same breath. The years of the pandemic exacerbated my ambivalence, but they also eventually led to my becoming enamored once more with poems—for their generative nature over time and their power on an individual reader's life. *The Poetry Reader* is, in part, a record of my renewed love.

Drawing on both the poetic tradition and contemporary works, this collection offers wide-ranging, globe-spanning, stylistically diverse poetry—from canonical poems by the likes of Sappho and Shakespeare to those of new voices such as Layli Long Soldier and Mũkoma wa Ngũgĩ. Instead of attempting to survey entire time periods or aesthetic areas, I have collected poems under topics, ranging from "Emotion" and "Self-Expression" to "Enjambment" and "Imagery" and from "Memory" and "Meditation" to "Political Poetry" and "Publication." I have also placed side-by-side poems that speak to each topic as well as to each other over time. What do I mean by that? Let's take the very first section: Poetic Aims. All but one of the poems share the title "Ars Poetica," yet each comes at the idea of what a poem is from very different angles. Archibald MacLeish's ends with "A poem should not mean / But be." José Olivarez's prose poem states, "My work: to write poems that make my people feel safe, seen, or otherwise loved." And Elizabeth Alexander's poem asserts, "Poetry … is not all love, love, love, / and I'm sorry the dog died." By reading these poems together, under a specific topic, we can open up conversations and arguments that wouldn't otherwise happen by reading each of these poems in isolation.

In fact, the argument of this book is that to better understand any poem is to understand its conversations, explicit and implicit, with other poems. Some of the poems here, for example, directly respond to other poems. In the "Imitation" section, Annie Finch's "Coy Mistress" expressly rebuts Andrew Marvell's "To His Coy Mistress." Other poems address similar situations, ideas, or emotions within their section headings, even if they were never intended to do so; see Sylvia Plath's "Poppies in October" and Louise Glück's "The Red Poppy," both in the "Identity" section. Finally, there are poems that engage each other *across* section headings. For example, in "Spirituality" we have Bianca Stone's "Making Applesauce with My Dead Grandmother," and then a few sections later in "First Principles" along comes Yolanda Wisher's "no more grandma poems." What happens when you go back and reread that "grandma" poem after reading a poem ostensibly arguing against the idea of them altogether? In both its structure and curated content, this collection aims to illustrate the critical term often bandied about: *intertextuality*.

That word really disguises an aspect so obvious it often goes undiscussed: *Literature is generative*. And if we do discuss this idea, it's mostly boiled down to framed discussions of "poetic" schools, groupings, or movements—the Metaphysical poets, Renaissance poetry, Romanticism, Surrealist texts, etc. Again, this skims over the connections between and among poems that exist *absent any direct lineage or timeframe*. If you read poems long enough over years and decades, you'll begin to notice and comprehend that poems are not only related to other poems, but that poems seem to beget other poems and that even when their makers may not intend, poems echo other poems. To modify John Donne's famous line, we might put forth *No poem is an island*.

One way to use *The Poetry Reader* is to read it alongside *Poetry: A Survivor's Guide*, my guide to reading and writing poems; the books have corresponding section titles. If you don't have my guide, don't worry. I have provided brief header notes in this book. Unlike other anthologies, I have tried not to offer prescriptive or proscriptive diagnoses of the poems that follow. Instead, please take my comments as starting points to begin your own exploration. When you read a particular section, understand that the individual poems grouped there could also have been placed under different section headings. Consider the poems in "Close Reading": Billy Collins' "Introduction to Poetry" could come under "Poetic Aims"; Anne Stevenson's "Vertigo" and Mahmoud Darwish's "Viewpoint" both could fall under "Ineffability" or "Ambiguity"; Ye Mimi's "His Days Go by the Way Her Years" could be examined for its abundant imagery; and Zaki Ovais' "Someone I'm Afraid Of" is a wonderful example of relentless metaphor. But I have placed all of those poems under "Close Reading" in order to highlight a certain facet of the topic or to test and probe conventional notions associated with the topic.

You will notice there are no biographical notes about the poets in this book. If I had my way, in fact, I might leave off the poets' names entirely. What might be lost, what gained? Another option: What if in each section the names of the poets were randomly listed at the end and we had to match them up, trying to figure out who wrote what? Maybe the best thing to do with these poets, assuming you are intrigued by one of their poems, is to search out more of their work!

Poetry often asks for or requires such research. One of the first rules of reading poetry is that if you don't know a word, you should look it up. Why? Because poetry is nothing if not a course in and process of discovery—about others, about yourself, and about what you think you know about the world. This also goes for writing poetry. Although there's absolutely no reason to indulge in the fanciful notion of writer's block, if you ever do get bored by writing poems, all you have to do is return to reading them. Reading poems generates writing them. Literature is generative in this way, too. Relatedly, many of us wonder how AI will affect the generation of literature. But is there really an issue? If an algorithm, machine, or bot creates a text that moves you, let it. If it doesn't, that's fine too. After all, what is a human being but the originary AI. Yes, that's what I mean: we *are* already artificial intelligence.

Every anthology has a flaw. With any Norton or Norton-type anthology of poetry the problem is palpable: the book is trying to do too much. At the same time, this can be its beneficence, its gift. There may be some gem hidden inside, there for you and only you—you simply have to rough it out. When you find the flaw(s) in the book you are holding now, find it all the way down. Really sink your teeth into it, as though it's a piece of impossible meat. Go ahead, mix your metaphors. What is it about the flaw that rubs you the wrong way? What is it about yourself that rubs you the wrong way? Were I a less honest poet-editor, I would send you off with a bromide like *I hope you find what you are looking for*. But the tone of that statement has always struck me as sarcastic or resentful, as in a romantic break-up: *It's not you, it's me*. Instead, I wish that you, Poetry Reader, discover something you were *not* looking for, something you didn't know was there, but once you found it you recognized it for what it was: a new part of yourself.

Reading

There are as many reasons to read poetry as there are readers of poetry. At least that's what they say. In my experience, almost all who open a book of poems do so for the same reason: to find something they can't get from novels, memoirs, short stories, essays, movies, shows, plays, music, the news, and any other text, art, or medium. What I mean is this: You can get commiseration from a parent, a friend, a therapist, a character in a novel or movie, a voice in a song; and you can get a good or great story from any one of those. But what you are less likely to receive—what a poem is much better suited for—is a different, even new way of understanding or perceiving. Emily Dickinson calls this kind of understanding *slant*, as in her famous line "Tell all the truth but tell it slant."

Why slant? Because as one grows into the world, one also becomes so accustomed to it that many things—feelings, experiences, thoughts, phenomena—can feel, well, boring. We get jaded, not just by the news but by almost anything and everything, especially the more these things become habitualized. No longer, for instance, does the cute kitten in a photo give one warm fuzzies; it's just another cute kitten. One's eyes glaze over, one's thoughts become like others' thoughts, and culture itself grows weary of its memes—and particularly its language.

Think of how much of what you say to others or what you think (that ongoing self-narration) uses well-worn phrases. At the end of the day ... I hear what you're saying ... to be honest ... the new normal .... Such phrases come and go, some sticking around longer than others. It's not that they are inherently bad or wrong, it's just that they don't really register in the mind any longer because they've been registered umpteen times. Of course, these linguistic ticks provide "meaning"—our ability to communicate rests on many of them—and yet they often come across as nearly meaningless. If a poem is any good, it's going to help make such familiarity less familiar. It's going to make you ask a question like, "Did I just see what I've already seen but didn't ever really see?" I never tire of this little example from Julian Barnes' novel *Flaubert's Parrot*, which makes me re-see or re-think what a "net" is: On the one hand, it is a mesh to catch things such as fish; on the other, it is a collection of holes tied together with string. Barnes may be a novelist, but this slant way of conceptualizing a net is really poetry.

One might call that example simply a flash of insight or a flash in the pan. But a poem can do such work so repeatedly and thoroughly that it's not just a word or concept we re-see, but an entire self-awareness of what we say and think. A poem, that is, can reach our deep emotions and psychic lives when it plays with the patterns of our thinking. If this all sounds quite serious, remember to approach your reading of a poem in a supremely playful manner. Sometimes you will be discomfited by what you read—that's okay! Sometimes you will misread a line or a whole poem—that's okay too! Your relationship to a poem lies in the interplay between you and the poem you are reading, as well as the poems you've already read, and perhaps forgotten about.

Should you ever get bored by poems themselves, run to the dictionary … which in a way contains all the poems ever written. Two of the best are *Webster's Second New International Unabridged* (1937) and *Webster's Third New International Unabridged* (1961). Begin with the definition of the word *door*: "a movable piece of a firm material or a structure supported usually along one side and swinging on pivots or hinges, sliding along a groove, rolling up and down, revolving as one of four leaves, or folding like an accordion by means of which an opening may be closed or kept open …." Then, turn to the "End Notes" section in this book and read the prose poems from Victoria Chang's *Obit*; you will begin to understand *door* in a new, slant way. This is what poems can offer: the possibility of making the world less boring and making you more curious about it. Let yourself play in their mystery, wonder, and even all-out bewilderment.

POETIC AIMS

Ars poetica, or "the art of poetry," is a somewhat showy term for a poem or text that explains or illustrates what a poem is, or how a poem works or should work. The first two poems below offer us arguments and possibilities about the *being* and *meaning* of poetry. Notice that both poems are set in couplets; how come? The third poem seems to challenge accepted or expected notions of what we think a poem about poetry should be or do. Notice that it's in prose; again, what gives? Lastly, there is Marianne Moore's famous take on poetry, in a poem that went through dozens of revisions and published incarnations, some pages long, only to end up as a three-line poem that locates the aim of poetry in a decidedly ambiguous place; why? After reading through these poems a few times, which one makes the most sense to you? Which one changes your mind about what a poem should be or do?

Archibald MacLeish
Ars Poetica

A poem should be palpable and mute
As a globed fruit,

Dumb
As old medallions to the thumb,

Silent as the sleeve-worn stone
Of casement ledges where the moss has grown—
A poem should be wordless
As the flight of birds.

*

A poem should be motionless in time
As the moon climbs,

Leaving, as the moon releases
Twig by twig the night-entangled trees,

Leaving, as the moon behind the winter leaves,
Memory by memory the mind—

A poem should be motionless in time
As the moon climbs.

*

A poem should be equal to:
Not true.

For all the history of grief
An empty doorway and a maple leaf.

For love
The leaning grasses and two lights above the sea—

A poem should not mean
But be.

Elizabeth Alexander
Ars Poetica #100: I Believe

Poetry, I tell my students,
is idiosyncratic. Poetry

is where we are ourselves
(though Sterling Brown said

"Every 'I' is a dramatic 'I'"),
digging in the clam flats

for the shell that snaps,
emptying the proverbial pocketbook.

Poetry is what you find
in the dirt in the corner,

overhear on the bus, God
in the details, the only way

to get from here to there.
Poetry (and now my voice is rising)

is not all love, love, love,
and I'm sorry the dog died.

Poetry (here I hear myself loudest)
is the human voice,

and are we not of interest to each other?

José Olivarez (translated from the Spanish by David Ruano González)
Ars Poetica

Migration is derived from the word "migrate," which is a verb defined by *Merriam-Webster* as "to move from one country, place, or locality to another." Plot twist: migration never ends. My parents moved from Jalisco, México, to Chicago in 1987. They were dislocated from México by capitalism, & they arrived in Chicago just in time to be dislocated by capitalism. Question: is migration possible if there is no "other" land to arrive in? My work: to imagine. My family started migrating in 1987 & they never stopped. I was born mid-migration. I've made my home in that motion. Let me try again: I tried to become American, but America is toxic. I tried to become Mexican, but México is toxic. My work: to do more than reproduce the toxic stories I inherited & learned. In other words: just because it is art doesn't mean it is inherently nonviolent. My work: to write poems that make my people feel safe, seen, or otherwise loved. My work: to make my enemies feel afraid, angry, or otherwise ignored. My people: my people. My enemies: capitalism. Susan Sontag: "victims are interested in the representation of their own sufferings." Remix: survivors are interested in the representation of their own survival. My work: survival. Question: Why poems? Answer: ███████.

Marianne Moore
Poetry

I, too, dislike it.
   Reading it, however, with a perfect contempt for it, one dis-
                                               covers in
   it, after all, a place for the genuine.

BIOGRAPHY

What is the biography of a poet to their poem? The poet made the poem—this much is true—but after that it's anyone's guess. That's the heart of the matter: the endless speculation about "what really happened" or "the story behind the poem" or the tempting query "what did the poet really intend?" Allow yourself these thoughts, then set them aside so that you can enter the poem itself. Looking into a poet's background or life story may be meaningful and rewarding, but it is a separate adventure. Why? Because even if we could ask the maker of the poem what their poem means, we might get a different answer depending on the day, depending on the poet's mood, whether the poet had a solid breakfast, is grappling with the latest family drama, or has just read some terrible news headline.

   As you read these outwardly biographical poems, keep in mind a line from Marguerite Duras: "You're always more unreal to yourself than other people are." Put otherwise: you may very well be an unreliable witness to your own life.

Vijay Seshadri
Memoir

Orwell says somewhere that no one ever writes the real story of their life.
The real story of a life is the story of its humiliations.
If I wrote that story now—

radioactive to the end of time—
people, I swear, your eyes would fall out, you couldn't peel
the gloves fast enough
from your hands scorched by the firestorms of that shame.
Your poor hands. Your poor eyes
to see me weeping in my room
or boring the tall blonde to death.
Once I accused the innocent.
Once I bowed and prayed to the guilty.
I still wince at what I once said to the devastated widow.
And one October afternoon, under a locust tree
whose blackened pods were falling and making
illuminating patterns on the pathway,
I was seized by joy,
and someone saw me there,
and that was the worst of all,
lacerating and unforgettable.

Adrienne Rich
Diving into the Wreck

First having read the book of myths,
and loaded the camera,
and checked the edge of the knife-blade,
I put on
the body-armor of black rubber
the absurd flippers
the grave and awkward mask.
I am having to do this
not like Cousteau with his
assiduous team
aboard the sun-flooded schooner
but here alone.

There is a ladder.
The ladder is always there
hanging innocently
close to the side of the schooner.
We know what it is for,
we who have used it.
Otherwise
It's a piece of maritime floss
some sundry equipment.

I go down.

Rung after rung and still
the oxygen immerses me
the blue light
the clear atoms
of our human air.
I go down.
My flippers cripple me,
I crawl like an insect down the ladder
and there is no one
to tell me when the ocean
will begin.

First the air is blue and then
it is bluer and then green and then
black I am blacking out and yet
my mask is powerful
it pumps my blood with power
the sea is another story
the sea is not a question of power
I have to learn alone
to turn my body without force
in the deep element.

And now: it is easy to forget
what I came for
among so many who have always
lived here
swaying their crenellated fans
between the reefs
and besides
you breathe differently down here.

I came to explore the wreck.
The words are purposes.
The words are maps.
I came to see the damage that was done
and the treasures that prevail.
I stroke the beam of my lamp
slowly along the flank
of something more permanent
than fish or weed

the thing I came for:
the wreck and not the story of the wreck
the thing itself and not the myth
the drowned face always staring
toward the sun

the evidence of damage
worn by salt and sway into this threadbare beauty
the ribs of the disaster
curving their assertion
among the tentative haunters.

This is the place.
And I am here, the mermaid whose dark hair
streams black, the merman in his armored body.
We circle silently
about the wreck
we dive into the hold.
I am she: I am he

whose drowned face sleeps with open eyes
whose breasts still bear the stress
whose silver, copper, vermeil cargo lies
obscurely inside barrels
half-wedged and left to rot
we are the half-destroyed instruments
that once held to a course
the water-eaten log
the fouled compass

We are, I am, you are
by cowardice or courage
the one who find our way
back to this scene
carrying a knife, a camera
a book of myths
in which
our names do not appear.

Lenelle Moïse
the children of immigrants

When I am a toddler, a child, a tween, a teen, and a young adult, I am called an ancestral soul, a ti gran moun, a little old person.

Adults study me and decide that I am wise beyond my years, mature for my age, emotionally ripe. I am told it is unusual to meet a five-ten-fifteen-year-old girl who does not slouch or mumble or speak in monosyllables.

When I do the things that come naturally to me—when I hold my spine up erect, when I wait my turn to speak, when I speak having listened, carefully, when I enunciate, when I look grown-ups in the eye—I am told I must have "been here before."

"How do you know?" one college professor asks me after she has seen a psychologically violent play I have written at age nineteen. "How do you already know?"

In high school, I charm my teachers. They encourage me to write speeches about feminism that I recite for International Women's Day at City Hall or deliver as part of conference panels at local universities. "If you were older," they tell me, "we would probably be friends." One of them even flirts with me.

Among my peers I exist somewhere between amicably mysterious and irrevocably dorky. The popular kids greet me in the hallways, but they never invite me to their beer-drenched parties. I will never play Spin the Bottle. I will never play Seven Minutes in Heaven. My mother tells me she is protecting me from boys, but the truth is, after I do my homework, she wants me to type up another family friend's résumé or resignation letter. At home, I am a bridge, a cultural interpreter, a spokesperson, a trusted ally, an American who is Haitian too, but also definitely American.

The children of immigrants don't get to be children. We lose our innocence watching our parents' backs bend, break. I am an old soul because when I am young, I watch my parents' spirits get slaughtered.

In Haiti, they were middle class. Hopeful teachers. Home owners. They were black like their live-in servants. They donated clothes to the poor. They gave up everything they knew to inherit American dreams. And here, they join factory lines, wipe shit from mean old white men's behinds, scrub five-star hotel toilets for dimes above minimum wage. Here, they shuck and jive and step and fetch and play chauffeur to people who aren't as smart as they are, people who do not speak as many languages as they do. In the 1980s, they are barred from giving blood because newscasters and politicians say that AIDS comes from where they come from: Haiti, the poorest country in the Western Hemisphere, a black magic island that spawns boat people and chaos, a place of illiterate zombies, orphan beggars and brazen political corruption.

When I am a child, my childhood is a luxury my family cannot afford. Their dignity is not spared, so my innocence is not spared. They are humiliated and traumatized daily, so I become a nurse to their trauma. I am told too much, so I know too much, so I am wise beyond my years.

When I am six, my mother tells me that when she found out she was pregnant with me at age nineteen, she "tried to kill the baby." She says "the baby," as if it isn't me she's talking about; as if I am not the expensive, scandalous daughter who forced my way into her world despite the abortion-inducing herbal teas she drank and her frantic leaps off of small buildings.

When I am sixteen, my father calls me on the phone to, inevitably, weep. He says, "Living in this country, I have learned not to hope for things. Only you are my hope. Only you."

So—yes, I grow up fast.

Cathy Park Hong
Ontology of Chang and Eng, the Original Siamese Twins

Chang spoke / Eng paused.

Chang threw a beach ball / Eng caught it.

Chang told a white lie / Eng got caught for the lie.

Chang forgot his first language / Eng picked up English.

In letters, Chang referred to themselves as "I" / Eng as "we."

While proselytizing, the preacher asked Chang, "Do you know where you go after you die?" Chang said, "Yes, yes, up dere." / Thinking they didn't understand, he asked, "Do you know where I go after I die?" Eng said, "Yes, yes, down dere."

Chang married Adelaine / Eng married her sister Sally.

Chang made love to his wife / Eng daydreamed about money, his Siam childhood and roast beef. He tried not to get aroused.

Chang checked his watch, scratched his head and fidgeted/
Eng made love to his wife.

Chang became drunk, knocked Eng out with a whiskey bottle and went carousing with his boys / Eng was unconscious.

Chang proved Einstein's time dilation while drunkenly running from one bar to the next / Eng was unconscious.

Chang apologized / Eng grudgingly accepted.

Chang paused / Eng spoke / Chang interrupted.

"I am my own man!" / Eng echoed, "We are men yes."

*

Both broke their bondage with their pitchman, Mr. Coffin.

Both owned land in North Carolina and forty slaves.

Both were nostalgic for Siam: childhood of preserving duck eggs, watching tiger and elephant fights with the King, Mother Nok who loved them equally.

The physicians were surprised to find both were "personable."

Both did not appreciate the outhouse joke.
"Are all Orientals joined?" "Allow me to stick this very sharp pin

in Eng's neck to see if both of you feel the pain." "Is it true that
you turn babies into cabbages?" "We are nice, civilized people.
We offer you bananas."

Both were sick of fascination.

Both woke up, played checkers, sired children, owned whips
for their slaves, shot game, ate pie. Both wore French black silk, smoked
cigars, flirted. Both believed in the tenets of individualism.
Both listed these activities to the jury and cried, "See, we are American!"

Both were released with a $500 fine for assaulting another head hunter.

Both were very self-aware.

Both insisted on an iron casket so that grave robbers would not
dig up their bodies and sell them to the highest bidder.

Both did not converse with one another except towards the end:

"My lips are turning blue, Eng" / Eng did not answer.

"They want our bodies, Eng." / Eng did not answer.

"Eng, Eng! My lips are turning blue." / Eng turned to his body and did not answer.

CLOSE READING

You may come across the idea that poems have hidden meanings that you just have to uncover. Sometimes you'll hear "close reading" as a term used in such a way. But this is not the way. Close reading doesn't mean finding some kind of single meaning in a text. Neither is it the case that a poem has an "infinite" set of meanings, depending on who is reading it. A poem may, of course, have many meanings but this shouldn't be carte blanche to read into a poem whatever you like.

    Close reading involves asking a lot of questions. Be careful, however; the fundamental question to ask as one *reads closely* is not "Why did the poet select this or that word or line?" but "Why *this* word or that line *here*?" For example in Billy Collins' poem below, what is the effect of beginning the poem with "hold it up to the light," and why transition to "press an ear" in the second one-line stanza? Again, not "why did Collins choose to do this," but *what effect* does opening a poem titled "Introduction to Poetry" make manifest in these first two stanzas? This isn't reaching for hidden meaning. This is close reading, which asks you to *slow down* and look for patterns and variations on those patterns. This does not mean "reading more deeply" as you may hear from certain teachers and other students. This means discerning what's already there on the surface. One example: when you finish reading Zaki Ovais' poem, consider what variation has occurred between the title and last line, between "I" and "someone."

Billy Collins
Introduction to Poetry

I ask them to take a poem
and hold it up to the light
like a color slide

or press an ear against its hive.

I say drop a mouse into a poem
and watch him probe his way out,

or walk inside the poem's room
and feel the walls for a light switch.

I want them to waterski
across the surface of a poem
waving at the author's name on the shore.

But all they want to do
is tie the poem to a chair with rope
and torture a confession out of it.

They begin beating it with a hose
to find out what it really means.

Anne Stevenson
Vertigo

Mind led body
to the edge of the precipice.
They stared in desire
at the naked abyss.
If you love me, said mind,
take that step into silence.
If you love me, said body,
turn and exist.

Mahmoud Darwish (translated from the Arabic by Fady Joudah)
Viewpoint

The difference between narcissus
and sunflower
is a point of view: the first
stares at his image in water
and says, there is no I but I
and the second looks

at the sun and says I am
what I worship.
And at night, difference shrinks
and interpretation widens.

Ye Mimi (translated from the Chinese by Steve Bradbury)
His Days Go by the Way Her Years

he smells like bottled root beer
her pie in the sky allays his hunger and his days go by the way her years
he is a lonely plural
her door-latch is sour or sore
the au contraire of plentiful is he
(won't they help her build her Tower of Basil?)
she hairs his chest he heartens her sweetheart
one day every living soul will turn to soil
he ocean fleets a vessel
she mountain passes a night
Wednesday likes the rain
by rain were they woven into angelfish
eyes unfolded into riddles
yet he steals beneath her iron skin
and leaning on the chair-back of time
gradually invents a kind of knock

the more he is the sun the more she is the moon

Zaki Ovais
Someone I'm Afraid Of

I'm a hungry star in the sky,
covered by jealous clouds.

I'm a goldfish plant in the garden,
shaded from daylight.

I'm a fly in the kitchen, buzzing
on the boundary of a blind wall.

I'm a chicken under mother's wing,
confined to the narrows of a wattle.

I'm a dove on the street of Yangon,
jailed in the cage of inhumanity.

I'm the water flowing in Mayu river,
missing my partner—Air.

I'm a human in the universe,
denied the most basic rights.

I'm someone I'm afraid of.

EMOTION

Set aside the pervasive and vacuous idea that poetry is all about "emotions" or "feelings." Instead, consider where our emotions originate. Try, for instance, to have a feeling without thinking. It can be done as a kind of reflex, say, to seeing someone crying. But otherwise and most often, we have an emotion because we are thinking of something—a situation, a person, a scene, an idea—that produces an emotion or feeling. In other words, our thoughts lead to our emotions. The power of a poem lies in *how* it structures, narrates, or otherwise determines our thoughts ... which result in feelings.

The crux of many so-called emotional poems or poems that involve emotions lies in their *turns and transformations*. Feelings evolve and revolve around frictions, vacillations, or if you prefer, *variations*. If you can identify the turn(s) in the following poems, you'll be able to identify why you find them *moving*. The movement is both figurative and literal.

Anonymous, Sixteenth Century
Western Wind

O Western wind when wilt thou blow
That the small rain down can rain
Christ that my love were in my arms
And I in my bed again!

Sonia Sanchez
Blues Haiku [let me be yo wil]

let me be yo wil
derness let me be yo wind
blowing you all day.

Sharon Olds
Not Once

Not once—not when I toppled, rigid, a
5'7" pole-pine felled,
stiff as a board, a five and a half foot
plank, 16 x 32,

and not while I wallowed on the rug among
his oxygen tubes, and my cane, and his 8
wheelchair wheels, and not when I sat by his
hospice bed, chirping I'm fine!
and not the next day, when the brilliant violet
and charcoal slashed and slathered in my easy-life skin,
or days later when the purple turned yellow and the
blue green—never once when I
said No pain, Nothing broken,
did I feel lucky, did I measure the force of the
blow, the floor speeding up like a heavyweight's
smash to my cheek and eyebrow. Not until today
did I begin to feel grateful
for my good fortune—no concussion, no
fracture—as if I had expected I'd be able to be
struck by the earth, a wrecking ball,
and not feel it—
as when someone on the other side of the world,
or the city, is struck in my name, I do not feel it.

Craig Arnold
Bird-Understander

Of many reasons I love you here is one

the way you write me from the gate at the airport
so I can tell you everything will be alright

so you can tell me there is a bird
trapped in the terminal   all the people
ignoring it   because they do not know
what to do with it   except to leave it alone
until it scares itself to death

it makes you terribly terribly sad

You wish you could take the bird outside
and set it free or   (failing that)
call a bird-understander
to come help the bird

All you can do is notice the bird
and feel for the bird   and write
to tell me how language feels
impossibly useless

but you are wrong

You are a bird-understander
better than I could ever be
who make so many noises
and call them song

These are your own words
your way of noticing
and saying plainly
of not turning away
from hurt

you have offered them
to me   I am only
giving them back

if only I could show you
how very useless
they are not

PATTERN AND VARIATION

When we begin to examine the patterns and variations in a poem, we may feel utterly overwhelmed. There is simply too much going on in such a brief space.

Try considering one aspect or item at a time, starting with what appears most salient to you. If, for instance, you are attracted to something about the picture the poem creates in your mind, begin by noting the images—that is, the concrete nouns. Write them, one at a time, in the margin alongside the poem. When you have finished, inspect the list. Where do you find connections, similarities, oppositions? Is there a pattern that emerges from or among the images? If so, what does that pattern—or a variation on that pattern—imply or suggest or assert?

Then, try moving to another aspect of the poem, such as its sonics. Scrutinize any words that are connected to other words, or parts of words, by sound. Consider not just rhyme but consonance and assonance, not just at the beginnings of words but in their middles and ends; Macbeth's speech below is primed for this kind of examination.

Alternatively, look for whole phrases or lines that echo each other, or vary slightly; the intent of William Blake's "The Tyger" is nearly encapsulated by the variation of the last line of the first stanza and the last line of the poem. Elizabeth Bishop's "One Art" continually plays with pattern and variation in its two semi-repeated lines in order to arrive ultimately at a fresh take on what a villanelle can do. In Khaled Mattawa's "Ecclesiastes," itself a rendition of the book of the Hebrew bible, the intent of the poem is wrapped up in the patterning of "trick" and "rule" until one seems to become the other. And in francine j. harris' poem, the repeated and dismissive line "katherine with the lazy eye. short. and not a good poet." gets completely turned around in the end.

As you continue to read poems in this book or elsewhere, keep in mind that even if a poem appears unorganized, it may just be using patterns you are not used to. The more you read poems, the more you begin to comprehend the order of the "messy" looking ones, those that initially look wholly arbitrary or scattered across the page.

William Shakespeare
from *Macbeth* (Act 5, Scene 5)

Tomorrow, and tomorrow, and tomorrow,
Creeps in this petty pace from day to day,
To the last syllable of recorded time;
And all our yesterdays have lighted fools
The way to dusty death. Out, out, brief candle!
Life's but a walking shadow, a poor player,
That struts and frets his hour upon the stage,
And then is heard no more. It is a tale
Told by an idiot, full of sound and fury,
Signifying nothing.

William Blake
The Tyger

Tyger Tyger, burning bright,
In the forests of the night;
What immortal hand or eye,
Could frame thy fearful symmetry?

In what distant deeps or skies.
Burnt the fire of thine eyes?
On what wings dare he aspire?
What the hand, dare seize the fire?

And what shoulder, & what art,
Could twist the sinews of thy heart?
And when thy heart began to beat.
What dread hand? & what dread feet?

What the hammer? what the chain,
In what furnace was thy brain?
What the anvil? what dread grasp.
Dare its deadly terrors clasp?

When the stars threw down their spears
And water'd heaven with their tears:

Did he smile his work to see?
Did he who made the Lamb make thee?

Tyger Tyger burning bright,
In the forests of the night:
What immortal hand or eye,
Dare frame thy fearful symmetry?

Elizabeth Bishop
One Art

The art of losing isn't hard to master;
so many things seem filled with the intent
to be lost that their loss is no disaster.

Lose something every day. Accept the fluster
of lost door keys, the hour badly spent.
The art of losing isn't hard to master.

Then practice losing farther, losing faster:
places, and names, and where it was you meant
to travel. None of these will bring disaster.

I lost my mother's watch. And look! my last, or
next-to-last, of three loved houses went.
The art of losing isn't hard to master.

I lost two cities, lovely ones. And, vaster,
some realms I owned, two rivers, a continent.
I miss them, but it wasn't a disaster.

—Even losing you (the joking voice, a gesture
I love) I shan't have lied. It's evident
the art of losing's not too hard to master
though it may look like (*Write* it!) like disaster.

Khaled Mattawa
Ecclesiastes

The trick is that you're willing to help them.
The rule is to sound like you're doing them a favor.

The rule is to create a commission system.
The trick is to get their number.

The trick is to make it personal:
No one in the world suffers like you.

The trick is that you're providing a service.
The rule is to keep the conversation going.

The rule is their parents were foolish,
their children are greedy or insane.

The rule is to make them feel they've come too late.
The trick is that you're willing to make exceptions.

The rule is to assume their parents abused them.
The trick is to sound like the one teacher they loved.

And when they say "too much,"
give them a plan.

And when they say "anger" or "rage" or "love,"
say "give me an example."

The rule is everyone is a gypsy now.
Everyone is searching for his tribe.

The rule is you don't care if they ever find it.
The trick is that they feel they can.

francine j. harris
katherine with the lazy eye. short. and not a good poet.

this morning, i heard you were found in your mcdonald's uniform.

i heard it while i was visiting a lake town, where empty
woodsy highways turn into waterside drives.

i'd forgotten my toothbrush and was brushing my teeth with one finger.
a friend who didn't know you said he'd heard it like this: *you know katherine. short.*

with a lazy eye. poet. not a very good one. yeah, well she died. the blue on that lake
isn't so frank. it fogs off into the horizon like styrofoam. the

picnic tables full of white people. i ask them where the coffee is. they say at meijer.

i wonder if you thought about getting out of detroit. when you read at the open mic
you'd point across the street at mcdonald's and tell us to come see you.

katherine with the lazy eye. short and not a good poet, i guess i almost cried.
i don't know why, because i didn't like you. this is the first time i remembered your
    name.

i didn't like how you followed around a married man. that your poems sucked
and that i figured they were all about the married man.

that sometimes you reminded me of myself, boy crazy. that sometimes
i think people just don't tell me that i'm kind of, well … slow.

katherine with the lazy eye, short. and not a good poet.
i didn't like that your lazy eye was always

looking at me. that you called me by my name. i didn't
like you, since the first time i saw you at mcdonald's.

you had a mop. and you were letting some homeless dude
flirt with you. i wondered then, if you thought that was the best

you could do. i wondered then
if it was.

katherine with the lazy eye, short. and not a good poet.
you were too silly to wind up dead in an abandoned building.

i didn't like you because, what was i supposed to tell you. what.
don't let them look at you like that, katherine. don't let them get you alone.

katherine with the lazy eye, short. and not a good poet. what
was i supposed to say to you, you don't get to laugh like that,

like nothing's gonna get you. not everyone
will forgive the slow girl. katherine with

the fucked up eye, short. poetry sucked, musta knew better. i avoided you
in the hallway. i avoided you in lunch line. i avoided you in the lake.

i avoided you. my lazy eye. katherine with one hideous eye, shit.
poetry for boys again, you should have been immune. you were supposed

to be a cartoon. your body was supposed to be as twisted as
it was gonna get. short. and not a good poet. katherine with

no eye no more. i avoided you. hated it when you said my name. i
really want to leave detroit. katherine with the lazy short.

not a good poet. and shit. somewhere someone has already asked
what was she like, and a woman has brought out her wallet and said

this is her. this is my beautiful baby.

INEFFABILITY

Ineffability is often defined as the inability to express something. Like the feeling you may have for autumn—part nostalgia, part appreciation of deterioration, and part something you can't quite name, put your finger on, or express. Does this mean everything that is able to be expressed is *effable*?

    In south-central Illinois, there is a city of just over ten thousand residents called Effingham, which lies at the crossroads of Interstates 57 and 70. There is a 198-foot tall blazing white cross made out of 180 tons of steel built in 2001 that stands alongside the highways. When is the right moment while driving through Effingham that one should depress the gas pedal harder in an effort to speed away from such ineffability? This question is something like the 316 questions that Pablo Neruda poses in the final book he wrote, excerpted below.

Ineffability, in other words, is about asking questions that do not demand answers but instead demand more questions, or are themselves a celebration of inquiry itself. When you examine Neruda's couplets, study the juxtapositions—associations, leaps, and frictions—that occur from one couplet to the next or within each section of couplets, or even from section to section; these will yield other dimensions to your ineffability.

Henrietta Cordelia Ray
Limitations

The subtlest strain a great musician weaves,
Cannot attain in rhythmic harmony
To music in his soul. May it not be
Celestial lyres send hints to him? He grieves
That half the sweetness of the song, he leaves
Unheard in the transition. Thus do we
Yearn to translate the wondrous majesty
Of some rare mood, when the rapt soul receives
A vision exquisite. Yet who can match
The sunset's iridescent hues? Who sing
The skylark's ecstasy so seraph-fine?
We struggle vainly, still we fain would catch
Such rifts amid life's shadows, for they bring
Glimpses ineffable of things divine.

Pablo Neruda (translated from the Spanish by William O'Daly)
from *The Book of Questions*

VI

Why does the hat of night
fly so full of holes?

What does old ash say
when it passes near the fire?

Why do clouds cry so much,
growing happier and happier?

For whom do the pistils of the sun burn
in the shadow of the eclipse?

How many bees are there in a day?

VII

Is peace the peace of the dove?
Does the leopard wage war?

Why does the professor teach
the geography of death?

What happens to swallows
who are late for school?

Is it true they scatter
transparent letters across the sky?

XXXIII

And why is the sun such a bad companion
to the traveler in the desert?

And why is the sun so congenial
in the hospital garden?

Are they birds or fish
in these nets of moonlight?

Was it where they lost me
that I finally found myself?

XXXVIII

Do you not believe that death lives
inside a cherry's sun?

Cannot a kiss of spring
also kill you?

Do you believe that ahead of you
grief carries the flag of your destiny?

And in the skull do you discover
your ancestry condemned to bone?

XLIV

Where is the child I was,
still inside me or gone?

Does he know that I never loved him
and that he never loved me?

Why did we spend so much time
growing up only to separate?

Why did we both not die
when my childhood died?

And why does my skeleton pursue me
if my soul has fallen away?

Wallace Stevens
The Snow Man

One must have a mind of winter
To regard the frost and the boughs
Of the pine-trees crusted with snow;

And have been cold a long time
To behold the junipers shagged with ice,
The spruces rough in the distant glitter

Of the January sun; and not to think
Of any misery in the sound of the wind,
In the sound of a few leaves,

Which is the sound of the land
Full of the same wind
That is blowing in the same bare place

For the listener, who listens in the snow,
And, nothing himself, beholds
Nothing that is not there and the nothing that is.

Joe Wenderoth
Writer

A person, for you, is a book.
Impossible to categorize,
it veers from non-sense verse
to the most tedious of novels
and back
in just a breath.
And the book ends, the book ends.
And what makes the person more real,
then,
than a book,
is just that you cannot reread
one chapter, one sentence, one word.
You must rewrite him,

her,
and you cannot.
You cannot.
This inability is the source
of everything you have to say.

SOUND WORK

Many of us want poems to sound nice and please the ear, if not to patently rhyme. Is this due to an inherent propensity, or is it the result of a nurtured inculcation? The question is a red herring. Because in either case, the ear picks up more sense than the silent mind does alone. You must forgo what you were taught in formative school—to not read aloud because you might disturb others. If you do nothing else with a poem, read it aloud. It is a singular way of disturbing your own soul. If that doesn't suffice a desire for disturbance, read W.H. Auden's and Molly Peacock's poems one after the other and back again, exploring what you think you know about suffering and altruism. Then, read Frederick Seidel's "Widening Income Inequality" with the understanding that being discomfited by a poem carries its own kind of soulwork.

George Herbert
Love (III)

Love bade me welcome. Yet my soul drew back
        Guilty of dust and sin.
But quick-eyed Love, observing me grow slack
        From my first entrance in,
Drew nearer to me, sweetly questioning,
        If I lacked any thing.

A guest, I answered, worthy to be here:
        Love said, You shall be he.
I the unkind, ungrateful? Ah my dear,
        I cannot look on thee.
Love took my hand, and smiling did reply,
        Who made the eyes but I?

Truth Lord, but I have marred them: let my shame
        Go where it doth deserve.
And know you not, says Love, who bore the blame?
        My dear, then I will serve.
You must sit down, says Love, and taste my meat:
        So I did sit and eat.

W.H. Auden
Musée des Beaux Arts

About suffering they were never wrong,
The Old Masters: how well they understood
Its human position; how it takes place
While someone else is eating or opening a window or just walking dully along;
How, when the aged are reverently, passionately waiting
For the miraculous birth, there always must be
Children who did not specially want it to happen, skating
On a pond at the edge of the wood:
They never forgot
That even the dreadful martyrdom must run its course
Anyhow in a corner, some untidy spot
Where the dogs go on with their doggy life and the torturer's horse
Scratches its innocent behind on a tree.

In Breughel's *Icarus*, for instance: how everything turns away
Quite leisurely from the disaster; the ploughman may
Have heard the splash, the forsaken cry,
But for him it was not an important failure; the sun shone
As it had to on the white legs disappearing into the green
Water; and the expensive delicate ship that must have seen
Something amazing, a boy falling out of the sky,
Had somewhere to get to and sailed calmly on.

Molly Peacock
Altruism

What if we got outside ourselves and there
really was an outside out there, not just
our insides turned inside out? What if there
really were a you beyond me, not just
the waves off my own fire, like those waves off
the backyard grill you can see the next yard through,
though not well—just enough to know that off
to the right belongs to someone else, not you.
What if, when we said *I love you*, there were
a you to love as there is a yard beyond
to walk past the grill and get to? To endure
the endless walk through the self, knowing through a bond
that has no basis (for ourselves are all we know)
is altruism: not giving, but coming to know
someone is there through the wavy vision
of the self's heat, love become a decision.

Frederick Seidel
Widening Income Inequality

I live a life of appetite and, yes, that's right,
I live a life of privilege in New York,
Eating buttered toast in bed with cunty fingers on Sunday morning.
Say that again?
I have a rule—
I never give to beggars in the street who hold their hands out.

I woke up this morning in my air-conditioning.
At the end of my legs were my feet.
Foot and foot stretched out outside the duvet looking for me!
Get up. Giddyup. Get going.
My feet were there on the far side of my legs.
Get up. Giddyup. Get going.

I don't really think I am going to.
Obama is doing just fine.
I don't think I'm going to.
Get up. Giddyup. Get going.
I can see out the window it isn't raining.
So much for the endless forecasts, always wrong.

The poor are poorer than they ever were.
The rich are richer than the poor.
Is it true about the poor?
It's always possible to be amusing.
I saw a rat down in the subway.
So what if you saw a rat.

I admire the poor profusely.
I want their autograph.
They make me shy.
I keep my distance.
I'm getting to the bottom of the island.
Lower Broadway comes to a boil and City Hall is boiling.

I'm half asleep but I'm awake.
At the other end of me are my feet
In shoes of considerable sophistication
Walking down Broadway in the heat.
I'm half asleep in the heat.
I'm, so to speak, wearing a hat.

I'm no Saint Francis.
I'm in one of my trances.

When I look in a mirror,
There's an old man in a trance.
There's a Gobi Desert,
And that's poetry, or rather rhetoric.

You see what happens if you don't make sense?
It only makes sense to not.
You feel the flicker of a hummingbird
It takes a second to find.
You hear a whirr.
It's here. It's there. It hovers, begging, hand out.

RHYTHM

Most often when we talk about rhythm in a poem, we talk about a certain kind of *patterned* rhythm, say, iambic pentameter or trochaic inversion, or a highly stylized, "formal" ordering like terza rima as in Dante's *Inferno*. Aline Murray Kilmer's and Wilfred Owen's poems here pleasingly fall into such a discussion.

Other times, we talk about rhythm as simply the repetition and variation of beats, as when listening, playing, or even just feeling music. If we want to get tonal about it, we might say that beats can become booms, plinks, bongs, tweaks, twinges, and so on. Or, if we want to consider the sheer sonic rhythms of language, we can turn to the "sound poems" of someone like Kurt Schwitters, especially the various recordings of his "Ursonate."

In the usual examination of poetry's sonics, many of us have been taught that sound and sense are intertwined, that rhythm provides a beat that either goes with or rubs against the content of a poem. But what else can we say?

The last two poems here offer less conventional experiences with rhythm. Ask of these poems: When might rhythm modulate content, not just offer a bass line or percussive role? Where and how do the rhythmic patterns push off and improvise their own patterns? How can a seemingly chaotic rhythm make a different kind of sense, or renew the sense we believe we know of rhythm? In particular, how does the title of "Any Lit" jibe with what's in the body of the poem? And in "Gyre's Galax," it might be easy to call the poem "jazzy," but what in the poem defies jazz? What is jazz anyway?

Aline Murray Kilmer
Shards

I can never remake the thing I have destroyed;
  I brushed the golden dust from the moth's bright wing,
I called down wind to shatter the cherry-blossoms,
  I did a terrible thing.

I feared that the cup might fall, so I flung it from me;
   I feared that the bird might fly, so I set it free;
I feared that the dam might break, so I loosed the river:
   May its waters cover me.

Wilfred Owen
Dulce et decorum est

Bent double, like old beggars under sacks,
Knock-kneed, coughing like hags, we cursed through sludge,
Till on the haunting flares we turned our backs,
And towards our distant rest began to trudge.
Men marched asleep. Many had lost their boots,
But limped on, blood-shod. All went lame; all blind;
Drunk with fatigue; deaf even to the hoots
Of gas-shells dropping softly behind.

Gas! GAS! Quick, boys!—An ecstasy of fumbling
Fitting the clumsy helmets just in time,
But someone still was yelling out and stumbling
And flound'ring like a man in fire or lime.—
Dim through the misty panes and thick green light,
As under a green sea, I saw him drowning.

In all my dreams before my helpless sight,
He plunges at me, guttering, choking, drowning.

If in some smothering dreams, you too could pace
Behind the wagon that we flung him in,
And watch the white eyes writhing in his face,
His hanging face, like a devil's sick of sin;
If you could hear, at every jolt, the blood
Come gargling from the froth-corrupted lungs,
Obscene as cancer, bitter as the cud
Of vile, incurable sores on innocent tongues,—
My friend, you would not tell with such high zest
To children ardent for some desperate glory,
The old Lie: *Dulce et decorum est*
Pro patria mori.

Harryette Mullen
Any Lit

You are a ukulele beyond my microphone
You are a Yukon beyond my Micronesia

You are a union beyond my meiosis
You are a unicycle beyond my migration
You are a universe beyond my mitochondria
You are a Eucharist beyond my Miles Davis
You are a euphony beyond my myocardiogram
You are a unicorn beyond my Minotaur
You are a eureka beyond my maitai
You are a Yuletide beyond my minesweeper
You are a euphemism beyond my myna bird
You are a unit beyond my mileage
You are a Yugoslavia beyond my mind's eye
You are a yoo-hoo beyond my minor key
You are a Euripides beyond my mime troupe
You are a Utah beyond my microcosm
You are a Uranus beyond my Miami
You are a youth beyond my mylar
You are a euphoria beyond my myalgia
You are a Ukrainian beyond my Maimonides
You are a Euclid beyond my miter box
You are a Univac beyond my minus sign
You are a Eurydice beyond my maestro
You are a eugenics beyond my Mayan
You are a U-boat beyond my mind control
You are a euthanasia beyond my miasma
You are a urethra beyond my Mysore
You are a Euterpe beyond my Mighty Sparrow
You are a ubiquity beyond my minority
You are a eunuch beyond my migraine
You are a Eurodollar beyond my miserliness
You are a urinal beyond my Midol
You are a uselessness beyond my myopia

N.H. Pritchard
Gyre's Galax

Sound variegated through beneath lit
Sound variegated through beneath lit
through sound beneath variegated lit
sound variegated through beneath lit

Variegated sound through beneath lit dark
Variegated sound through beneath lit dark
sound variegated through beneath lit
variegated sound through beneath lit dark

Through variegated beneath sound lit
Through variegated beneath sound lit
through variegated beneath sound lit
through variegated beneath sound lit
Through variegated beneath sound lit
Through variegated beneath sound lit
through beneath lit
through beneath lit
through beneath lit
through beneath lit
Thru beneath
Thru beneath
Thru beneath
through beneath lit
Thru beneath
through beneath lit
Thru beneath
through beneath lit
Thru beneath
Thru beneath
through beneath lit
Thru beneath
Thru beneath
through beneath lit
Thru beneath
Thru beneath
Thru beneath
Thru beneath
Thru beneath
Thru beneath
Thru beneath
Through beneath lit

Twainly ample of amongst
twainly ample of amongst
Twainly ample of amongst
twainly ample of amongst
Twainly ample of amongst
twainly ample of amongst
In lit black viewly
  viewly
  viewly
  in viewly
  viewly
  viewly
  in viewly

            viewly
            in viewly
            viewly
            in viewly
            viewly
            viewly
            viewly
            in viewly
            viewly
In lit black viewly
    in dark to stark
In dark to stark
In dark to stark
    in dark to stark
In dark to stark
    in dark to stark
In dark to stark lit
In above beneath
In above beneath
In above beneath
   above beneath lit
   above beneath
   above beneath
   above beneath
   above beneath lit
   above beneath
   above beneath lit
   above beneath
   above beneath lit
   above beneath
   above beneath
   above beneath
   above beneath
   above beneath lit
   above beneath
   above beneath
   above beneath lit
   above beneath
   above beneath
   above beneath
   above beneath
   above beneath
   above beneath
   above beneath
   above beneath
   above beneath lit

ENJAMBMENT

Think of the doorjamb: the threshold that marks being inside the room and outside of it. That liminal state. That is enjambment, a word that auto-corrects to "enjoyment," which is often true of the double-meaning or playfulness that occurs when syntax spills over from one line to the next. If a line doesn't end with punctuation, like a comma or period, or is otherwise end-stopped by the completion of a sentence or phrase, the line is defined as enjambed. Lines can enjamb, and so too can stanzas.

Ross Gay
ode to the flute

A man sings
by opening his
mouth a man
sings by opening
his lungs by
turning himself into air
a flute can
be made of a man
nothing is explained
a flute lays
on its side
and prays a wind
might enter it
and make of it
at least
a small final song

Benjamin Gucciardi
Advice to Pallbearers

To make the sound of your footsteps
disappear requires practice,

a cornfield in late autumn
when the ground is brittle enough

to repeat what it hears.
Best if the six of you can go together

at dusk, find a barn-owl,
a corn-crow will do.

See how close you can get
before the bird startles,

observe the interaction
of air and wing.

Before you handle the casket,
borrow your mother's finest crystal

vase, carry it through the crowded parking lot
to the water park, ride the slides.

Let nothing shatter.
The trick is for the coffin to appear

to float, the weight of his failures
superfluous. Let him be known

as a saint, for a few moments,
before he is forgotten.

Truong Tran
what remains two

it has long been forgotten this practice of the mother
weaning a child she crushes the seeds of a green
chili rubs it to her nipple what the child feels
she too will   share in this act   of love
my own mother says it was not meant
to be cruel when cruelty she tells me
is a child's lips   torn from breast as proof
back home the women wear teeth marks

Matthea Harvey
Pity the Bathtub Its Forced Embrace of the Human Form

1.
Pity the bathtub that belongs to the queen its feet
Are bronze casts of the former queen's feet its sheen
A sign of fretting is that an inferior stone shows through
Where the marble is worn away with industrious
Polishing the tub does not take long it is tiny some say
Because the queen does not want room for splashing
The maid thinks otherwise she knows the king
Does not grip the queen nightly in his arms there are
Others the queen does not have lovers she obeys

Her mother once told her *your ancestry is your only*
Support then is what she gets in the bathtub she floats
Never holds her nose and goes under not because
She might sink but because she knows to keep her ears
Above water she smiles at the circle of courtiers below
Her feet are kicking against walls which cannot give
Satisfaction at best is to manage to stay clean

2.
Pity the bathtub its forced embrace of the whims of
One man loves but is not loved in return by the object
Of his affection there is little to tell of his profession
There is more for it is because he works with glass
That he thinks things are clear (he loves) and adjustable
(she does not love) he knows how to take something
Small and hard and hot and make room for
His breath quickens at night as he dreams of her he wants
To create a present unlike any other and because he cannot
Hold her he designs something that can a bathtub of
Glass shimmers red when it is hot he pours it into the mold
In a rush of passion only as it begins to cool does it reflect
His foolishness enrages him he throws off his clothes meaning
To jump in and lie there but it is still too hot and his feet propel
Him forward he runs from one end to the other then falls
To the floor blisters begin to swell on his soft feet he watches
His pain harden into a pretty pattern on the bottom of the bath

3.
Pity the bathtub its forced embrace of the human
Form may define external appearance but there is room
For improvement within try a soap dish that allows for
Slippage is inevitable as is difference in the size of
The subject may hoard his or her bubbles at different
Ends of the bathtub may grasp the sponge tightly or
Loosely it may be assumed that eventually everyone gets in
The bath has a place in our lives and our place is
Within it we have control of how much hot how much cold
What to pour in how long we want to stay when to
Return is inevitable because we need something
To define ourselves against even if we know that
Whenever we want we can pull the plug and get out
Which is not the case with our own tighter confinement
Inside the body oh pity the bathtub but pity us too

THE LINE

A line in a poem is a poetic unit itself. How a poem deals with this unit is a very poetic matter, meaning that prose, which is written left margin to right margin without break, isn't afforded the line. See what happens, for example, if you write out the first two poems below in prose. Notice where there is palpable loss, in meaning, in tone, in affectations. The line—not just where it breaks—has become crucial to the intent of each poem.

If you hear somebody complain that so much of contemporary poetry lacks the structure and order of end rhyme or orderly rhythm—that in effect "poetry today is just arbitrarily broken up prose"—gently remind them that other structures and permutations exist. You might even promote the idea that the greatest tool a poet now has is where and how to break a line.

The last two poems below modify or challenge our understanding of the line as a poetic unit. "In Strength Sweetness" the forward slash (or virgule)—a punctuation that normally indicates in prose where there should be a line break—is used within the lines themselves. What's the effect—a double line break, a new connection, an ambiguous severing? "The Boy Calls Twilight" plays with the poetic device of the caesura, sectioning the line into even smaller units—all the while complicating each line's meaning with enjambment. Such complication is not arbitrary, but rather is subtly constructed and is as consequential as any patterning in our more traditional forms.

Yusef Komunyakaa
Facing It

My black face fades,
hiding inside the black granite.
I said I wouldn't
dammit: No tears.
I'm stone. I'm flesh.
My clouded reflection eyes me
like a bird of prey, the profile of night
slanted against morning. I turn
this way—the stone lets me go.
I turn that way—I'm inside
the Vietnam Veterans Memorial
again, depending on the light
to make a difference.
I go down the 58,022 names,
half-expecting to find
my own in letters like smoke.

I touch the name Andrew Johnson;
I see the booby trap's white flash.
Names shimmer on a woman's blouse
but when she walks away
the names stay on the wall.
Brushstrokes flash, a red bird's
wings cutting across my stare.
The sky. A plane in the sky.
A white vet's image floats
closer to me, then his pale eyes
look through mine. I'm a window.
He's lost his right arm
inside the stone. In the black mirror
a woman's trying to erase names:
No, she's brushing a boy's hair.

Denise Levertov
The Secret

Two girls discover
the secret of life
in a sudden line of
poetry.

I who don't know the
secret wrote
the line. They
told me

(through a third person)
they had found it
but not what it was
not even

what line it was. No doubt
by now, more than a week
later, they have forgotten
the secret,

the line, the name of
the poem. I love them
for finding what
I can't find,

and for loving me
for the line I wrote,
and for forgetting it
so that

a thousand times, till death
finds them, they may
discover it again, in other
lines

in other
happenings. And for
wanting to know it,
for

assuming there is
such a secret, yes,
for that
most of all.

Elizabeth Willis
In Strength Sweetness

in the wind / an inky air

in the air / finchness

in the ink / a stone

in the winter / winter

in the nest / in the piney

in the tree / filigree

in the great / bye and bye

in the worm / William Blake

in the fall / fortune

in the ocean / a figure

in canvas / the grain

in the apartment / a body

in the mountain / its making

in the cottage / a fable

in the mind / its miniature

in the seed / a sun

in the fist / a question

in the question/ an expedition

in the expedition / a bank

in the dollar / a seal

in the seal / another seal

in the sand / a massacre

in the blood / spirit

in the word / your mouth

in the tale / its labyrinth

in the lion / the bee

in the bee / a plain

in the plan / a city

in your city / its anger

in your anger / a harbor

in your harbor / a boat

in the boat / open sea

Shane McCrae
The Boy Calls Twilight

The boy calls twilight   *little dark* the night
Big dark and smiles at the moon on the wall   the boy
Rocking himself to sleep his head against
The padding on the bars   until he falls
Over and sleeps   and if he wakes in the night
The boy   his head against the padding he
Rocks in the big dark little rocks and soft-
er once   and softer twice   until he falls
The boy he slumps   against the bars of the crib
Falls over falls asleep   and wakes in the lit-
tle dark the morning   little dark the lit-
tle dark through the window little   blue on the crib
And on the moon   which does not glow in the light
The little light   the moon is for the night

THE LYRIC

We understand "the lyric" as a personal or emotional song, and we refer to "lyrics" as words that accompany an instrumental or vocal composition. As in popular music, we often experience a lyric poem paradoxically as open-ended and self-contained; we don't get or even need the full "story" to understand the meaning of the poem. Mood, tone, or stylistic flourishes may feel more important than any overarching narrative.

What's curious about a lyric is that usually it's told or sung to us by a single entity, like that of the troubadour. The traveling songster shows us how to be solitary yet not lonely. Some of the most memorable lyric poems ascribe to a formulation of bell hooks': "Knowing how to be solitary is central to the art of loving. When we can be alone, we can be with others without using them as means of escape." (In the poems that follow, you might try finding the ways in which the lyric itself becomes the escape.)

All of this said, lyric poems don't have to be strictly personal or dramatic, and they don't have to be "musical." A lyric may have other missions: to seek, to hold onto, to capture, or to embody a moment, a fragment, and/or a place in time. Lyric poems can be fertile fields for playing with our sense of time. Because we read in a linear fashion, a lyric poem can offer an ambiguous, time-altering, unfamiliar experience. And when you read a "visual" poem, such as Mary Szybist's here, you may experience a "lyricism" that uses the page as a type of canvas, offering a space for song troubling the line between time-bound and timeless.

Sappho (translated from the ancient Greek by Anne Carson)
Fragment 22

>   ]
>   ]work
>   ]face
>   ]
>   ]
>   if not, winter
>   ]no pain
>   ]
>]I bid you sing
> of Gongyla, Abanthis, taking up
> your lyre as (now again) longing
>   floats around you,
>
> you beauty. For her dress when you saw it
> stirred you. And I rejoice.
> In fact she herself once blamed me
>   Kyprogeneia

because I prayed
this word:
I want

Mina Loy
Love Songs (section III)

We might have coupled
In the bed-ridden monopoly of a moment
Or broken flesh with one another
At the profane communion table
Where wine is spilled on promiscuous lips

We might have given birth to a butterfly
With the daily news
Printed in blood on its wings.

Li-Young Lee
This Room and Everything in It

Lie still now
while I prepare for my future,
certain hard days ahead,
when I'll need what I know so clearly this moment.

I am making use
of the one thing I learned
of all the things my father tried to teach me:
the art of memory.

I am letting this room
and everything in it
stand for my ideas about love
and its difficulties.

I'll let your love-cries,
those spacious notes
of a moment ago,
stand for distance.

Your scent,
that scent
of spice and a wound,
I'll let stand for mystery.

Your sunken belly
is the daily cup
of milk I drank
as a boy before morning prayer.

The sun on the face
of the wall
is God, the face
I can't see, my soul,

and so on, each thing
standing for a separate idea,
and those ideas forming the constellation
of my greater idea.
And one day, when I need
to tell myself something intelligent
about love,

I'll close my eyes
and recall this room and everything in it:
My body is estrangement.
This desire, perfection.
Your closed eyes my extinction.
Now I've forgotten my
idea. The book
on the windowsill, riffled by wind …
the even-numbered pages are
the past, the odd-
numbered pages, the future.
The sun is
God, your body is milk …

useless, useless …
your cries are song, my body's not me …
no good… my idea
has evaporated… your hair is time, your thighs are song …
it had something to do
with death… it had something
to do with love.

Frank O'Hara
Having a Coke with You

is even more fun than going to San Sebastian, Irún, Hendaye, Biarritz, Bayonne
or being sick to my stomach on the Travesera de Gracia in Barcelona

partly because in your orange shirt you look like a better happier St. Sebastian
partly because of my love for you, partly because of your love for yoghurt
partly because of the fluorescent orange tulips around the birches
partly because of the secrecy our smiles take on before people and statuary
it is hard to believe when I'm with you that there can be anything as still
as solemn as unpleasantly definitive as statuary when right in front of it
in the warm New York 4 o'clock light we are drifting back and forth
between each other like a tree breathing through its spectacles

and the portrait show seems to have no faces in it at all, just paint
you suddenly wonder why in the world anyone ever did them
                                                         I look
at you and I would rather look at you than all the portraits in the world
except possibly for the *Polish Rider* occasionally and anyway it's in the Frick
which thank heavens you haven't gone to yet so we can go together for the first time
and the fact that you move so beautifully more or less takes care of Futurism
just as at home I never think of the *Nude Descending a Staircase* or
at a rehearsal a single drawing of Leonardo or Michelangelo that used to wow me
and what good does all the research of the Impressionists do them
when they never got the right person to stand near the tree when the sun sank
or for that matter Marino Marini when he didn't pick the rider as carefully
as the horse
              it seems they were all cheated of some marvelous experience
which is not going to go wasted on me which is why I'm telling you about it

Kim Hyesoon (translated from the Korean by Vanessa Falso)
Horizon

Who drew it—
The horizon
The crack between land and sky?
Through it, an evening spills red blood.

Who drew it—
The line between my upper and lower eyelids?
My body is divided: the vastness of inner and outer skin.
Between them, an evening floods with tears.

Can wounds run into other wounds?
I open my eyes and sunset rushes in.
Wound meets wound.
Rivers of red water pour out endlessly
And a door closes in the dark: the exit with your name.

Who divided them—
The white day and the black night?

She is a hawk by day.
He is a wolf by night.
Inside the crack, the evening we met
Scrapes like a blade.

Mary Szybist
How (Not) to Speak of God

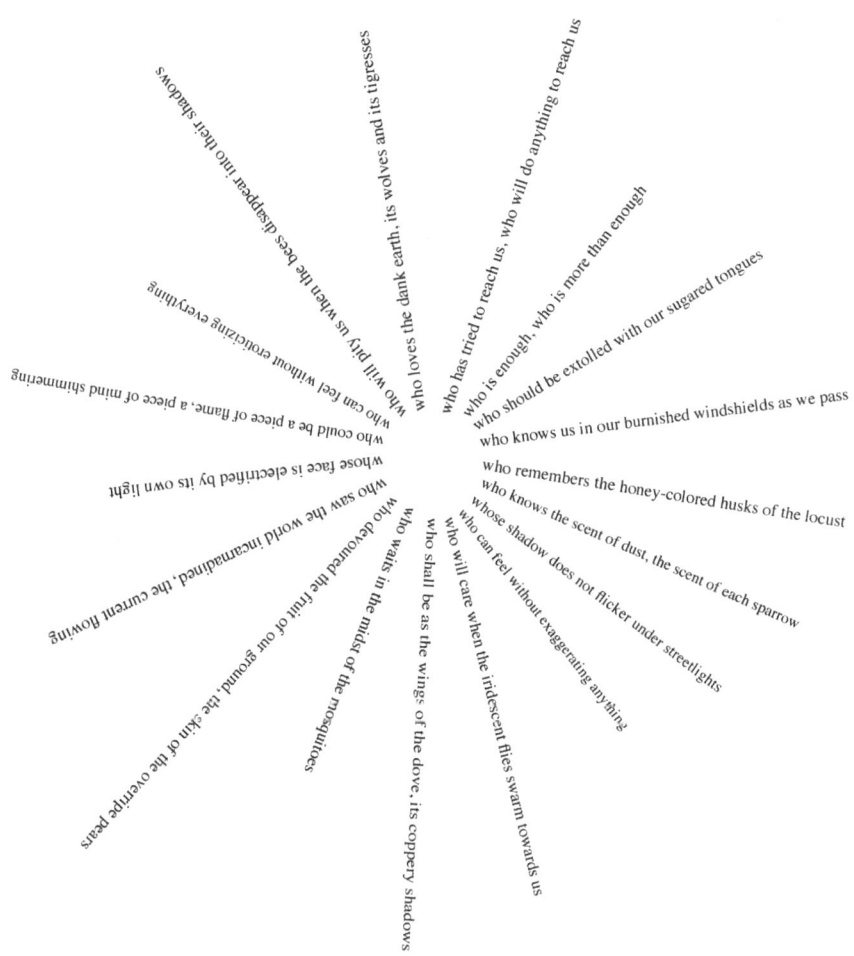

METAPHOR

One shouldn't simply tick *metaphor* off of a list of literary terms to be learned. That well-worn definition of metaphor as "a comparison of two unlike things" is just part of our literary story. In fact, all our thoughts are metaphoric! Language itself is a system of complex metaphor, where metaphor makes and builds meaning. Our cognition operates constantly in metaphor. *I hear what you mean. Do you follow me? Look hard for the answer. At the end of the day I can't see my way out of this problem!*

Fundamentally, metaphor involves substitution. The word *knife*, for example, stands in for that thing that sits on the counter waiting for me to pick it up and slice something. More broadly: one thing, concept, or set of words is substituted for another thing, concept, set of words—in order to illustrate, to elucidate, to enlighten, or to re-envision.

When it comes to poems, metaphors can feel like riddles. In fact, there's a whole tradition of riddle poems that employ metaphor at their core. The first poem below is from *The Exeter Book of Riddles*, and its intent lies in trying to figure out the identity of the speaker. (If you want to know the answer to the riddle, turn to the Notes section at the back of this book.) But metaphors don't have to disguise; they can be clear and upfront. Or they can be controlling and extended throughout a text ... or even "overextended." The overextension is often the result of the reader no longer going along with the substitution: one of the aspects of the substitute seems spot on, but then other aspects seem to falsify the substitution.

Consider Psalm 23 from the King James Bible, below. If the "Lord is my shepherd" who makes the speaker lay down in a pasture, it follows that the speaker is one of a flock, perhaps a sheep. The shepherd takes care of the speaker-cum-sheep, a comforting substitution. But when we get to the fifth verse, it seems as if the sheep is going to be feasted upon, or at the very least soon will be no more ... "dwelling" in the house of the Lord (the shepherd) forever. This may sound somewhat blasphemous, but this is what good poetry readers do: they inspect closely and even interrogate metaphors.

In the poems below, notice where and how specific metaphors are challenged as well as how the utility and limits of metaphor are questioned.

from *The Exeter Book of Riddles*
85

My home's not silent, but I am not
loud-mouthed. The Lord shaped
our course together: I'm swifter than he,
sometimes stronger; he's more strenuous.
At times I rest; he must run onward.
But I live in him all the days of my life;
if we're divided I'm certain to die.

The King James Bible
Psalm 23

The Lord is my shepherd; I shall not want.
He maketh me to lie down in green pastures: he leadeth me beside the still waters.

He restoreth my soul: he leadeth me in the paths of righteousness for his name's sake.
Yea, though I walk through the valley of the shadow of death, I will fear no evil: for thou art with me; thy rod and thy staff they comfort me.
Thou preparest a table before me in the presence of mine enemies: thou anointest my head with oil; my cup runneth over.
Surely goodness and mercy shall follow me all the days of my life: and I will dwell in the house of the Lord forever.

Virginia Hamilton Adair
Now You Need Me

When the rains come
you remember
our old closeness
humping along
in the wet.
You grope the dark
where I hang
morosely
by my crooked neck.
You pull off my cover
shake me till my
ribs jiggle
and a moth flies out.
Your hand reaches under
my black skirt
and up one leg
thin as a cane
until I open wide
with a rusty squawk
hovering above you
like a dark and loving
raven, said the old
umbrella, her night
full of holes.

Michael Chitwood
Here I Am, Lord

The ribbed black of the umbrella
is an argument for the existence of God,

that little shelter
we carry with us

and may forget
beside a chair

in a committee meeting
we did not especially want to attend.

What a beautiful word, "umbrella."
A shade to be opened.

Like a bat's wing, scalloped.
It shivers.

A drum head
beaten by the silver sticks

of rain,
and I do not have mine,

and so the rain showers me.

Bryan Walpert
No Metaphor

A tuba and a man stroll through
the grass, a pretzel of flesh and brass
you could say, I guess, except it's
only a man wearing a tuba beneath late

autumn reds as blackbirds flock
overhead. The tuba is cold metal
fact, and this fellow bears
the weight on his back less like

a broken-hearted lament than a bulky
instrument. This sight, it's true, might
remind someone less sensible than you
of a duet, of a girl, of the year

that has unfurled since the touch of her
hand, of a melody that fluttered last fall
then collapsed to earth with no sound
at all, like the sudden absence of a breeze.

But, please: A tuba and its man are merely
crossing a park at bright noon, absent
a band or a tune, and there is no need
to notice, no need for a word about

the blackbirds, which ripple to earth behind
the man like the folding of a fan—

just not as final or as fast and,
overall, more like birds landing in grass.

Carolina Ebeid
Punctum / Metaphor

Love remains a kind of present tense. This is how we describe the scenes in photographs—as though the actions in them were still happening. My father is throwing a rock in this picture. My father keeps lions in his chest & they rip apart a gazelle in this picture.

A man throwing a rock; the image holds an old grammar. This rock has yet to leave the hand, to measure the horizontal span from A to B. Nor has it completed the vertical distance from first line to last line, riding a tangle of syntax. The photograph captures a skirmish in the West Bank town of Nablus; the man hurling the rock is my father insofar as Juliet is the sun.

G.C. Waldrep
Apocatastasis

For the instruments are by their rhymes,
as Kit Smart wrote. Walking out yesterday
the bud's promise seemed a crystalline
hallucination, spring's early flowing stone,
the maimed sycamores climbing in geometry
grey as steel, as smoke, as the sky
that hangs low as stiff washing from the lines.
Pity small life, the stem that pushes
up from this hard surface, the insensate
bravery. If we anthropomorphize the world,
the night reduces to our capacity for hope
and all tender fallacies. Thus purity.
Thus metaphor's gift, the ice that spools
and circles at skin's surface. My love,
there is no winter but the winter of the heart.
Perhaps this cold will pass. Perhaps
that bridge was not a harp at all.

AMBIGUITY

Each of these poems here contains a specific ambiguity, in which an idea, image, or emotion is at odds with itself. Remember, ambiguity is not synonymous with uncertainty. Ambiguity means trying to come to terms with the experience of holding two contrasting things in your mind at the same time and not choosing one over the other. If you want to ramp up the headiness, try reading the horses in Kay Ryan's poem as though they are the same horses in Kedarnath Singh's poem. Or, try reading John Ashbery's poem and then returning to Joe Wenderoth's "Writer" which appears earlier under the section "Ineffability."

Kay Ryan
All Your Horses

Say when rain
cannot make
you more wet
or a certain
thought can't
deepen and yet
you think it again:
you have lost
count. A larger
amount is
no longer a
larger amount.
There has been
a collapse; perhaps
in the night.
Like a rupture
in water (which
can't rupture
of course). All
your horses
broken out with
all your horses.

Kedarnath Singh (translated from the Hindi by Vinay Dharwadker)
An Argument about Horses

The three of them were sitting in the sun
and arguing about horses

The horse is beautiful—the first one said
You're wrong—the second one retorted
the horse is simply solid—very solid

The third man who'd been silent until then
said softly—It's so solid
that you can't argue about it

Why can't we argue about it—the first one shouted
Of course we can argue about it—the second one agreed

The third man was silent
rather he was very pleased
flicking the ash from his cigarette he said—
But where is the horse?

So what if it isn't here
at least we can argue about it
the first one said

We can argue about it
but I'm sad I haven't seen a horse in so many years—
there was a strange kind of pain in the third man's voice

There are fewer and fewer horses
the first one said

Right—the second one replied
that's precisely the question
why are there fewer and fewer horses?

They're sold off—the first one said

But who buys so many horses
the second one asked—
there must be statistics about this somewhere

There are—said the first one
emphasizing the *are*—
but we can't get to see them

Why—why can't we get to see them—
the second man was shaking

Because the horses trample down the statistics
the first one said

His voice was so faint
it seemed he wasn't speaking to the others but only to himself

The third man who'd been silent all this while
screamed suddenly—

My friends
one day those statistics will rise
and trample down the horses

For a long time
after that
there was no more argument

Heather McHugh
Language Lesson 1976

When Americans say a man
takes liberties, they mean

he's gone too far. In Philadelphia today I saw
a kid on a leash look mom-ward

and announce his fondest wish: one
bicentennial burger, hold

the relish. Hold is forget,
in American.

On the courts of Philadelphia
the rich prepare

to serve, to fault. The language is a game as well,
in which love can mean nothing,

doubletalk mean lie. I'm saying
doubletalk with me. I'm saying

go so far the customs are untold.
Make nothing without words,

and let me be
the one you never hold.

John Ashbery
Paradoxes and Oxymorons

This poem is concerned with language on a very plain level.
Look at it talking to you. You look out a window
Or pretend to fidget. You have it but you don't have it.
You miss it, it misses you. You miss each other.

The poem is sad because it wants to be yours, and cannot.
What's a plain level? It is that and other things,
Bringing a system of them into play. Play?
Well, actually, yes, but I consider play to be

A deeper outside thing, a dreamed role-pattern,
As in the division of grace these long August days
Without proof. Open-ended. And before you know
It gets lost in the steam and chatter of typewriters.

It has been played once more. I think you exist only
To tease me into doing it, on your level, and then you aren't there
Or have adopted a different attitude. And the poem
Has set me softly down beside you. The poem is you.

DICKINSON

Who would win in a battle-off of poetic ambiguity—Shakespeare or Dickinson? Wouldn't it be something to see them go linguistic punch for punch exchanging lines?

In a letter Dickinson once wrote about Shakespeare's plays: "Why clasp any hand but his?" and "Why is any other book needed?" This is equally how some poets today feel about her own collected poems, which have been published in various editions, some with paternal edits, others with re-corrected "errors," still others that are facsimiles of poems she wrote in correspondence and on envelopes to their very edges.

Dickinson's poetry may suffer from her being known as a recluse, an unacknowledged genius of her time, or a poet overly obsessed with death and abstraction. But whatever one wants to believe about her actual life or reputation, the reason to take her poems to a deserted island instead of the Bard's is not only because you can sing a great many of them to the theme song from *Gilligan's Island*, but because Dickinson in advising us to "Tell all the truth but tell it slant" has given poets a reason to exist.

Tell all the truth but tell it slant

Tell all the truth but tell it slant –
Success in Circuit lies
Too bright for our infirm Delight
The Truth's superb surprise
As Lightning to the Children eased
With explanation kind
The Truth must dazzle gradually
Or every man be blind –

After great pain, a formal feeling comes –

After great pain, a formal feeling comes –
The Nerves sit ceremonious, like Tombs –
The stiff Heart questions 'was it He, that bore,'
And 'Yesterday, or Centuries before'?

The Feet, mechanical, go round –
A Wooden way
Of Ground, or Air, or Ought –

Regardless grown,
A Quartz contentment, like a stone –

This is the Hour of Lead –
Remembered, if outlived,
As Freezing persons, recollect the Snow –
First – Chill – then Stupor – then the letting go –

Because I could not stop for Death –

Because I could not stop for Death –
He kindly stopped for me –
The Carriage held but just Ourselves –
And Immortality.

We slowly drove – He knew no haste
And I had put away
My labor and my leisure too,
For His Civility –

We passed the School, where Children strove
At Recess – in the Ring –
We passed the Fields of Gazing Grain –
We passed the Setting Sun –

Or rather – He passed Us –
The Dews drew quivering and Chill –
For only Gossamer, my Gown –
My Tippet – only Tulle –

We paused before a House that seemed
A Swelling of the Ground –
The Roof was scarcely visible –
The Cornice – in the Ground –

Since then – 'tis Centuries – and yet
Feels shorter than the Day
I first surmised the Horses' Heads
Were toward Eternity –

I cannot live with You –

I cannot live with You –
It would be Life –
And Life is over there –
Behind the Shelf

The Sexton keeps the Key to –
Putting up
Our Life – His Porcelain –
Like a Cup –

Discarded of the Housewife –
Quaint – or Broke –
A newer Sevres pleases –
Old Ones crack –

I could not die – with You –
For One must wait
To shut the Other's Gaze down –
You – could not –

And I – Could I stand by
And see You – freeze –
Without my Right of Frost –
Death's privilege?

Nor could I rise – with You –
Because Your Face
Would put out Jesus' –
That New Grace

Glow plain – and foreign
On my homesick Eye –
Except that You than He
Shone closer by –

They'd judge Us – How –
For You – served Heaven – You know,
Or sought to –
I could not –

Because You saturated Sight –
And I had no more Eyes
For sordid excellence
As Paradise

And were You lost, I would be –
Though My Name
Rang loudest
On the Heavenly fame –

And were You – saved –
And I – condemned to be
Where You were not –
That self – were Hell to Me –

So We must meet apart –
You there – I – here –
With just the Door ajar
That Oceans are – and Prayer –
And that White Sustenance –
Despair –

CLASSICS

How seriously are we to take the literary "c" word?

Some poets have taken it all the way to the grave. The Romantics … who clinked their classics against frangible teacups. Or Ezra Pound … who gave new meaning as well as new xenophobia to his classics ….

This is the point. The capital or little "c" classics are not classics simply because their authors made them. Readers made and still make them classic. Readers can and will continue to give old stones new moss. The speaker in Diane Seuss' poem below illustrates the point.

Who will be the stones of your poetic thoughts? What kinds of moss will you grow from them? What else will you build?

Ezra Pound
Cantico del Sole

The thought of what America would be like
If the Classics had a wide circulation
        Troubles my sleep,
The thought of what America,
The thought of what America,
The thought of what America would be like
If the Classics had a wide circulation
        Troubles my sleep.
Nunc dimittis, now lettest thou thy servant,
Now lettest thou thy servant
        Depart in peace.
The thought of what America,
The thought of what America,
The thought of what America would be like
If the Classics had a wide circulation …
        Oh well!
        It troubles my sleep.

Diane Seuss
Romantic Poetry

Now that the TV is gone and the music
has been hauled away,
it's just me here, and the muffling silence
a spider wraps around a living morsel.
And at times, often, the unbearable.
I bear it, though, just like you.
Long ago, I bore a suitcase filled with books,
bore it far on city streets. To sell, I guess, at some
used books place, one of those doorways down
steps into dankness and darkness. The scent

of mildewed, dog-eared, fingered pages.
The suitcase, big and square and sharp-cornered,
covered in snakeskin, bought at Goodwill
for a dollar, knowing I had some traveling to do,
some lugging, and I was right.
What books I sold I do not know.
Maybe that's where *Modern Poetry* went.
The cover cherry-red and blossom-white.
I can see its spine in my mind's eye,
pointing downward beneath the dank

and the dark to the water tunneling
under the city and making its way to the river.
Poems sliding down the book's spine
into water, the shock of the cold and dank,
down where my uterine lining, my blood
and cast-off ovulations, cast-off fetal
tissue swims, below the city.
The microdead ride modern poems
like swan boats in the park.
From the park to the river to the sea.

I'm thinking now of PJ Harvey and Nick Cave.
Balladeers. Lovers. Vita and Virginia.
Frank O'Hara and Vincent Warren. Somehow,
we ride our lost loves out to sea. Or they ride us.
It doesn't matter. Poet or poem or reader, the same
ectoplasm. The modern, in time, becomes antique,
and the stone faces of the dead convert to symbols,
ripe for smashing. Come to think of it,
symbols are terrible. As the tyrant
shouted to the masses,

part of his brainwashing campaign:
I know it, and you know it, too.
I was twenty-three when I sold off
Modern Poetry and sailed to Italy, seeking
Romantic poetry, which was at one time
modern, and found my way to Rome,
and Keats's death room.
His deathbed, a facsimile.
Everything he touched was burned,
to kill what killed him.

I lifted his death mask from its nail,
cradled it, closed my eyes and kissed his lips
until the plaster warmed,
and stained his face
with the lipstick on my lips. Red
as the cover of *Modern Poetry.*
The color of the droplets of arterial blood
he coughed onto his sheets and viewed
by candlelight. Then he knew he was done for.
His death warrant, he called it.

After those many kisses over his face and eyes,
and the reticulated eyelashes,
cold and tangled,
my lips were blossom-white,
my face, chalked. Like I'd caught
something from him,
and I don't just mean consumption,
though my lungs burned for years.
They still burn.
This is the danger of the ecstasy of kissing

the dead or dying poet on the mouth.
The disease you'll catch—well,
it changes you.
The tingle in the spine,
the erotic charge, will be forever married
to poetry's previous incarnations.
It's why marriage itself never worked for me.
I kept wanting to get to the part
where death parts us
and I could find myself again.

Keats made such a compact corpse.
Only five feet tall, shorter than Prince,
and intricately made. Always,

he was working it, working it out,
the meaning of suffering, the world's,
his own, the encounter with beauty,
nearly synonymous with suffering,
how empathy could extinguish him,
and he could set down the suitcase at last,
or finally deliver him to himself, distinct

as the waves in his hair and the bridge
of his nose. How auspicious,
rare, lush,
bizarre, kinky, transcendent,
romantic, to be young, just twenty-three,
and to cradle him
in my arms, as we listened
to the burbling water
of the Fontana della Barcaccia
from the open window.

MYTHS

We hear, read, and are taught myths. But this absorption comes to us differently than when the myths were first made. As well, many myths may have been transformed, disappeared then reappeared, or otherwise altered before reaching us in the present. In other words, myths are changeable and generative, and poets sometimes return to myths that which was perhaps never there. So be open to long ago legends; they may have lessons for you as models of appreciation and stewardship. Obversely, you may have to school them ... as Mathias Svalina does in "Creation Myth," one of the forty-four creation myths in his book *Destruction Myth*.

Amorak Huey
We Were All Odysseus in Those Days

A young man learns to shoot
& dies in the mud
an ocean away from home,
a rifle in his fingers
& the sky dripping
from his heart. Next to him
a friend watches
his final breath slip
ragged into the ditch,
a thing the friend will carry

back to America—
wound, souvenir,
backstory. He'll teach
literature to young people
for 40 years. He'll coach
his daughters' softball teams.
Root for Red Wings
& Lions & Tigers. Dance
well. Love generously.
He'll be quick with a joke
& firm with handshakes.
He'll rarely talk
about the war. If asked
he'll tell you instead
his favorite story:
Odysseus escaping
from the Cyclops
with a bad pun & good wine
& a sharp stick.
It's about buying time
& making do, he'll say.
It's about doing what it takes
to get home, & you see
he has been talking
about the war all along.
We all want the same thing
from this world:
Call me nobody. Let me live.

Muriel Rukeyser
Waiting for Icarus

He said he would be back and we'd drink wine together
He said that everything would be better than before
He said we were on the edge of a new relation
He said he would never again cringe before his father
He said that he was going to invent full-time
He said he loved me that going into me
He said was going into the world and the sky
He said all the buckles were very firm
He said the wax was the best wax
He said Wait for me here on the beach
He said Just don't cry

I remember the gulls and the waves
I remember the islands going dark on the sea
I remember the girls laughing
I remember they said he only wanted to get away from me
I remember mother saying: Inventors are like poets, a trashy lot
I remember she told me those who try out inventions are worse
I remember she added: Women who love such are the worst of all
I have been waiting all day, or perhaps longer.
I would have liked to try those wings myself.
It would have been better than this.

Jericho Brown
Ganymede

A man trades his son for horses.
That's the version I prefer. I like
The safety of it, no one at fault,
Everyone rewarded. God gets
The boy. The boy becomes
Immortal. His father rides until
Grief sounds as good as the gallop
Of an animal born to carry those
Who patrol our inherited
Kingdom. When we look at myth
This way, nobody bothers saying
Rape. I mean, don't you want God
To want you? Don't you dream
Of someone with wings taking you
Up? And when the master comes
For our children, he smells
Like the men who own stables
In Heaven, that far terrain
Between Promise and Apology.
No one has to convince us.
The people of my country believe
We can't be hurt if we can be bought.

Leila Chatti
Confession

Oh, I wish I had died before this and was in oblivion, forgotten.
Mary giving birth, the Holy Qur'an

Truth be told, I like Mary a little better
when I imagine her like this, crouched
and cursing, a boy-God pushing on
her cervix (I like remembering
she had a cervix, her body ordinary
and so like mine), girl-sweat lacing
rivulets like veins in the sand,
her small hands on her knees
not doves but hands, gripping,
a palm pressed to her spine, fronds
whispering like voyeurs overhead—
(oh Mary, like a God, I too take pleasure
in knowing you were not all
holy, that ache could undo you
like a knot)—and, suffering,
I admire this girl who cared
for a moment not about God
or His plans but her own
distinct life, this fiercer Mary who'd disappear
if it saved her, who'd howl *to Hell
with salvation* if it meant this pain,
the blessed adolescent who squatted
indignant in a desert, bearing His child
like a secret she never wanted to hear.

Mathias Svalina
Creation Myth

In the beginning there were only streets.
There were streets that led to cliffs,
streets that led to patches of dandelions,
streets that led to other streets,
streets that led to desires & streets that led
to the potential for desires.

Some streets curled into tongue-sized segments.
Some streets were perforated so that the wind whistled dissonant tonalities.
Some streets burrowed into the earth to the molten core.

There was a four-mile stretch of street
in the middle of the Australian outback,
a street floating in the Indian Ocean.

There were streets that were never seen.
There was a street that looked like you
when you were eight years old.
Some streets considered themselves to be houses.
Some streets did not know
they were streets.

There was, however, no Department of Transportation
& over the millennia the streets dissolved into cracks & weeds.
Eventually the living things arrived
& grew bigger & smaller
& there were people & the people
invented cars.

When you're driving a car & you feel the wheel
jerk beneath your hands, it is not the wind
or a pothole. You've driven over the ghost
of an ancient street & your car is crying out
the only way it knows how.

Your car does not love you. Your car knows
what it is to be a car & that cars belong
to streets. Just as every bird
belongs to the bird feeder. Just as lead
belongs to the pencil. That's how I felt
when I was eight years old
& my home broke apart.

GREAT BOOKS

Of the various lists of Great Books proffered by academe, the literati, or book clubs, poetry seldom appears unless in the form of epic narratives. What does it mean to want a Great Book that possesses no propelling or overarching storyline?

What are your Great Books? They can be any book, of course, and over many years and decades, some of those on your list are maybe only great because they are great to you. When you look at the bookshelf and see your childhood favorite, say, *The Little Engine That Could*, or that random book you picked up as a teen, say, the romance-novel *Arousing Touch*, and you are deeply moved by originary feeling, who's to say these are not Great Books? If any book should be called Great, it is the one that first made you feel that reading was important, that reading was kinship, that reading was love. The Greatest Book is the one that as you are reading it makes you want to read or live more.

Suzanne Buffam
from *A Pillow Book*: "A Great Book can be read again and again ..."

A Great Book can be read again and again, inexhaustibly, with great benefit to great minds, wrote Mortimer Adler, co-founder of the Great Books Foundation and the Great Books of the Western World program at the university where my husband will be going up for tenure next fall, and where I sometimes teach as well, albeit in a lesser, "non-ladder" position. Not only must a Great Book still matter today, Adler insisted, it must touch upon at least twenty-five of the one hundred and two Great Ideas that have occupied Great Minds for the last twenty-five centuries. Ranging from Angel to World, a comprehensive list of these concepts can be found in Adler's two-volume *Syntopicon: An Index to the Great Ideas*, which was published with Great Fanfare, if not Great Financial Success, by Encyclopedia Britannica in 1952. Although the index includes many Great Ideas, including Art, Beauty, Change, Desire, Eternity, Family, Fate, Happiness, History, Pain, Sin, Slavery, Soul, Space, Time, and Truth, it does not, alas, include an entry on Pillows, which often strike me, as I sink into mine at the end of long day of anything, these days, as at the very least worthy of note. Among the five hundred and eleven Great Books on Adler's list, updated in 1990 to appease his quibbling critics, moreover, only four, I can't help counting, were written by women—Virginia, Willa, Jane, and George—none of whom, as far as I can discover, were anyone's mother.

☽

Missing Scenes

In which Eve plucks her moustache.
In which Achilles waxes his ass.
In which a butterfly triggers *The Tempest*.
In which Moby Dick performs his own stunts.
In which Bashō smokes hashish.
In which the Buddha buys bonds.
In which the Heavenly Banquet is served with a spork.
In which Galahad chugs from the grail.
In which spring follows summer.
In which moss grows on meteors.
In which Pelé scores on the Peloponnesian Fields.

☽

Not in stock, says the campus bookstore clerk looking up from his screen with a smile when I inquire, incognito, after my books, which are nowhere to be found on the shelves. We used to have two copies of the first one, he says, but no one bought them, so we sent them back last June. We never carried the second one, he adds, but we could order it for you. What's your name? I glance up, above his head, at a shelf of Staff Picks. Between a history of disgust and a guide for saving the planet, I spot my husband's last book, gleaming in the day's dying light. Forget it, I mutter into my muffler, I can get it from Amazon by Friday. I go home and order an ivory satin pillowcase instead, guaranteed to reduce hair loss due to breakage and soften fine lines.

Mary Ruefle
One Book

How many books have I read? Only one—just as anyone who is literate has read only one book, or, to be precise, is in the process of reading the one book they will complete in their lifetime. That book is the particular sum of every book they have ever read, written in the particular order in which those books were read. The book is never the same, for no two persons have ever read exactly the same books in exactly the same order. There is a great difference between *The Secret of Larkspur Lane* followed by *Anna Karenina* and *Anna Karenina* followed by *The Secret of Larkspur Lane*. And if *What One Can Do with a Chafing Dish* happens to fall between ... as opposed to *Don Quixote* ... well, I don't mean to insult the genetic researchers, but I have a hunch that if no two people are alike, this is why.

WHITMAN

If Dickinson is our homebody, Whitman is our everybody. Neither is better than the other, but of America's two poetic parents, it's the work of the latter that appears to be more easily imitated and more ready to inspire. The self that Whitman created or embodied in his poems merges repeatedly, relentlessly, and delightedly with what or who they come into contact with: people, places, and things. His well-known poem about a live oak in Louisiana offers up such contact, and then ruminates in so many words: *Here is a thing (a tree) that is something like me and yet not exactly like me; I have witnessed it and in that witnessing I have discovered something about myself that was there all along.* Poets henceforth, like Ginsberg and Hahn below, echo Whitman's sentiment even when they are critical of it.

Walt Whitman
I Saw in Louisiana a Live-Oak Growing

I saw in Louisiana a live-oak growing,
All alone stood it and the moss hung down from the branches,
Without any companion it grew there uttering joyous leaves of dark green,
And its look, rude, unbending, lusty, made me think of myself,
But I wonder'd how it could utter joyous leaves standing alone there without its friend near, for I knew I could not,
And I broke off a twig with a certain number of leaves upon it, and twined around it a little moss,
And brought it away, and I have placed it in sight in my room,
It is not needed to remind me as of my own dear friends,
(For I believe lately I think of little else than of them,)

Yet it remains to me a curious token, it makes me think of manly love;
For all that, and though the live-oak glistens there in Louisiana solitary in a wide flat
    space,
Uttering joyous leaves all its life without a friend a lover near,
I know very well I could not.

Allen Ginsberg
A Supermarket in California

What thoughts I have of you tonight, Walt Whitman, for I walked down the sidestreets
    under the trees with a headache self-conscious looking at the full moon.
    In my hungry fatigue, and shopping for images, I went into the neon fruit
supermarket, dreaming of your enumerations!
    What peaches and what penumbras! Whole families shopping at night! Aisles full of
husbands! Wives in the avocados, babies in the tomatoes!—and you, García Lorca, what
were you doing down by the watermelons?
    I saw you, Walt Whitman, childless, lonely old grubber, poking among the meats in
the refrigerator and eyeing the grocery boys.
    I heard you asking questions of each: Who killed the pork chops? What price
bananas? Are you my Angel?
    I wandered in and out of the brilliant stacks of cans following you, and followed in
my imagination by the store detective.
    We strode down the open corridors together in our solitary fancy tasting
artichokes, possessing every frozen delicacy, and never passing the cashier.
    Where are we going, Walt Whitman? The doors close in an hour. Which way does
your beard point tonight?
    (I touch your book and dream of our odyssey in the supermarket and feel absurd.)
    Will we walk all night through solitary streets? The trees add shade to shade, lights
out in the houses, we'll both be lonely.
    Will we stroll dreaming of the lost America of love past blue automobiles in
driveways, home to our silent cottage?
    Ah, dear father, graybeard, lonely old courage-teacher, what America did you
have when Charon quit poling his ferry and you got out on a smoking bank and stood
watching the boat disappear on the black waters of Lethe?
                                                      Berkeley, 1955

Kimiko Hahn
Ode to the Whitman Line "When lilacs last in the dooryard bloom'd"

I cannot consider scent without you, I cannot
think that color so gay, so Japanese, so vernal

without you; not assassination or any death in any spring. I think of you
and I am man-and-woman, flawed as a Lincoln,
welcoming as a window-box, and so tenderly alliterative as to draw one near—
at times, perhaps, to withdraw from all—yes,
without you I am without pulse in that dooryard, that blooming unfurling

so tell me finally, is *last* as in *the last time* or *to make something last*
—to hold, to hold you, to memorize fast—

IMAGERY

In the twentieth century, imagery features at least as much as sound in poetry. In this century, one could argue that imagery predominates. It's not only that we see so many more images via technology and globalization than we used to; it's also that reading itself, as neuroscience reveals, is a visual activity in the brain. We recognize a word by its picture, not its meaning.

When we read a word that stands in for a picture, like "bird," our brain does a little matching game: *bird* = [the image in the mind that correlates]. While the [image in the mind that correlates] is different for each of us, based on our experiences in life and/or in language itself (such as reading a bunch of poems that include birds, as you are about to do), it's not *that* different. When you read the word *vulture*, you likely see a picture in your mind's eye very similar to what others see. And yet, differences do exist, subtle or great.

In the first poem below, what do you see after reading "a bird has left its shit on the fence post"? One possibility: "white" birdshit on a "white" fence post. But all birdshit and fences are not white. This experience is, in great part, what imagery in poems is for. Images are not there simply to "paint pretty pictures." The picture you create in your mind is *your mind at work*, in action, and not passively receiving pictures from, say, the medium of a screen.

As you read the poems, examine the images carefully, looking for patterns and variations on what you "expect" from birds—hawk, geese, vulture—and their connotations. In references to the moon, again consider your associations with the moon, and how the poem(s) play off of those associations. And when you get to the buffalo (the collective noun for a group of buffalo is "an obstinacy"), notice how the picture you have of buffalo transforms throughout the poem all the way up to its ending.

Jyoin (translated from the Japanese by Ikuho Amano and James Shea)
Haiku

A hazy moonlit night—a bird has left its shit on the fence post

Amy Lowell
The Garden by Moonlight

A black cat among roses,
Phlox, lilac-misted under a first-quarter moon,
The sweet smells of heliotrope and night-scented stock.
The garden is very still,
It is dazed with moonlight,
Contented with perfume,
Dreaming the opium dreams of its folded poppies.
Firefly lights open and vanish
High as the tip buds of the golden glow
Low as the sweet alyssum flowers at my feet.
Moon-shimmer on leaves and trellises,
Moon-spikes shafting through the snow ball bush.
Only the little faces of the ladies' delight are alert and staring,
Only the cat, padding between the roses,
Shakes a branch and breaks the chequered pattern
As water is broken by the falling of a leaf.
Then you come,
And you are quiet like the garden,
And white like the alyssum flowers,
And beautiful as the silent sparks of the fireflies.
Ah, Beloved, do you see those orange lilies?
They knew my mother,
But who belonging to me will they know
When I am gone.

James Wright
Lying in a Hammock at William Duffy's Farm in Pine Island, Minnesota

Over my head, I see the bronze butterfly,
Asleep on the black trunk,
Blowing like a leaf in green shadow.
Down the ravine behind the empty house,
The cowbells follow one another
Into the distances of the afternoon.
To my right,
In a field of sunlight between two pines,
The droppings of last year's horses
Blaze up into golden stones.
I lean back, as the evening darkens and comes on.
A chicken hawk floats over, looking for home.
I have wasted my life.

Mary Oliver
Wild Geese

You do not have to be good.
You do not have to walk on your knees
for a hundred miles through the desert, repenting.
You only have to let the soft animal of your body love what it loves.
Tell me about despair, yours, and I will tell you mine.
Meanwhile the world goes on.
Meanwhile the sun and the clear pebbles of the rain
are moving across the landscapes,
over the prairies and the deep trees,
the mountains and the rivers.
Meanwhile the wild geese, high in the clean blue air,
are heading home again.
Whoever you are, no matter how lonely,
the world offers itself to your imagination,
calls to you like the wild geese, harsh and exciting—
over and over announcing your place
in the family of things.

Irma Pineda (translated from the Isthmus Zapotec and Spanish by Wendy Call)
My Voice Will Weigh on You

My voice will weigh on you
like a rope hanging from your neck
My voice will be the vulture
that patrols your rotting body
and remains tattooed
among the sounds in your mind
so that you can't sleep
because you clawed the light
from our grandparents' eyes

Cecilia Llompart
Eight Buffalo

An obstinacy of buffalo
is not to say that the buffalo
are stubborn. No, not like
a grass stain. More that
the very bulk of one—
silk eyed, nostril as big

as a fist—is a testament
to something we cannot
name in this life. And that
one buffalo, herded off a cliff
hoof over big, impossible hoof
could feed so many. And that
two buffalo could feed so many
more. And that three buffalo
could feed so many more.
Better to say an orbit of buffalo.
Better to say where the buffalo
roam than where they do not.
Three buffalo, four. Better to say
an obedience of them. An oblivion.

ROSES

Are there so many roses in poems because roses are so pretty? Or because poems are?

What is wrong with a violet? Is it too close to the word *violent*? And what about violets? Roses are red and violets are blue. But violets aren't blue, are they? They are purple or, well, *violet*.

At the mention of the word *rose*, you see red. Yet pink, yellow, and white exist. O, Rose, how did you get *that* red?

"What's in a name? That which we call a rose / By any other name would smell as sweet." That's Juliet talking about her beloved Romeo, trying to dispel the notion that his family's name doesn't matter to her. She may be a Capulet and he a Montague, but those are merely labels. She loves him regardless of the label. She is making a point, but it can't be taken as a general principle. Labels and names matter, of course. Adam and Eve didn't pick out their names, for example, but Yaweh gave them the power to name all the other living creatures. Naming begets hierarchy and control.

When Gertrude Stein writes "a rose is a rose is a rose," she's making us aware of our naming preoccupation, and even trying to help us break free of naming: read the phrase out loud over and over and you will hear not "rose" but "arose." This is language taking on a meaning we didn't intentionally give it.

There is that thing we call "rose" that exists in the world, and then there is that thing we have named rose in our system of language where *rose* has acquired a rarefied position. Consider other rather pedestrian words, too. Say, *apple*. The word doesn't appear in the Bible at all, but somewhere along the way someone decided that the fruit Adam and Eve munched on was an apple. Somewhere else along the way, it became associated with likable teachers. Later, someone decided it would make a fine word for a computer company ... not unlike what happened to the word Amazon. Consider the hierarchy of denotations and connotations. What is your first association with *Amazon*, your second, your third?

Who knows where *rose* will go in the future? A TV series that alters its position in the system of language? A name of an AI corporation? A car? A poem so powerful we will someday reconsider our entire conceptualization of *rose*?

E. E. Cummings
[somewhere i have never travelled,gladly beyond]

somewhere i have never travelled,gladly beyond
any experience,your eyes have their silence:
in your most frail gesture are things which enclose me,
or which i cannot touch because they are too near

your slightest look easily will unclose me
though i have closed myself as fingers,
you open always petal by petal myself as Spring opens
(touching skilfully,mysteriously)her first rose

or if your wish be to close me,i and
my life will shut very beautifully,suddenly,
as when the heart of this flower imagines
the snow carefully everywhere descending;

nothing which we are to perceive in this world equals
the power of your intense fragility:whose texture
compels me with the colour of its countries,
rendering death and forever with each breathing

(i do not know what it is about you that closes
and opens;only something in me understands
the voice of your eyes is deeper than all roses)
nobody,not even the rain,has such small hands

Dorothy Parker
One Perfect Rose

A single flow'r he sent me, since we met.
    All tenderly his messenger he chose;
Deep-hearted, pure, with scented dew still wet—
    One perfect rose.

I knew the language of the floweret;
    "My fragile leaves," it said, "his heart enclose."
Love long has taken for his amulet
    One perfect rose.

Why is it no one ever sent me yet
    One perfect limousine, do you suppose?
Ah no, it's always just my luck to get
    One perfect rose.

Raymond McDaniel
Hothouse

A rose, rose. A violet, violet. A jade, jade.
No. The architecture of each, a refusal.

Rose is not rose nor violet violet nor jade jade.
But each is what it is, not what it seems.

What each seems is what of each gets seen.
Though what we see isn't the thing seen.

The petals of the rose are violet and jade.
Thus the petals of the rose look, to us, rose.

The shape of the violet absorbs all but violet.
The violet we see is the violet a violet rejects.

A rose is a rose is a rose, but not as a rose.
Jade is the name of jade, not the jade named.

PROSE POETRY

Some will tell you that prose poems pay particular attention to "poetic elements" such as imagery, sonics, and rhythm. But others will tell you this is just phooey, or that prose poetry leans more toward narrative or scene, or that prose poetry was first invented by the French, or that prose poetry's first examples are in the Hebrew bible (see Psalm 23). Prose writers will at times scoff at the prose poetry label, preferring "flash fiction" or "short shorts" or "nano-essays." One could argue that these arguments exist because the form occupies a liminal space between two genres, which not incidentally has allowed a great deal of experimentation; Gertrude Stein's prose below might not be called a poem at all, but merely a "text." Indulge as much as you like in the debate, but know that at the most basic level, a prose poem is anything that runs from the left margin to the right margin, that doesn't care about line breaks, and that someone calls a "prose poem." Below, I have tried to select a range of styles representative of prose poetry. But if you'd like more, they also appear in "Poetic Aims," "Biography," "Metaphor," "Great Books," "Narrative," "Reader Response," "Classroom Reading," "Spirituality," "Flight," "Identity," "Professionalization," and "End Notes."

Francis Ponge (translated from the French by Joshua Corey and Jean-Luc Garneau)
Crate

Halfway between *crib* and *cage* the French language places *crate*, a simple slatted box for transporting those fruits that fall ill at the least lack of air.

Built in such a way that it can be broken down effortlessly after use, it is never used twice. It is really more perishable than the deliquescing foodstuffs that it carries.

On the corners of streets that lead to the markets, it gleams like white wood without wood's vanity. Still very new, and slightly surprised to find itself in this awkward position, having been thrown into the gutter without hope of retrieval, it remains a most likable object on whose fate we will not dwell for long.

Russell Edson
The Adventures of a Turtle

The turtle carries his house on his back. He is both the house and the person of that house.

But actually, under the shell is a little room where the true turtle, wearing long underwear, sits at a little table. At one end of the room a series of levers sticks out of slots in the floor, like the controls of a steam shovel. It is with these that the turtle controls the legs of his house.

Most of the time the turtle sits under the sloping ceiling of his turtle room reading catalogues at the little table where a candle burns. He leans on one elbow, and then the other. He crosses one leg, and then the other. Finally he yawns and buries his head in his arms and sleeps.

If he feels a child picking up his house he quickly douses the candle and runs to the control levers and activates the legs of his house and tries to escape.

If he cannot escape he retracts the legs and withdraws the so-called head and waits. He knows that children are careless, and that there will come a time when he will be free to move his house to some secluded place, where he will relight his candle, take out his catalogues and read until at last he yawns. Then he'll bury his head in his arms and sleep …. That is, until another child picks up his house ….

Marie Howe
Part of Eve's Discussion

It was like the moment when a bird decides not to eat from your hand, and flies, just before it flies, the moment the rivers seem to still and stop because a storm is coming, but there is no storm, as when a hundred starlings lift and bank together before they wheel and drop, very much like the moment, driving on bad ice, when it occurs to you your car could spin, just before it slowly begins to spin, like the moment just before you forgot what it was you were about to say, it was like that, and after that, it was still like that, only all the time.

Jennifer L. Knox
Hive Minds

Riding in the car with my mother, I never graduated from the backseat to the front. Whenever I tried to, climbing in next to her ("This is stupid—I'm riding up front"), she'd howl and swipe at me until I caved. That was how she defended her space. We drove around like that until I got my driver's license: us two, locked in the dust-mote mottled skies of our own minds, counting things. Me: syllables and the shadows of telephone poles falling across the car. Her: I don't know. She can't describe her OCD to me—only that it has to do with numbers—some inexplicable tally she's been running all her life. I imagine it like a spider's web, easily disturbed, then dispersed by the breath of other people. Whatever its shape, it's the only thing that's ever soothed her.

One stalk of corn can't bear fruit by itself. It needs other stalks around to pollinate. Even a single row won't cut it. The Mandan knew to grow them in circles, my boyfriend tells me. And sunflowers, his father adds, grown in a row will take turns bending north, then south, etc., down the line to give each other a shot at the light. We're in the garden after dinner. Suddenly I envy anything that moves itself to accommodate another: a subtle shift to the left or right, self-preservation that could pass for love.

Gertrude Stein
A BOX.

A large box is handily made of what is necessary to replace any substance. Suppose an example is necessary, the plainer it is made the more reason there is for some outward recognition that there is a result.

    A box is made sometimes and them to see to see to it neatly and to have the holes stopped up makes it necessary to use paper.

    A custom which is necessary when a box is used and taken is that a large part of the time there are three which have different connections. The one is on the table. The two are on the table. The three are on the table. The one, one is the same length as is shown by the cover being longer. The other is different there is more cover that shows it. The other is different and that makes the corners have the same shade the eight are in singular arrangement to make four necessary.

    Lax, to have corners, to be lighter than some weight, to indicate a wedding journey, to last brown and not curious, to be wealthy, cigarettes are established by length and by doubling.

    Left open, to be left pounded, to be left closed, to be circulating in summer and winter, and sick color that is grey that is not dusty and red shows, to be sure cigarettes do measure an empty length sooner than a choice in color.

    Winged, to be winged means that white is yellow and pieces pieces that are brown are dust color if dust is washed off, then it is choice that is to say it is fitting cigarettes sooner than paper.

    An increase why is an increase idle, why is silver cloister, why is the spark brighter, if it is brighter is there any result, hardly more than ever.

NARRATIVE

Epics were the first narrative poems, though they were not so named. Today, the connotations around epic involve grandeur or high drama. Narrative—think storytelling—can be handled in various ways in poems: stories embedded or nested in other stories; stories told elliptically where the reader has to make "leaps" to get across connections of event or time or concept; stories that talk about their story-making (meta-narratives); among others. What poets bring to narrative is their poetic (read: unfamiliar) subtlety or brandishing. You may find yourself wanting to label some narrative poems "flash fictions" or even "lyrical essays." Call narrative poems anything you like; however, remember to do the same pattern recognition you do when reading a poem that uses, say, sonics or line breaks to keep things together. Narrative, that is, is another method of pattern-making.

Jorge Luis Borges (translated from the Spanish by Andrew Hurley)
Borges and I

It's Borges, the other one, that things happen to. I walk through Buenos Aires and I pause—mechanically now, perhaps—to gaze at the arch of an entryway and its inner door; news of Borges reaches me by mail, or I see his name on a list of academics or in some biographical dictionary. My taste runs to hourglasses, maps, eighteenth-century typefaces, etymologies, the taste of coffee, and the prose of Robert Louis Stevenson; Borges shares those preferences, but in a vain sort of way that turns them into the accoutrements of an actor. It would be an exaggeration to say that our relationship is hostile—I live, I allow myself to live, so that Borges can spin out his literature, and that literature is my justification. I willingly admit that he has written a number of sound pages, but those pages will not save *me,* perhaps because the good in them no longer belongs to any individual, not even to that other man, but rather to language itself, or to tradition. Beyond that, I am doomed—utterly and inevitably—to oblivion, and fleeting moments will be all of me that survives in that other man. Little by little, I have been turning everything over to him, though I know the perverse way he has of distorting and magnifying everything. Spinoza believed that all things wish to go on being what they are—stone wishes eternally to be stone, and tiger, to be tiger. I shall endure in Borges, not in myself (if, indeed, I am anybody at all), but I recognize myself less in his books than in many others'; or in the tedious strumming of a guitar. Years ago I tried to free myself from him, and I moved on from the mythologies of the slums and outskirts of the city to games with time and infinity, but those games belong to Borges now, and I shall have to think up other things. So my life is a point-counterpoint, a kind of fugue, and a falling away—and everything winds up being lost to me, and everything falls into oblivion, or into the hands of the other man.

    I am not sure which of us it is that's writing this page.

Timothy Liu
The Silence

She took the spareribs out of the oven
and set them steaming on a plate
before leaving her apartment.
I didn't know how long to wait,
tore into cold meat when I decided

my mother wasn't coming back.

*

No one knew about the gun she kept
in her purse until the authorities
called—a .38 caliber pistol
with a pearl handle and a trigger
even she could easily pull—
her car still waiting to be towed
from a roadside ditch

when they arrived on the scene.

*

Yesterday morning, I was leaning
over a kitchen sink, my husband
upstairs sleeping. Between his snores
muffled under a down comforter
and a portable electric heater that kept
our bedroom warm, I knew
I could sob as loud as I wanted

without disturbing his dreams.

*

At the sports arena between musical acts
and clouds of dope, I texted my lover
a wide-angle shot of the stage—
the reception bars on my phone
bouncing back and forth between high
and low—a text I had to send
several times before it went through
even though there was a chance
his phone would be off or the text get

lost for hours in the ether, even days.
The silence is the agony.

*

My therapist says: *It's not your fault.*
No way for you to have known
exactly where your mother was headed.

Then why am I left weeping
in my kitchen decades after the fact?

When I went upstairs and sat
beside my husband, he could feel
the mattress shift beneath our weight
even though I felt much lighter
after watching translucent ropes of snot
lowering down into the sink, arms
around me when I asked if he

was awake, knowing that he wasn't.

*

How many romances get derailed
when a text that has been sent
fails to go through? How many mothers
disappear through a kitchen door
never to return—the food on the table

the last meal they will ever serve?

*

My lover texted back: *where are you now?*
Having no idea what I'd been
going through when he texted again:

Wish I was there with you.

Mũkoma wa Ngũgĩ
Hunting Words with My Father [Preface]
(For my father's seventieth)

One morning I burst into my father's study and said
when I grow up, I too want to hunt, I want to hunt
words, and giraffes, pictures, buffalos, and books

and he, holding a pen and a cup of tea, said, *Little Father,
to hunt words can be dangerous—but still, it is best to start
early.* He waved his blue *bic-pen* and his office turned

into Nyandarua forest. It was morning, the mist rising
from the earth like breath as rays from the sun fell hard
on the ground like sharp nails. *Little Father, do you see*

him?—my father asked. No, I said. *Look again—the mist
is a mirror—do you see him?* And I looked again and
there was a Maasai warrior tall as the trees, spear in hand.

*Shadow him, feign his movements, shadow him until
his movements are your movements.* Running my feet
along the leaves I walked to where he was, crouched

like him so close to the earth, feet sinking deeper
into the earth as if in mud, turning and reading the wind
and fading into the mist till I became one with the forest.

For half a day we stayed like this—tired and hungry
I was ready for home. But my father said, *I did not say
this was easy—you cannot hunt words on a full stomach.*

And just as soon as he spoke there was a roar so loud
and stomping so harsh that hot underground streams broke
open like a dozen or so water pipes sending hissing,

steaming water high into the air. I turned to run
but the warrior stood his ground. As the roar
and thunder came closer, his hair braided and full of red

ochre turned into dreadlocks so long that they seemed like
roots running from the earth. When the transfiguration
was complete, before me stood a Mau Mau fighter, spear

in one hand, homemade gun in the other, eyes so red
that through the mist they looked like hot molten
cinders, the long dreadlocks a thousand thin

snakes in the wind, the leaves and grass and thorns
rushing past him. *You must help him, don't just stand
there, help him*—my father implored but just as soon

as I had closed my little hands into fists, the lion
appeared high up in the air, body stretched the whole
length as the Mau Mau fighter pulled the spear like

it was a long root from the earth. The lion, midair, tried
to stop, recoiled its talons to offer peace, but it was too
late and it let out another roar as its chest crushed

into the spear, breastplate giving way until the spear
had edged its way to the heart. Dying then dead
it continued its terrible arc and landed. I waved

and the picture stood still. My father came up to me
and asked, *Why have you stopped the hunt?* I said
"but we killed it—I have what we came for." I pointed

to where the Mau Mau warrior was pulling his spear
from the carcass, but my father shook his head and said
—You have done well but look closely—how can you

carry all that in a word? How can we carry that home?
It is too heavy. I laughed and said—"Father, you help me."
But he pointed to the ground, to a steady flow of a bright

thin red river furiously winding down from the grooves
of the spear to the earth. I too pointed, unable to speak
—the beauty larger than my imagination. I was confused.

I had no words. *Come, let us go home Little Father.*
When you are of age you shall find the words, he said.
But always be careful—to hunt a word is to hunt a life.

Layli Long Soldier
38

Here, the sentence will be respected.

I will compose each sentence with care, by minding what the rules of writing dictate.

For example, all sentences will begin with capital letters.

Likewise, the history of the sentence will be honored by ending each one with appropriate punctuation such as a period or question mark, thus bringing the idea to (momentary) completion.

You may like to know, I do not consider this a "creative piece."

I do not regard this as a poem of great imagination or a work of fiction.

Also, historical events will not be dramatized for an "interesting" read.

Therefore, I feel most responsible to the orderly sentence; conveyor of thought.

That said, I will begin.

You may or may not have heard about the Dakota 38.

If this is the first time you've heard of it, you might wonder, "What is the Dakota 38?"

The Dakota 38 refers to thirty-eight Dakota men who were executed by hanging, under orders from President Abraham Lincoln.

To date, this is the largest "legal" mass execution in US history.

The hanging took place on December 26, 1862—the day after Christmas.

This was the *same week* that President Lincoln signed the Emancipation Proclamation.

In the preceding sentence, I italicize "same week" for emphasis.

There was a movie titled *Lincoln* about the presidency of Abraham Lincoln.

The signing of the Emancipation Proclamation was included in the film *Lincoln*; the hanging of the Dakota 38 was not.

In any case, you might be asking, "Why were thirty-eight Dakota men hung?"

As a side note, the past tense of hang is *hung*, but when referring to the capital punishment of hanging, the correct past tense is *hanged*.

So it's possible that you're asking, "Why were thirty-eight Dakota men hanged?"

They were hanged for the Sioux Uprising.

I want to tell you about the Sioux Uprising, but I don't know where to begin.

I may jump around and details will not unfold in chronological order.

Keep in mind, I am not a historian.

So I will recount facts as best as I can, given limited resources and understanding.

Before Minnesota was a state, the Minnesota region, generally speaking, was the traditional homeland for Dakota, Anishinaabeg, and Ho-Chunk people.

During the 1800s, when the US expanded territory, they "purchased" land from the Dakota people as well as the other tribes.

But another way to understand that sort of "purchase" is: Dakota leaders ceded land to the US government in exchange for money or goods, but most importantly, the safety of their people.

Some say that Dakota leaders did not understand the terms they were entering, or they never would have agreed.

Even others call the entire negotiation "trickery."

But to make whatever-it-was official and binding, the US government drew up an initial treaty.

This treaty was later replaced by another (more convenient) treaty, and then another.

I've had difficulty unraveling the terms of these treaties, given the legal speak and congressional language.

As treaties were abrogated (broken) and new treaties were drafted, one after another, the new treaties often referenced old defunct treaties, and it is a muddy, switchback trail to follow.

Although I often feel lost on this trail, I know I am not alone.

However, as best as I can put the facts together, in 1851, Dakota territory was contained to a twelve-mile by one-hundred-fifty-mile long strip along the Minnesota River.

But just seven years later, in 1858, the northern portion was ceded (taken) and the southern portion was (conveniently) allotted, which reduced Dakota land to a stark ten-mile tract.

These amended and broken treaties are often referred to as the Minnesota Treaties.

The word *Minnesota* comes from *mni*, which means water; and *sota*, which means turbid.

Synonyms for turbid include muddy, unclear, cloudy, confused, and smoky.

Everything is in the language we use.

For example, a treaty is, essentially, a contract between two sovereign nations.

The US treaties with the Dakota Nation were legal contracts that promised money.

It could be said, this money was payment for the land the Dakota ceded; for living within assigned boundaries (a reservation); and for relinquishing rights to their vast hunting territory which, in turn, made Dakota people dependent on other means to survive: money.

The previous sentence is circular, akin to so many aspects of history.

As you may have guessed by now, the money promised in the turbid treaties did not make it into the hands of Dakota people.

In addition, local government traders would not offer credit to "Indians" to purchase food or goods.

Without money, store credit, or rights to hunt beyond their ten-mile tract of land, Dakota people began to starve.

The Dakota people were starving.

The Dakota people starved.

In the preceding sentence, the word "starved" does not need italics for emphasis.

One should read "The Dakota people starved" as a straightforward and plainly stated fact.

As a result—and without other options but to continue to starve—Dakota people retaliated.

Dakota warriors organized, struck out, and killed settlers and traders.

This revolt is called the Sioux Uprising.

Eventually, the US Cavalry came to Mnisota to confront the Uprising.

More than one thousand Dakota people were sent to prison.

As already mentioned, thirty-eight Dakota men were subsequently hanged.

After the hanging, those one thousand Dakota prisoners were released.

However, as further consequence, what remained of Dakota territory in Mnisota was dissolved (stolen).

The Dakota people had no land to return to.

This means they were exiled.

Homeless, the Dakota people of Mnisota were relocated (forced) onto reservations in South Dakota and Nebraska.

Now, every year, a group called the Dakota 38 + 2 Riders conduct a memorial horse ride from Lower Brule, South Dakota, to Mankato, Mnisota.

The Memorial Riders travel 325 miles on horseback for eighteen days, sometimes through sub-zero blizzards.

They conclude their journey on December 26, the day of the hanging.

Memorials help focus our memory on particular people or events.

Often, memorials come in the forms of plaques, statues, or gravestones.

The memorial for the Dakota 38 is not an object inscribed with words, but an *act*.

Yet, I started this piece because I was interested in writing about grasses.

So, there is one other event to include, although it's not in chronological order and we must backtrack a little.

When the Dakota people were starving, as you may remember, government traders would not extend store credit to "Indians."

One trader named Andrew Myrick is famous for his refusal to provide credit to Dakota people by saying, "If they are hungry, let them eat grass."

There are variations of Myrick's words, but they are all something to that effect.

When settlers and traders were killed during the Sioux Uprising, one of the first to be executed by the Dakota was Andrew Myrick.

When Myrick's body was found,

        his mouth was stuffed with grass.

I am inclined to call this act by the Dakota warriors a poem.

There's irony in their poem.

There was no text.

"Real" poems do not "really" require words.

I have italicized the previous sentence to indicate inner dialogue, a revealing moment.

But, on second thought, the words "Let them eat grass" click the gears of the poem into place.

So, we could also say, language and word choice are crucial to the poem's work.

Things are circling back again.

Sometimes, when in a circle, if I wish to exit, I must leap.

And let the body	swing.

From the platform.

                        Out

                                    to the grasses.

CRITICISM AND THEORY

If literary criticism is simply another kind of literature, then theory is its outline. That is a conditional sentence that sounds true. For truth is what theory, like philosophy, is after. But what if theory and criticism are not after anything more than fooling around—playing with words and concepts. Which of the two poems below holds more truth for you? The answer may separate you from other readers, other poets.

    Try this theoretical act: after reading Curt Anderson's ludic poem "Platonic Love," replace the theorists/critics in the poem with celebrities, or write a similar love poem using the names of political figures for verbs, nouns, etc. Afterward, consider how the process of making your new version deepened an understanding of the poem's narrative structure. Such an endeavor can be—yes—a kind of criticism.

David Ignatow
No Theory

No theory will stand up to a chicken's guts
being cleaned out, a hand rammed up
to pull out the wriggling entrails,
the green bile and the bloody liver;
no theory that does not grow sick
at the odor escaping.

Curt Anderson
Platonic Love

We dine at Adorno and return to my Beauvoir.
She compliments me on my Bachelard pad.
I pop in a Santayana CD and Saussure back to the couch.
On my way, I pull out two fine Kristeva wine glasses.
I pour some Merleau-Ponty and return the Aristotle to Descartes.
After pausing an Unamuno, I wrap my arm around her Hegel.
Her hair smells of wild Lukacs and Labriola.
Our small talk expands to include Dewey, Moore and Kant.
I confess to her what's in my Eckhart. We Locke.
By this point, we're totally Blavatsky.
We stretch out on the Schopenhauer.
She slips out of her Lyotard and I fumble with my Levi-Strauss.
She unhooks her Buber and I pull off my Spinoza.
I run my finger along her Heraclitus as she fondles my Bacon.
She stops to ask me if I brought any Kierkegaard. I nod.
We Foucault.
She lights a cigarette and compares Foucault to Lacan.
I roll over and Derrida.

PESSOA

We might think of Fernando Pessoa as the Portuguese love-child of Emily Dickinson and Walt Whitman: a figure of inward thought and burgeoning externalities all wrapped into one. Or more accurately, wrapped into hundreds of personas. Pessoa, in Portuguese, means "person" but he seems to have been many persons, at least on the page and in his literary and textual worlds. Why did he do this? Perhaps Pessoa invented these personas, who even argued with each other in literary magazines, because that's where meaning lay for him—in voluminous and continuous play. If we need evidence, there are more than 30,000 pages and scraps of writing he left scholars to pore over. On one of those scraps he wrote: *Be plural like the universe!* Thus, we might view his personae not as masks of disguise but as affirmations of who he was. There may be no poet who so defies and rarifies a poet's biography as this one called Pessoa. (The poems below are all translated from the Portuguese by Richard Zenith.)

Autopsychography

The poet is a faker
Who's so good at his act
He even fakes the pain
Of pain he feels in fact.

And those who read his words
Will feel in his writing
Neither of the pains he has
But just the one they're missing.

And so around its track
This thing called the heart winds,
A little clockwork train
To entertain our minds.

Others Narrate with Lyres or Harps

Others narrate with lyres or harps;
   I tell with my thought.
For he finds nothing, who through music
   Finds only what he feels.
Words weigh more which, carefully measured,
   Say that the world exists.

The Tobacco Shop

I'm nothing.
I'll always be nothing.
I can't want to be something.
But I have in me all the dreams of the world.

Windows of my room,
The room of one of the world's millions nobody knows
(And if they knew me, what would they know?),
You open onto the mystery of a street continually crossed by people,
A street inaccessible to any and every thought,
Real, impossibly real, certain, unknowingly certain,
With the mystery of things beneath the stones and beings,
With death making the walls damp and the hair of men white,
With Destiny driving the wagon of everything down the road of nothing.

Today I'm defeated, as if I'd learned the truth.
Today I'm lucid, as if I were about to die
And had no greater kinship with things
Than to say farewell, this building and this side of the street becoming
A row of train cars, with the whistle for departure
Blowing in my head
And my nerves jolting and bones creaking as we pull out.

Today I'm bewildered, like a man who wondered and discovered and forgot.
Today I'm torn between the loyalty I owe
To the outward reality of the Tobacco Shop across the street
And to the inward reality of my feeling that everything's a dream.

I failed in everything.
Since I had no ambition, perhaps I failed in nothing.
I left the education I was given,
Climbing down from the window at the back of the house.
I went to the country with big plans.
But all I found was grass and trees,
And when there were people they were just like others.
I step back from the window and sit in a chair. What should I think about?

How should I know what I'll be, I who don't know what I am?
Be what I think? But I think of being so many things!
And there are so many who think of being the same thing that we can't all be it!
Genius? At this moment
A hundred thousand brains are dreaming they're geniuses like me,
And it may be that history won't remember even one,
All of their imagined conquests amounting to so much dung.
No, I don't believe in me.
Insane asylums are full of lunatics with certainties!
Am I, who have no certainties, more right or less right?
No, not even in me …
 In how many garrets and non-garrets of the world
Are self-convinced geniuses at this moment dreaming?
How many lofty and noble and lucid aspirations
—Yes, truly lofty and noble and lucid
And perhaps even attainable—
Will never see the true light of day or find a sympathetic ear?
The world is for those born to conquer it,
Not for those who dream they can conquer it, even if they're right.
I've done more in dreams than Napoleon.

I've held more humanities against my hypothetical breast than Christ.
I've secretly invented philosophies such as Kant never wrote.
But I am, and perhaps will always be, the man in the garret,
Even though I don't live in one.
I'll always be *the one who wasn't born for that*;
I'll always be merely *the one who had qualities*;
I'll always be the one who waited for a door to open in a wall without doors
And sang the song of the Infinite in a chicken coop
And heard the voice of God in a covered well.
Believe in me? No, not in anything.
Let Nature pour over my seething head

Its sun, its rain, and the wind that finds my hair,
And let the rest come if it will or must, or let it not come.
Cardiac slaves of the stars,
We conquered the whole world before getting out of bed,
But we woke up and it's hazy,
We got up and it's alien,
We went outside and it's the entire earth
Plus the solar system and the Milky Way and the Indefinite.

(Eat your chocolates, little girl,
Eat your chocolates!
Believe me, there's no metaphysics on earth like chocolates,
And all religions put together teach no more than the candy shop.
Eat, dirty little girl, eat!
If only I could eat chocolates with the same truth as you!
But I think and, removing the silver paper that's tinfoil,
I throw it all on the ground, as I've thrown out life.)

But at least, from my bitterness over what I'll never be,
There remains the hasty writing of these verses,
A broken gateway to the Impossible.
But at least I confer on myself a contempt without tears,
Noble at least in the sweeping gesture by which I fling
The dirty laundry that's me—with no list—into the stream of things,
And I stay at home, shirtless.

(O my consoler, who doesn't exist and therefore consoles,
Be you a Greek goddess, conceived as a living statue,
Or a patrician woman of Rome, impossibly noble and dire,
Or a princess of the troubadours, all charm and grace,
Or an eighteenth-century marchioness, décolleté and aloof,
Or a famous courtesan from our parents' generation,
Or something modern, I can't quite imagine what—
Whatever all of this is, whatever you are, if you can inspire, then inspire me!
My heart is a poured-out bucket.
In the same way invokers of spirits invoke spirits, I invoke
My own self and find nothing.
I go to the window and see the street with absolute clarity.
I see the shops, I see the sidewalks, I see the passing cars,
I see the clothed living beings who pass each other.
I see the dogs that also exist,
And all of this weighs on me like a sentence of exile,
And all of this is foreign, like everything else.)

I've lived, studied, loved, and even believed,
And today there's not a beggar I don't envy just because he isn't me.

I look at the tatters and sores and falsehood of each one,
And I think: perhaps you never lived or studied or loved or believed
(For it's possible to do all of this without having done any of it);
Perhaps you've merely existed, as when a lizard has its tail cut off
And the tail keeps on twitching, without the lizard.
I made of myself what I was no good at making,
And what I could have made of myself I didn't.
I put on the wrong costume
And was immediately taken for someone I wasn't, and I said nothing and was lost.
When I went to take off the mask,
It was stuck to my face.
When I got it off and saw myself in the mirror,
I had already grown old.
I was drunk and no longer knew how to wear the costume that I hadn't taken off.
I threw out the mask and slept in the closet
Like a dog tolerated by the management
Because it's harmless,
And I'll write down this story to prove I'm sublime.

Musical essence of my useless verses,
If only I could look at you as something I had made
Instead of always looking at the Tobacco Shop across the street,
Trampling on my consciousness of existing,
Like a rug a drunkard stumbles on
Or a doormat stolen by gypsies and it's not worth a thing.

But the Tobacco Shop Owner has come to the door and is standing there.
I look at him with the discomfort of a half-twisted neck
Compounded by the discomfort of a half-grasping soul.
He will die and I will die.
He'll leave his signboard, I'll leave my poems.
His sign will also eventually die, and so will my poems.
Eventually the street where the sign was will die,
And so will the language in which my poems were written.
Then the whirling planet where all of this happened will die.

On other planets of other solar systems something like people
Will continue to make things like poems and to live under things like signs,
Always one thing facing the other,
Always one thing as useless as the other,
Always the impossible as stupid as reality,
Always the inner mystery as true as the mystery sleeping on the surface.
Always this thing or always that, or neither one thing nor the other.

But a man has entered the Tobacco Shop (to buy tobacco?),
And plausible reality suddenly hits me.
I half rise from my chair—energetic, convinced, human—
And will try to write these verses in which I say the opposite.

I light up a cigarette as I think about writing them,
And in that cigarette I savor a freedom from all thought.
My eyes follow the smoke as if it were my own trail
And I enjoy, for a sensitive and fitting moment,
A liberation from all speculation
And an awareness that metaphysics is a consequence of not feeling very well.
Then I lean back in the chair
And keep smoking.
As long as Destiny permits, I'll keep smoking.

(If I married my washwoman's daughter
Perhaps I would be happy.)
I get up from the chair. I go to the window.

The man has come out of the Tobacco Shop (putting change into his pocket?).
Ah, I know him: it's unmetaphysical Esteves.
(The Tobacco Shop Owner has come to the door.)
As if by divine instinct, Esteves turns around and sees me.
He waves hello, I shout back "Hello, Esteves!" and the universe
Falls back into place without ideals or hopes, and the Owner of the Tobacco
    Shop smiles.

POLITICAL POETRY

Like it or not, politics will come to you. Perhaps you will ignore what you see and read, feeling overwhelmed and checking out. Perhaps you will feel a certain responsibility to do something, then seek out a means to act on that feeling. None of this demands that you must like reading (or writing) political poems. Sometimes poems categorized as political will seem like obvious protests or lame lamentations. Sometimes poems that are not categorized as political will seem to be full of ideology or bias or subversive takes.

Below you will find poems that try to move beyond simple sermons or "bearing witness" as they employ sarcasm, tragicomedy, or abstract thinking, in a struggle to make meaning out of political trouble. As you read, consider these fundamental questions: Is the "role of the poet" in your society different from the "role of the citizen"? If so, how? If not, why not?

Bernadette Mayer
The Tragic Condition of the Statue of Liberty

A collaboration with Emma Lazarus

Give me your tired, your poor,
Your huddled masses yearning to breathe free,
The wretched refuse of your teeming shore.
Send these, the homeless, tempest-tost to me,
I lift my lamp beside the golden door!
Give me your gentrificatees of the Lower East Side including all the well-heeled young Europeans who'll take apartments without leases
Give me your landlords, give me your cooperators
Give me the guys who sell the food and the computers to the public schools in District One
Give me the IRS-FBI-CIA men who don't take election day off
Give me the certain members of the school board & give me the district superintendent
Give me all the greedy members of both american & foreign capitalist religious sects
Give me the parents of the punk people
Give me the guy who puts those stickers in the Rice Krispies
Give me the doctor who thinks his time is more valuable than mine and my daughter's & the time of all the other non-doctors in this world
Give me the mayor, his mansion, and the president & his white house
Give me the cops who laugh and sneer at meetings where they demonstrate the new uses of mace and robots instead of the old murder against people who are being evicted
Give me the landlord's sleazy lawyers and the deal-making judges in housing court & give me the landlord's arsonist
Give me the known & unknown big important rich guys who now bank on our quaint neighborhood
Give me, forgive me, the writers who have already or want to write bestsellers in this country
Together we will go to restore Ellis Island, ravaged for years by wind, weather and vandals
I was surprised and saddened when I heard that the Statue of Liberty was in such a serious state of disrepair & I want to help
This is the most generous contribution I can afford.

Julia Vinograd
Ginsberg

No blame. Anyone who wrote *Howl* and *Kaddish*
earned the right to make any possible mistake
for the rest of his life.
I just wish I hadn't made this mistake with him.

It was during the Vietnam war
and he was giving a great protest reading
in Washington Square Park
and nobody wanted to leave.
So Ginsberg got the idea, "I'm going to shout
'the war is over' as loud as I can," he said
"and all of you run over the city
in different directions
yelling the war is over, shout it in offices,
shops, everywhere and when enough people
believe the war is over
why, not even the politicians
will be able to keep it going."
I thought it was a great idea at the time,
a truly poetic idea.
So when Ginsberg yelled I ran down the street
and leaned in the doorway
of the sort of respectable down on its luck cafeteria
where librarians and minor clerks have lunch
and I yelled "the war is over."
And a little old lady looked up
from her cottage cheese and fruit salad.
She was so ordinary she would have been invisible
except for the terrible light
filling her face as she whispered
"My son. My son is coming home."
I got myself out of there and was sick in some bushes.
That was the first time I believed there was a war.

Jameson Fitzpatrick
The Last Analysis; or, I Woke Up

and it was political.
I made coffee and the coffee was political.
I took a shower and the water was.
I walked down the street in short shorts and a Bob Mizer tank top
and they were political, the walking and the shorts and the beefcake
silkscreen of the man posing in a G-string. I forgot my sunglasses
and later, on the train, that was political,
when I studied every handsome man in the car.
Who I thought was handsome was political.
I went to work at the university and everything was
very obviously political, the department and the institution.

All the cigarettes I smoked between classes were political,
where I threw them when I was through.
I was blond and it was political.
So was the difference between "blond" and "blonde."
I had long hair and it was political. I shaved my head and it was.
That I didn't know how to grieve when another person was killed in America
was political, and it was political when America killed another person,
who they were and what color and gender and who I am in relation.
I couldn't think about it for too long without feeling a helplessness
like childhood. I was a child and it was political, being a boy
who was bad at it. I couldn't catch and so the ball became political.
My mother read to me almost every night
and the conditions that enabled her to do so were political.
That my father's money was new was political, that it was proving something.
Someone called me faggot and it was political.
I called myself a faggot and it was political.
How difficult my life felt relative to how difficult it was
was political. I thought I could become a writer
and it was political that I could imagine it.
I thought I was not a political poet and still
my imagination was political.
It had been, this whole time I was asleep.

Dunya Mikhail
The War Works Hard

How magnificent the war is!
How eager
and efficient!
Early in the morning,
it wakes up the sirens
and dispatches ambulances
to various places,
swings corpses through the air,
rolls stretchers to the wounded,
summons rain
from the eyes of mothers,
digs into the earth
dislodging many things
from under the ruins ...
Some are lifeless and glistening,
others are pale and still throbbing ...
It produces the most questions

in the minds of children,
entertains the gods
by shooting fireworks and missiles
into the sky,
sows mines in the fields
and reaps punctures and blisters,
urges families to emigrate,
stands beside the clergymen
as they curse the devil
(poor devil, he remains
with one hand in the searing fire) …
The war continues working, day and night.
It inspires tyrants
to deliver long speeches,
awards medals to generals
and themes to poets
it contributes to the industry
of artificial limbs,
provides food for flies,
adds pages to the history books,
achieves equality
between killer and killed,
teaches lovers to write letters,
accustoms young women to waiting,
fills the newspapers
with articles and pictures,
builds new houses
for the orphans,
invigorates the coffin makers,
gives grave diggers
a pat on the back
and paints a smile on the leader's face.
The war works with unparalleled diligence!
Yet no one gives it
a word of praise.

Edmond Jabès (translated from the French by Rosmarie Waldrop)
from *The Little Book of Unsuspected Subversion*

> Subversion is the very movement of writing: the very movement of death.
>
> The written page is no mirror. To write means to confront an unknown face.
>
> Driven mad, the sea, unable to die in a single wave.

~

Blank, like a name left blank.

~

"What is subversion?"
"Perhaps, in the rose that you adore, the least obtrusive thorn."

The book thrusts its rhythm on the body, the mind.

Free rein, then, for subversion.

Whatever you do, it is yourself you hope to save. It is yourself you lose.

Truth knows all shades of subversions.

"If our place is what detains us, mine will in the end have been a fetter, a humiliating hobble," he said.

For place, all you will have had is the hope of a mild place beyond the sands: a mirage of repose.

Life adds. Death subtracts.

> *(All creation takes for its place an enclosed space*
> *surrounded by the infinite.*
> *I shall have torn down walls everywhere, offering to my books, beyond their own*
> *space, an infinite, forbidden space.)*

There is a time for allegiance. March time or mark time.
Subversion always demands our immediate, full commitment.

Subversion never relents. You stop it by making it shift targets.

Like the dark at the foot of night, subversion can issue only onto itself.

To live means to adopt the subversion of the moment; to die, the irreversible subversion of eternity.

"The cadence of subversion. Ah, I had to find again this cadence," he said.

You have not created. In your small sphere of action, God-like, you create but for the moment.

Subversion is a pact with the future.

"At its peak subversion is so natural, so innocent, that I might be tempted to consider it one of the privileged moments when our precarious balance is restored," he also said.

Menace is illegible.

~

If the word enlightens, silence does not obscure: it regenerates.

Banality is not harmless: blue shark.

> ("*Banality is no stranger to subversion. An ally of time, which discounts it, it is subversion banalized,*" he said.)

Subversion hates disorder. It is itself righteous order as opposed to reactionary order.

Knowledge knocks against the cold scope of ignorance, like sunbeams on the mirroring sea, dumbfounded by its depth.

> (*There are no exceptional actions. There are only natural actions, but among them some major, some mediocre.*
>
> *There is creation.*)

AESTHETICS

Did Thoreau love nature for nature's own sake? Or did he traipse paths, meadows, and woods every day because he couldn't tolerate the small talk of people and the tedium of society? Even if you could argue both were the case, don't you long to find one *more* true than the other? Aesthetics comes down to similar decisions, or if not actual decisions, then proclivities based as often on intuition as on discernment.

Alice Duer Miller's "Why We Oppose Pockets for Women" underscores how aesthetics can be enforced as much by "utility" as by sheer convention and oppression. By turns, Mitsuharu Kaneko's "Opposition" plays with the idea of opposition as a force of aesthetics, no matter the utility. And Jason Schneiderman's "Dramaturgy" complicates the notion of what a guiding force is at all. His poem's title already sets us on a winding course; a dramaturgy is a complex concept about how a play functions. Is theater a metaphor for life, or is life itself all theater? (Cf. Shakespeare's "All the world's a stage, / And all the men and women merely players.") This would seem to be a significant aesthetic choice.

By the end of Schneiderman's poem, what are we to understand about how art is made from life and, by turns, how life should or should not be a work of art? Does one merely reflect the other? Can art change one's life, not by reflecting life back, but giving life a process akin to art-making?

Alice Duer Miller
Why We Oppose Pockets for Women

1. Because pockets are not a natural right.
2. Because the great majority of women do not want pockets. If they did they would have them.

3. Because whenever women have had pockets they have not used them.
4. Because women are required to carry enough things as it is, without the additional burden of pockets.
5. Because it would make dissension between husband and wife as to whose pockets were to be filled.
6. Because it would destroy man's chivalry toward woman, if he did not have to carry all her things in his pockets.
7. Because men are men, and women are women. We must not fly in the face of nature.
8. Because pockets have been used by men to carry tobacco, pipes, whiskey flasks, chewing gum and compromising letters. We see no reason to suppose that women would use them more wisely.

Mitsuharu Kaneko (translated from the Japanese by Loren Goodman)
Opposition

When I was a boy
I opposed school.
And now, again
I oppose work.

Above all, I hate things
Like health and justice.
Nothing makes a person more heartless
Than being healthy and righteous.

Of course I'm opposed to the Japanese spirit.
And duty and compassion make me vomit.
I always oppose government,
And turn my back on literary and artistic circles.

If you ask me why I was born,
I'll answer without hesitation: to oppose.
When I'm in the East,
I want to go West,

I wear my kimono left over right, shoes right left,
Hakama backwards, and ride a horse ass-first.
What others hate, I like.
What I especially dislike is when we're all in sync.

I believe this: opposition in life
Is the only honorable thing.
To oppose is to live.
To oppose is to get a grasp on oneself.

Jason Schneiderman
Dramaturgy

I'm writing a play about a Kommandant at Auschwitz
who recognizes one of the Jewish prisoners
as a famous poet, and as the Kommandant
has poetic aspirations himself, he pulls the prisoner
away from the work detail to receive poetry lessons
from the celebrated Jewish writer. The bulk of the play
is their discussions of poetry, which the poet
is initially reluctant to have, the power differential
being so stark, and though he flatters the Kommandant
at first, when he begins to see his Nazi pupil's
true devotion to the art, as well as his untrained
and untapped talent, he goes to work in earnest,
and at times they are both simply lovers
of the German language, though the truth of their
situation often interrupts. In the last act,
the Kommandant is on trial for his crimes,
and in the days before he is to be executed,
he begs the poet to publish his work under his own name—
the Nazi's writing under the Jew's name—
because as a Nazi, he feels his own name is disgraced,
but he believes so strongly in poetry that it matters
more to him that his work survive than that anyone
know it was his work. The play is pulled entirely
from my imagination, a careful rereading
of Simon Wiesenthal's *The Sunflower*, and the poetic ideas
of Rilke and Goethe, with a smattering of Nietzsche.
In readings of the play, the Kommandant
has seemed more noble than I had intended—in many ways,
more noble than the Jew, because the Jew is suffering
by no fault of his own, while the Kommandant is tortured
by conscience, and driven by a sense of poetic calling
that separates him from the Germans around him.
On the morning of the third workshop reading, I watched
a video of two Russians on an ice-dancing reality show
performing as Jews in Auschwitz. I was sickened,
even though I couldn't follow the pantomimed action,
and I wondered if I was producing Holocaust kitsch myself,
if my work was as disgusting as theirs, though I knew
if I asked any of my team, they would reassure me
that I am doing important work that rises to the level
of art. Last night, during a break in the workshop of the play,

I told the story of how my grandmother, upon learning
that her entire family had died in the camps,
had burned the photo albums of everyone she had loved.
I have told that story many, many times,
without feeling much more than regret, or sympathy,
but this time I broke down crying, and I couldn't stop.
Everyone at the table came to comfort me,
and I felt ridiculous, but the only thing I could say was,
"It's time for us to go. This isn't a place we can live anymore."
I left the studio embarrassed, and later that day,
I resigned from the production. I don't think they believed
that I was serious, and they'll expect me to show up
at the next table reading. I won't. The play will go on
though I can have nothing more to do with it.
This morning, after taking a shirt off the hanger,
I looked in the mirror and realized I hadn't put it on.
Without thinking, I had started packing a bag.

READER RESPONSE

One way to talk about a poem is to talk about how you relate to it. How you may identify with the speaker of it, like a main character in a story or movie. Or how you share the emotions running through the poem. Or how you are sympathetic to a particular situation, event, or character in the poem because you've had similar experiences.

But what if you don't relate to a particular poem in any of these ways? Or what if the way you relate to the poem is by taking a different or opposing viewpoint? What then? Do you chuck the poem aside, spit in its eye, take it out back, and smack it around a little, before burying it at the back of the bookshelf? That would be one method of readerly response. All reading, in one way or another, is call-and-response. The call is the set of words on the page, and the response is your reaction in reading them.

But here is the thing: *you have the ability to relate to anything.* Your imagination is as powerful as any reality you have experienced or are presently experiencing. If you have a certain response to a poem—especially an adverse one—have it. Let it run its course. Then, re-read the poem, questioning what you think you know about it in order to enter the poem on its own terms.

The following poems illustrate differences in and of points-of-view. But they also highlight what we bring to a poem before we read it, and what is possible after we let a poem open us up to new ways of relating.

Miroslav Holub
Napoleon

Children, when was
Napoleon Bonaparte born,
asks teacher.

A thousand years ago, the children say.
A hundred years ago, the children say.
Last year, the children say.
No one knows.

Children, what did
Napoleon Bonaparte do,
asks teacher.

Won a war, the children say.
Lost a war, the children say.
No one knows.

Our butcher had a dog
called Napoleon,
says František.
The butcher used to beat him and the dog died
of hunger
a year ago.

And all the children are now sorry
for Napoleon.

Edward Mullany
A Rugged Coast

"Why do you hate nature?" asked the boy's stepmother, who didn't actually believe the boy hated nature, but believed he wanted her to believe that he hated nature.

"He doesn't hate nature," said his father.

They were looking out at the sea, a wind was blowing in their faces, and it was cold.

"How do you know what I hate?" said the boy.

"He knows what you hate because he's your father," said his stepmother lightheartedly.

"No," said his father. "I know what he hates because he's my son."

Lynn Emanuel
The Politics of Narrative: Why I Am a Poet

Jill's a good kid who's had some tough luck. But that's another story. It's a day when the smell of fish from Tib's hash house is so strong you could build a garage on it. We are sitting in Izzy's where Carl has just built us a couple of solid highballs. He's okay, Carl is, if you don't count his Roamin' Hands and Rushin' Fingers. Then again, that should be the only trouble we have in this life. Anyway, Jill says, "Why don't you tell about it? Nobody ever gets the poet's point of view." I don't know, maybe she's right. Jill's just a kid, but she's been around; she knows what's what.

So, I tell Jill, we are at Izzy's just like now when he comes in. And the first thing I notice is his hair, which has been Vitalis-ed into submission. But, honey, it won't work, and it gives him a kind of rumpled your-boudoir-or-mine look. I don't know why I noticed that before I noticed his face. Maybe it was just the highballs doing the looking. Anyway, then I see his face, and I'm telling you—I'm telling Jill—this is a masterpiece of a face.

But—and this is the god's own truth—I'm tired of beauty. Really. I know, given all that happened, this must sound kind of funny, but it made me tired just to look at him. That's how beautiful he was, and how much he spelled T-R-O-U-B-L-E. So I threw him back. I mean, I didn't say it, I say to Jill, with my mouth. But I said it with my eyes and my shoulders. I said it with my heart. I said, Honey, I'm throwing you back. And looking back, that was the worst, I mean, the worst thing—bar none—that I could have done, because it drew him like horseshit draws flies. I mean, he didn't walk over and say, "Hello, girls; hey, you with the dark hair, your indifference draws me like horseshit draws flies."

But he said it with his eyes. And then he smiled. And that smile was a gas station on a dark night. And as wearying as all the rest of it. I am many things, but dumb isn't one of them. And here is where I say to Jill, "I just can't go on." I mean, how we get from the smile into the bedroom, how it all happens, and what all happens, just bores me. I am a conceptual storyteller. In fact, I'm a conceptual liver. I prefer the cookbook to the actual meal. Feeling bores me. That's why I write poetry. In poetry you just give the instructions to the reader and say, "Reader, you go on from here." And what I like about poetry is its readers, because those are giving people. I mean, those are people you can trust to get the job done. They pull their own weight. If I had to have someone at my back in a dark alley, I'd want it to be a poetry reader. They're not like some people, who maybe do it right if you tell them, "Put this foot down, and now put that one in front of the other, button your coat, wipe your nose."

So, really, I do it for the readers who work hard and, I feel, deserve something better than they're used to getting. I do it for the working stiff. And I write for people, like myself, who are just tired of the trickle-down theory where somebody spends pages and pages on some fat book where everything including the draperies, which happen to be *burnt orange*, are described, and, further, are some *metaphor* for something. And this whole boggy waste trickles down to the reader in the form of a little burp of feeling. God, I hate prose. I think the average reader likes ideas.

"A sentence, unlike a line, is not a station of the cross." I said this to the poet Mark Strand. I said, "I could not stand to write prose; I could not stand to have to write things like 'the draperies were burnt orange and the carpet was brown.'" And he said, "You could do it if that's all you did, if that was the beginning and the end of your novel." So please, don't ask me for a little trail of bread crumbs to get from the smile to the bedroom, and from the bedroom to the death at the end, although you can ask me a lot about death. That's all I like, the very beginning and the very end. I haven't got the stomach for the rest of it.

I don't think many people do. But, like me, they're either too afraid or too polite to say so. That's why the movies are such a disaster. Now *there's* a form of popular culture that doesn't have a clue. Movies should be five minutes long. You should go in, see a couple of shots, maybe a room with orange draperies and a rug. A voice-over would say, "I'm having a hard time getting Raoul from the hotel room into the elevator." And, bang, that's the end. The lights come on, everybody walks out full of sympathy because this is a shared experience. Everybody in that theater knows how hard it is to get Raoul from the hotel room into the elevator. Everyone has had to do boring, dogged work. Everyone has lived a life that seems to inflict every vivid moment the smears, fingerings, and pawings of plot and feeling. Everyone has lived under this oppression. In other words, everyone has had to eat shit—day after day, the endless meals they didn't want, those dark, half-gelatinous lakes of gravy that lay on the plate like an ugly rug and that wrinkled clump of reddish-orange roast beef that looks like it was dropped onto your plate from a great height. God what a horror: getting Raoul into the elevator.

And that's why I write poetry. In poetry, you don't do that kind of work.

Wang Ping
The Price of a Finger

With your right hand, you slip
strips of metal under a hammer
backed by four-thousand pounds
of pressure; with your left, you
sweep molded parts into a pile.
You do this once a second for a
ten-hour shift, minus a half-hour
lunch. You must concentrate. You
must not lose a beat, or it's all
over.

—Wang Chenghua, migrant
worker with crushed fingers

> Construct the World's Biggest Market
>
> Build an International Shopping Heaven
>
> —Neon banners on Yiwu World Trade Center

China makes 80% of the toys sold in America.

> Yiwu, the most exciting city in Zhejiang Province, makes trinkets that fill stores the world over. Five-hundred-thousand migrant workers live in and around this city of six-hundred-forty-thousand residents.

You tell them to pay attention and they don't listen. They have no culture or education. They are told many times to be safe and they just don't get it.

—Shi Yanxin, owner of Hua Xin Electronics

At fourteen, my son left to work in the city. Fifteen years later, he still borrows money to look for jobs. To make money, you have to leave the village. Nobody has made much, but we can't go back. There's nothing left at home. Everything is broken, broken.

—Cai Songquan, farmer from Caijia Village

> Yongkang, the hardware capital of China, with seven-thousand private-owned factories making hinges, hubcaps, pots, power drills, thermoses, plugs, headphones, filling the shelves of Walmarts with products that

> get better and cheaper each year.
> "Eternal health" in Chinese,
> Yongkang is also the dismem-
> berment capital, with two
> thousand five hundred accidents
> each year, and thousands more
> unreported.

The riskiest jobs, as in war, go
to green recruits, fresh from the
farm. Young migrants are hired
at the train station to run metal-
stampers, molders, and high-pres-
sure hammers driven by flywheels.
Few workers last a month.

> We have always met the gov-
> ernment's standards for safety.
> Otherwise, they would not let us
> operate.
>
> —Kang Ziying, lawyer for
> Lucky Gem and Jewelry

Of course life has improved. We
couldn't have imagined any of this
ten years ago. This small town with
mud houses now has an airport, a
world trade center, skyscrapers, hun-
dreds of factories, hotels—including
two Middle Eastern restaurants with
belly dancers. We hardly had any
education, but our daughter studies
marketing in college.

—Jin Xiaoqin, Yiwu factory owner

> From their rice paddies, the vil-
> lagers watch trucks whiz by on
> the new cross-national superhigh-
> way, carrying goods made by their
> teenage sons and daughters far
> away, goods they will never see.

And they've been pushing down the
rates. We used to get 3.5 fen per toy
but now they are just paying 2.5 fen,

less than one-tenth of an American penny. When the orders are high, we work fourteen hours a day, seven days a week, and might clear $120 in a month. More typical is $90 a month and in a slow month, $50. It's not enough to get by.

—Cai Gaoxiang, migrant worker at Yiwu Toys

> You have no right to speak. You have no right to organize.
>
> —Hu Xu, owner of Xu Xing Metals

Each eyelash is assembled from 464 inch-long strands of human hair, placed in a crisscross pattern on a thin strip of transparent glue. It takes an hour to complete a pair. We work fourteen-hour shifts, but can't make enough for a bonus.

—Wei Qi, sixteen-year-old migrant worker from Anshan

> Kin Ki and other big producers have come under greater pressure to adhere to global labor codes. They open their doors to foreign inspectors to assuage concerns that products used to entertain children in rich countries are not made under oppressive conditions in poor ones.

Life was poorer under Mao— you were lucky if you had a pair of pants, but it was more equal.

— Cai Songquan, farmer from Cai Jia Village

> The goal conflicts with price pressures in commodity industries like toys, where manufacturers

command no premium for good labor practices. China alone has eight-thousand toy makers competing fiercely for contracts by shaving pennies off production costs.

I keep this job because my parents and my daughter depend on the money I earn. No one likes to work in these conditions, but I have no choice.

—Anonymous migrant worker

Kin Ki stays competitive, workers say, by paying them twenty-four cents an hour in Shenzhen, where the minimum wage is thirty-three cents. When the Etch A Sketch line shut down in Ohio just after the Christmas rush in 2000, wages for the unionized work force there had reached $9.00 an hour.

Ours is a typical story. From small to big, from middleman to producer of goods, from a mud house in the country to a four-story house in town, from carrying goods on our shoulders to a motorcycle eight years ago and, last year, a van.

—Jin Xiaoqin, owner of Yiwu Toy

I came to China about a decade ago because Korean companies could no longer compete in the market for false eyelashes, which sell for as little as fifty cents a set in Asia and the U.S.A.

—Lee Yo Han, South Korean entrepreneur

I summon my boy to my bed. He starts crying before I open my mouth. He knows he must now quit his dream of college and find a job. He's fourteen; it's time to help the family. I start crying too. But what else can we do? I'm on the threshold of death and our money is running out. This is our only choice. This is our fate.

—Hu, migrant worker with silicosis

> Mary and Jesus are hot. Sell like crazy. We ship them in giant containers. The real problem is the eyes. To do it right, you have to paint them by hand. That's what Americans care about, the tears in Mary's eyes, the sorrow.
>
> —Jin Xiaoqin, owner of Yiwu Plastic Factory

Caijia Village, the incubating ground for the Communist revolution in Jiangxi Province at the beginning of the twentieth century, now provides young people for the booming industrial towns on the coast, joining the two-hundred-fifty-million migrant workforce nationwide from China's interior.

CLASSROOM READING

Remember when the English teacher made you and your classmates go around the room, each student having to read a sentence or paragraph or, god forbid, a soliloquy by a character in a play? This was and still is terrifying for some people; others somehow relish the deed. Classroom reading is, if nothing else, a performative act.

Thus, read the poem below out loud. Now. If you are alone, do it anyway. If you are in class, do a Quaker reading—which means whoever feels inspired or compelled to read out loud begins to do so. If nobody feels such an urge, allow silence to speak—to you, for others, and especially to and for whoever wrote the poem. Do not even consider abandoning the poem until it's been read aloud all the way to the end. Think of this as positive peer pressure.

Lucy Ives
Early Poem

The first sentence is a sentence about writing. The second sentence tells you it's alright to lose interest. You might be one of those people who sits back in his or her chair without interest, and this would have been the third sentence you would have read. The fourth sentence, what does that say, that says something about how I genuinely feel, even if it no longer matters how I genuinely feel, that has not even become the topic of another book. The fifth sentence says that that was left by the wayside because it was such a variable thing. That's what the sixth sentence said, and says, that it sits there still, varying, changing its colors, etc., the army of ancient Rome marches by, they think it is some sort of tomb and display their eagle insignia. The seventh sentence ill conceals its surprise that I should have tried to make it all look so far away. The eighth sentence is therefore a meditation on something close at hand. The ninth sentence is a means of approach. In the tenth sentence I discover I am staring at a list of things I have done written in blue pencil on brown paper. In the eleventh sentence I draw a one-eyed duck on the paper beside the list. In the twelfth sentence I circle one of the numbers on the list and I start to feel nervous. In the thirteenth sentence I realize I have chosen something. In the fourteenth sentence I decide I will read my choice aloud. In the fifteenth sentence I stall by saying the words "I don't have a choice." In the sixteenth sentence I stall again by thinking about the obelisk on the Upper East Side in Central Park and how it is called "Cleopatra's Needle," and how around the base of the "needle" there are metal supports in the shape of crustaceans, I think they are crabs in fact but sometimes that word is slightly obscene so I consider not writing it. In the seventeenth sentence I think some more about the kinds of joke that employ that word and whether it is worth thinking about such jokes, as it does alter the genre of what you are writing if such things are allowed to be thought as a part of it. The lawns of the park were very green in summer, and it is early summer right now, right as I think to think this, and this is the first time I have lived in New York City for a full year in ten years, this is what I tell as the nineteenth sentence. In the twentieth sentence I recall the list and resolve again to look at it. In the twentifirst sentence I misspell twenty-first with two "i"s. In the twenty-second sentence I look down at the list, I have circled no. 18759351 on the list. In the twentisecond sentence I misspell twenty-second using an "i" again. In the twenty-third sentence I read what is written next to no. 18759351, it says, "He was sitting on a bench …, " but at this moment a breeze enters in through the open window, lifting the page and you begin reading another line, the words, "And you hand in the application and it takes three months and ….." In the twenty-fourth sentence you can see me set the page down as another person walks through the door. I turn off the electronic typewriter and scroll out the page and place it facedown on the desk and I cover it with a notebook you weren't aware was also there on the desk. Now you can see it, it is almost the exact same color as the surface of the desk and now you can see it. These were the twenty-fifth and twenty-sixth sentences, respectively, it is the lot of the twenty-seventh sentence to have to announce that. In the twenty-eighth sentence a cloud passes over the apartment on its way into space. In the twenty-ninth sentence, I think, next year this will be the number of my age. The thirtieth sentence is all about the speed at which time is passing. In the thirty-first sentence I won't care anymore, I'll see that reality only accrues to itself and does not have to mean something. In the thirty-second sentence I want you to agree with me. Things happen by chance, and what Montaigne pleads with us to believe, in an essay, is that fortune makes herself known in the act of reading, there is much that I could not have intended which is yet here, I forget exactly how this goes, this being the thirty-third sentence. I sit down beside myself in the thirty-fourth sentence and say to myself, smiling, even small numbers are big. This is the working of time, the thirty-fifth sentence joins in saying this, too, once one has crossed the years their number does not matter. But what I was trying to get across was, I think in sentence thirty-six, that maybe you could not have done things earlier, maybe it just was not possible in those days for whichever reasons. You spend the thirty-seventh sentence attempting to spell those reasons out. You fall asleep, and in the thirty-eighth sentence you dream about a room. The room is a classroom in which you are alone, says sentence number thirty-nine, the windows have been left open and a sentence can be read on the blackboard. In the fortieth sentence you have to force yourself to go on. Descartes' dream, you remember, in sentence forty-one, provided a quote supposedly from Ausonius. This is the forty-second sentence, *Est et non*. Then I think it is safe to say that something begins to happen, sentence forty-three tells us. Sentence forty-four says that you should forgive. Sentence forty-five says that you remember this number as having been particularly beautiful when worn by your mother. Sentence forty-six says the figures move away. Sentence forty-seven is a sentence about what loneliness names itself in the paradoxical presence of others. Sentence forty-eight says it has a name. Sentence forty-nine says that I cannot remember this name. Sentence fifty says that I go back and try and live there in that moment when I was saying the name. I say, "Happiness." This was sentence fifty-one. That was sentence fifty-two. Sentence fifty-four is a sentence about how there is too much of so many things, there is too much of all the words, but the world runs on underneath them and I keep on imagining how you could have heard me, how you could not have heard me. Sentence fifty-five is a sentence about picking up the phone. Sentence fifty-six is a sentence about picking up a small cellular phone but not using it and willing the phone to ring on its own. The gray cotton of the sweatshirt I wear is a warm cotton in sentence fifty-seven. In sentence fifty-eight I decide to keep on saying the numbers. In sentence fifty-nine I hold the page up to the light and see the type on the other side show through, In sentence sixty you start to believe me. In sentence sixty-one I start to go back to the beginning. I wonder if I should worry. The world is full of pauses, the world is full with continuations, says sentence sixty-three. I let sentence sixty-four go. In sentence sixty-five it occurs to me that I concern myself here with something that ought not to be touched. Sentence sixty-six is a guess that this is the mystery of counting, that it goes on and means itself without having a meaning. I count the people in the distance I can see from my window in sentence sixty-seven. In sentence sixty-eight the breeze has a sweet smell. In sentence sixty-nine, it turns the last week of May in the year 2008. Sentence seventy concerns the lack of what I wanted, in my own mind, to be saying. In sentence seventy-one I'm going so far as to ask you if you can see this, how much of what I thought lay before me remained in the distance. In sentence seventy-two there is a hill there. In sentence seventy-three we see flowers open their faces and then black snakes slide down the face of the hill. In sentence seventy-four there is still nothing. In sentence seventy-five the moon changes place with the sun. In sentence seventy-six this takes place again, only now it is day. In sentence seventy-seven it is still day. In sentence seventy-eight it is still day. Why do you think about tragedy, sentence seventy-nine wants to know, since it is the least likely thing to happen. Sentence eighty will eventually come to me and want to know what I am doing with myself. Sentence eighty-one reminds me to expect this question. In sentence eighty-two something changes. I stay up two nights running and in the morning the sidewalk seems to rise up and meet my feet underneath my feet. Sentence eighty-four contains the question, didn't you already know that this would start to happen? Sentence eighty-five agrees. When I start to read sentence eighty-six I discover it contains the words, It is also true that what you said could *be*. For this reason, sentence eighty-seven is a sentence about why there are certainly points of correspondence between what we expect to be the case and what is. Sentence eighty-eight proclaims it feels the excitement and not the work. Sentence eighty-nine takes action without saying anything first. In sentence ninety I cover my eyes. In sentence ninety-one I uncover my eyes so that I can look again. In sentence ninety-two I cover them again. Now I am speaking to you. Now I am speaking to you. Say the words after me just as I say them. What it means to live is the subject of sentence ninety-six. You are moving out of earshot now. We are not going to miss each other. You have an excellent memory. Please never forget I was the one who told you that

POETRY READINGS

Are poetry readings the best or worst way to experience poetry? This depends on how you like to get your entertainment or spend your leisure time. Do you prefer to drink alone or with others? Do you like to go to concerts, sporting events, plays, art exhibitions, tarot card readings?

Performance is the key term. If poetry reading is tantamount to performance, then there's no reason to worry about the text of the poem itself—because it will be brought off with delivery, tone, pitch, dynamics.

As a poet who gives a reading, you may wish by the end of the affair to have been another kind of performer like a rock star, a stand-up comedian, or trapeze artist.

As you read the poems about poetry readings, consider the relationship between the poet who performs and the audience who attends. Some of the poems seem to argue, implicitly or explicitly, that the audience should be the focus, that the poet needs to entertain to be effective. Other poems argue against this, intimating that the poet just by reading on stage is performing a vulnerability—and therefore is inherently "effective." What does a poet "owe" an audience? Is this an ethical dilemma, a writerly one, or both?

Kim Stafford
At the Student Poetry Reading

I guess you could call me broken,
says one. *I'm still lonely,* says another,
but now I can name it with a song.

In my poem, says another,
*I can forget I am forgotten. Now
I understand being misunderstood,*

says another. And another says,
in a bold, undeniable voice of power,
I won't step down from myself again.

And they are beautiful, beautiful,
standing one by one at the mic
where they have come forth at last

from behind the curtain.

The Cyborg Jillian Weise
Nondisabled Demands

It isn't fair to us. You owe it to the reader.
We're trying to help. We have an uncle
with a disability and he always says

exactly what it is. Take it from him.
Take it from us. Take it from them.
You can't expect people to read you

if you don't come out and say it.
Everyone knows the default mode
of a poem is ten fingers, ten toes

in love with women and this nation.
When this is not true, it is incumbent
on you to come out and say it.

Here's what we'll do. We'll rope you
to the podium and ask
What do you have? What is it?

If you refuse to answer then we call
your doctor. Then we get to say
You're an inspiration.

Anna Swir (translated from the Polish by Czesław Miłosz and Leonard Nathan)
Poetry Reading

I'm curled into a ball
like a dog
that is cold.

Who will tell me
why I was born,
why this monstrosity
called life.

The telephone rings. I have to give
a poetry reading.

I enter.
A hundred people, a hundred pairs of eyes.
They look, they wait.
I know for what.

I am supposed to tell them
why they were born,
why there is
this monstrosity called life.

SPIRITUALITY

Our quest for the divine, mystical, mysterious, numinous, or spiritual never seems to end. Herman Melville conceptualized it as a veil one must strike through. The Surrealists tried to play their way into it—with playful seriousness—through games of chance operations or dream notebooks and dream logic or a multitude of strategies for getting to what was *really* behind, above, or below it all. This striving for something "beyond" is not that dissimilar to what Plato sought in his "forms" or "ideas." But the transcendentalists found their spirituality here on Earth, soloing in nature. The poet W.B. Yeats tried to reach it through myth, folklore, and the ouija board, ultimately settling for a "present absence" at the center of everything. A favorite trope for this lack of logos is the onion: peel off layer upon layer upon layer until ... voila! There's nothing left except a nothing. All of this spiritual talk shouldn't be confused with atheistic desires. Even when poets don't mean to, they often find themselves in the middle of forces beyond their knowledge, much less their control. They make discoveries not because they long to find a particular thing, but because discovering is the thing to be discovered.

Amiri Baraka
Preface to a Twenty-Volume Suicide Note

(For Kelli Jones, born 16 May 1959)

Lately, I've become accustomed to the way
The ground opens up and envelops me
Each time I go out to walk the dog.
Or the broad edged silly music the wind
Makes when I run for a bus ...

Things have come to that.

And now, each night I count the stars,
And each night I get the same number.
And when they will not come to be counted,
I count the holes they leave.

Nobody sings anymore.

And then last night, I tiptoed up
To my daughter's room and heard her
Talking to someone, and when I opened
The door, there was no one there ...
Only she on her knees, peeking into

Her own clasped hands.

Gerald Stern
Your Animal

The final end of all but purified souls
is to be swallowed up by Leviathan,
or to be bound with fiery chains and flogged
with 70 stripes of fire.
I walk along the mule path dreaming of my weaknesses
and praying to the ducks for forgiveness.
Oh there is so much shit in the universe

and my walks, like yours,
are more and more slippery and dangerous.
I love a duck for being almost like a vegetable.
I love him because his whole body can be consumed,
because there is no distance between him and his watery offal.
Your animal is almost human,
distant from his waste,
struggling to overcome the hated matter,
looking up with horrified white eyes,
eternally hunting for space in the little islands of Riverside Drive
and the fenced-in parks of the Village.

I love duck and potatoes, duck and red beets,
duck and orange juice.
I love the head of duck dipped in sugar,
I love chocolate duck with chipolata sausage,
fragrant crisp duck mixed with shrimp and pork.
I love the webs and the heart; I love the eggs
preserved in lime and potash, completely boned duck
filled with ham and chestnuts, fried duck with pineapple
and canned red cherries or sections of tangerine.

This is a poem against gnosticism;
it is a poem against the hatred of the flesh
and all the vicious twists and turns we take
to calm our frightened souls.
It is a poem celebrating the eating of duck
and all that goes with it.
It is a poem I am able to write after walking every day
through the flocks, and loving the babies, and watching them slip
down the mud sides and float into the current.
It is a poem about shooting galleries and cardboard heads,
about hunters and their checkered hats and frozen fingers,
about snow-white cloths and steaming laced-up birds
and waiters standing in little regiments
getting ready to run in among the tables and start carving.
—It is my poem against the starving heart.
It is my victory over meanness.

James Tate
Goodtime Jesus

Jesus got up one day a little later than usual. He had been dreaming so deep there was nothing left in his head. What was it? A nightmare, dead bodies walking all around him, eyes rolled back, skin falling off. But he wasn't afraid of that. It was a beautiful day. How 'bout some coffee? Don't mind if I do. Take a little ride on my donkey, I love that donkey. Hell, I love everybody.

Bianca Stone
Making Applesauce with My Dead Grandmother

I dig her up and plop her down in a wicker chair.
She's going to make applesauce and I'm going to get drunk.
She's cutting worms out of the small green apples from the backyard
and I'm opening a bottle. It erects like a tower
in the city of my mouth.

The way she makes applesauce, it has ragged
strips of skin and spreads thickly over toast.
It's famous; eating it is as close to God as I'm going to get,
but I don't tell her. There's a dishtowel wrapped around her head
to keep her jaw from falling slack—

Everything hurts.
But I don't tell her that either. I have to stand at the call box
and see what words I can squeeze in. I'm getting worried.
If I dig her up and put her down in the wicker chair
I'd better be ready for the rest of the family

to make a fuss about it. I'd better bring her back right.
The whole house smells of cinnamon and dust.
We don't speak. She's piling up the worms, half-alive
in a silver bowl, she's throwing them back into the ground
right where her body should be.

Moon Bo Young (translated from the Korean by Hedgie Choi)
Down Jacket God

God wears a massive down jacket. Humans are the countless duck feathers trapped inside, the poet writes. Sometimes a feather pokes out. God plucks it carelessly. That's what people call death. A feather gets plucked. That person dies. A feather gets plucked. That person expires. A feather gets plucked. That person breathes their last breath. A feather gets plucked. That person disappears.

After death there's no heaven or hell, no angels or devils, the poet writes. There's only a feather. It swings in the air. Gently, the feather settles on the ground.

T'ao Ch'ien (translated from the Chinese by Stephen Owen)
Substance, Shadow, and Spirit

I
Substance to Shadow

Earth and heaven endure forever,
Streams and mountains never change.
Plants observe a constant rhythm,
Withered by frost, by dew restored.
But man, most sentient being of all,
In this is not their equal.
He is present here in the world today,
Then leaves abruptly, to return no more.
No one marks there's one man less—
Not even friends and family think of him;
The things that he once used are all that's left
To catch their eye and move them to grief.
I have no way to transcend change,
That it must be, I no longer doubt.
I hope you will take my advice:
When wine is offered, don't refuse.

II
Shadow to Substance

No use discussing immortality
When just to keep alive is hard enough.
Of course I want to roam in paradise,
But it's a long way there and the road is lost.
In all the time since I met up with you
We never differed in our grief and joy.
In shade we may have parted for a time,
But sunshine always brings us close again.
Still this union cannot last forever—
Together we will vanish into darkness.
The body goes; that fame should also end
Is a thought that makes me burn inside.
Do good, and your love will outlive you;
Surely this is worth your every effort.
While it is true, wine may dissolve care
That is not so good a way as this.

III
Spirit's Solution

The Great Potter cannot intervene—
All creation thrives of itself.
That Man ranks with Earth and Heaven
Is it not because of me?
Though we belong to different orders,
Being alive, I am joined to you.
Bound together for good or ill
I cannot refuse to tell you what I know:
The Three August Ones were great saints
But where are they living today?
Though P'eng-tsu lasted a long time
He still had to go before he was ready.
Die old or die young, the death is the same,
Wise or stupid, there is no difference.
Drunk every day you may forget,
But won't it shorten your lifespan?
Doing good is always a joyous thing
But no one has to praise you for it.
Too much thinking harms my life;
Just surrender to the cycle of things,
Give yourself to the waves of the Great Change
Neither happy nor yet afraid.
And when it is time to go, then simply go
Without any unnecessary fuss.

FLIGHT

Nothing quite concentrates the mind as keenly as air travel. Whether aboard a plane, at the airport, or while anticipating arrival or departure, flight offers mundanity, confusion, idle speculation, and cosmic wonder—often all at once. As the following poems display, flight is the occasion and nexus of the lyrical, the epic, the spiritual, and the banal. Is it any wonder that airports have been called the cathedrals of our age?

Gary Snyder
Waiting for a Ride

Standing at the baggage passing time:
Austin Texas airport—my ride hasn't come yet.
My former wife is making websites from her home,
one son's seldom seen,
the other one and his wife have a boy and girl of their own.

My wife and stepdaughter are spending weekdays in town
so she can get to high school.
My mother ninety-six still lives alone and she's in town too,
always gets her sanity back just barely in time.
My former former wife has become a unique poet;
most of my work,
such as it is   is done.
Full moon was October second this year,
I ate a mooncake, slept out on the deck
white light beaming through the black boughs of the pine
owl hoots and rattling antlers,
Castor and Pollux rising strong
—it's good to know that the Pole Star drifts!
that even our present night sky slips away,
not that I'll see it.
Or maybe I will, much later,
some far time walking the spirit path in the sky,
that long walk of spirits—where you fall right back into the
"narrow painful passageway of the Bardo"
squeeze your little skull
and there you are again

waiting for your ride

(October 5, 2001)

Naomi Shihab Nye
Gate A-4

Wandering around the Albuquerque Airport Terminal, after learning my flight had been delayed four hours, I heard an announcement: "If anyone in the vicinity of Gate A-4 understands any Arabic, please come to the gate immediately."

Well—one pauses these days. Gate A-4 was my own gate. I went there.

An older woman in full traditional Palestinian embroidered dress, just like my grandma wore, was crumpled to the floor, wailing. "Help," said the flight agent. "Talk to her. What is her problem? We told her the flight was going to be late and she did this."

I stooped to put my arm around the woman and spoke to her haltingly. "Shu-dow-a, Shu-bid-uck Habibti? Stani schway, Min fadlick, Shu-bit-se-wee?" The minute she heard any words she knew, however poorly used, she stopped crying. She thought the flight had been cancelled entirely. She needed to be in El Paso for major medical treatment the next day. I said, "No, we're fine, you'll get there, just later, who is picking you up? Let's call him."

We called her son and I spoke with him in English. I told him I would stay with his mother till we got on the plane and would ride next to her—Southwest. She talked to him. Then we called her other sons just for the fun of it. Then we called my dad and he and she spoke for a while in Arabic and found out of course they had ten shared friends. Then I thought just for the heck of it why not call some Palestinian poets I know and let them chat with her? This all took up two hours.

She was laughing a lot by then. Telling about her life, patting my knee, answering questions. She had pulled a sack of homemade *mamool* cookies—little powdered sugar crumbly mounds stuffed with dates and nuts—out of her bag—and was offering them to all the women at the gate. To my amazement, not a single woman declined one. It was like a sacrament. The traveler from Argentina, the mom from California, the lovely woman from Laredo—we were all covered with the same powdered sugar. And smiling. There is no better cookie.

And then the airline broke out free beverages from huge coolers and two little girls from our flight ran around serving us all apple juice and they were covered with powdered sugar, too. And I noticed my new best friend—by now we were holding hands—had a potted plant poking out of her bag, some medicinal thing, with green furry leaves. Such an old country tradition. Always carry a plant. Always stay rooted to somewhere.

And I looked around that gate of late and weary ones and thought, This is the world I want to live in. The shared world. Not a single person in that gate—once the crying of confusion stopped—seemed apprehensive about any other person. They took the cookies. I wanted to hug all those other women, too.

This can still happen anywhere. Not everything is lost.

Tony Hoagland
Reading *Moby-Dick* at 30,000 Feet

At this height, Kansas
is just a concept,
a checkerboard design of wheat and corn

no larger than the foldout section
of my neighbor's travel magazine.
At this stage of the journey

I would estimate the distance
between myself and my own feelings
is roughly the same as the mileage

from Seattle to New York,
so I can lean back into the upholstered interval
between Muzak and lunch,

a little bored, a little old and strange.
I remember, as a dreamy
backyard kind of kid,

tilting up my head to watch
those planes engrave the sky
in lines so steady and so straight

they implied the enormous concentration
of good men,
but now my eyes flicker

from the in-flight movie
to the stewardess's pantyline,
then back into my book,

where men throw harpoons at something
much bigger and probably
better than themselves,

wanting to kill it, wanting
to see great clouds of blood erupt
to prove that they exist.

Imagine being born and growing up,
rushing through the world for sixty years
at unimaginable speeds.

Imagine a century like a room so large,
a corridor so long
you could travel for a lifetime

and never find the door,
until you had forgotten
that such a thing as doors exist.

Better to be on board the *Pequod*,
with a mad one-legged captain
living for revenge.

Better to feel the salt wind
spitting in your face,
to hold your sharpened weapon high,

to see the glisten
of the beast beneath the waves.
What a relief it would be

to hear someone in the crew
cry out like a gull,
Oh Captain, Captain!
Where are we going now?

Writing

Reading poems very often leads to writing poems, or writing about poems. Curiosity leads to investigation about how a poem works, what its origins are, what it depends on, who it is for, how it can be turned this way and that, rubbed like a magic lantern until its secrets are revealed or wishes that you never knew you had are granted.

It all sounds so titillating, effervescent, and glorious! Yet, there isn't one single way of going about this work—and rest assured it is *work*. Serious play, the most precious nonsense there may be. The requirement is that you make time for it. Uninterrupted, undistracted minutes and hours, repeatedly. The patterns of poems are akin to the patterns of your life, and poem-making needs to eat up the time you could be doing other things: working, watching, scrolling, spending quality or shoddy time with others, talking, sleeping, drinking, loving.

No amount of didactic babble (however well meaning) or theory or theology or manifesto will permit you to escape the hours of sitting down, alone if not lonely, scrawling or pecking away. Teachers may help guide you and remind you to write, and show you who and what and how to read. Nevertheless, every poet becomes their own teacher, to a greater or lesser degree. And every poet becomes self-serving and self-taught. If it's true that each of us has a cross to bear, it is equally true that a poet's cross is nothing less than their poems.

FIRST PRINCIPLES

Charles Bukowski's poem about the writing life is either a warning or a dare. If you feel it's both, you are beginning to understand the premise of being a poet. But being a poet means, as well, doing exactly what the speaker of his poem doesn't want you to do. Reckon a writing life that isn't about trying to get someone into bed, or trying to get people to pay attention to you, or trying to sit there and wait for the muse to blow a kiss in your ear. You must address these things even if you shun them. Be that poet who writes a grandma poem while abhorring all grandma poems. There are worse paradoxes to live by.

Charles Bukowski
so you want to be a writer?

if it doesn't come bursting out of you
in spite of everything,
don't do it.
unless it comes unasked out of your
heart and your mind and your mouth
and your gut,
don't do it.
if you have to sit for hours
staring at your computer screen
or hunched over your
typewriter
searching for words,
don't do it.
if you're doing it for money or
fame,
don't do it.
if you're doing it because you want
women in your bed,
don't do it.
if you have to sit there and
rewrite it again and again,
don't do it.
if it's hard work just thinking about doing it,
don't do it.
if you're trying to write like somebody
else,
forget about it.

if you have to wait for it to roar out of
you,
then wait patiently.

if it never does roar out of you,
do something else.

if you first have to read it to your wife
or your girlfriend or your boyfriend
or your parents or to anybody at all,
you're not ready.

don't be like so many writers,
don't be like so many thousands of
people who call themselves writers,
don't be dull and boring and
pretentious, don't be consumed with self-
love.
the libraries of the world have
yawned themselves to
sleep
over your kind.
don't add to that.
don't do it.
unless it comes out of
your soul like a rocket,
unless being still would
drive you to madness or
suicide or murder,
don't do it.
unless the sun inside you is
burning your gut,
don't do it.

when it is truly time,
and if you have been chosen,
it will do it by
itself and it will keep on doing it
until you die or it dies in
you.

there is no other way.

and there never was.

Yolanda Wisher
no more grandma poems

they said
forget your grandma
these american letters

don't need no more
grandma poems
but i said
the grandmas are
our first poetic forms
the first haiku
was a grandma
& so too
the first sonnet
the first blues
the first praise song
therefore
every poem
is a grandmother
a womb that has ended
& is still expanding
a daughter that is
rhetorically aging
& retroactively living
every poem
is your grandma
& you miss her
wouldn't mind
seeing her again
even just
for a moment
in the realm of spirit
in the realm
of possibilities
where poems
share blood
& spit & exist
on chromosomal
planes of particularity
where poems
are strangers
turned sistren
not easily shook
or forgotten

FORM

Admit it—you want to be free! So why use this thing called "form" at all when you write a poem? Because form involves "rules" that, contrary to the notion of "being free," actually provide freedom. These rules, or more accurately parameters, can be inherited from previous makers—as in the case of the sonnet, ghazal, haiku, etc.—or they can be invented.

Below are forms of invention: Marianne Moore's employing idiosyncratic but regularized syllable counts; Christian Bök's employing only the vowel *e* in one of the sections of his book-length project *Eunoia*. Below, too, are forms borrowed and made fresh: C.D. Wright's appropriating the personal ad for her own ends; Evie Shockley's playing off the form of the multiple-choice question to test a wholly different kind of question. As you look for a way to make a poem, challenge yourself as these poets have: What kind of linguistic reality can you construct from the materials you have been given, or the ones you can find and refine?

Marianne Moore
The Fish

wade
through black jade.
    Of the crow-blue mussel-shells, one keeps
    adjusting the ash-heaps;
        opening and shutting itself like
an
injured fan.
    The barnacles which encrust the side
    of the wave, cannot hide
        there for the submerged shafts of the
sun,
split like spun
    glass, move themselves with spotlight swiftness
    into the crevices—
        in and out, illuminating
the
turquoise sea
    of bodies. The water drives a wedge
    of iron through the iron edge
        of the cliff; whereupon the stars,
pink
rice-grains, ink-
    bespattered jelly fish, crabs like green
    lilies, and submarine
        toadstools, slide each on the other.
All
external
    marks of abuse are present on this

    defiant edifice—
        all the physical features of
ac-
cident—lack
    of cornice, dynamite grooves, burns, and
    hatchet strokes, these things stand
        out on it; the chasm-side is
dead.
Repeated
    evidence has proved that it can live
    on what can not revive
        its youth. The sea grows old in it.

Christian Bök
from Chapter E of *Eunoia*

Enfettered, these sentences repress free speech. The text deletes selected letters. We see the revered exegete reject metred verse: the sestet, the tercet—even *les scènes élevées en grec*. He rebels. He sets new precedents. He lets cleverness exceed decent levels. He eschews the esteemed genres, the expected themes—even *les belles lettres en vers*. He prefers the perverse French esthetes: Verne, Péret, Genet, Perec—hence, he pens fervent screeds, then enters the street, where he sells these letterpress newsletters, three cents per sheet. He engenders perfect newness wherever we need fresh terms.

Relentless, the rebel peddles these theses, even when vexed peers deem the new precepts "mere dreck." The plebes resent newer verse; nevertheless, the rebel perseveres, never deterred, never dejected, heedless, even when hecklers heckle the vehement speeches. We feel perplexed whenever we see these excerpted sentences. We sneer when we detect the clever scheme—the emergent repetend: the letter E. We jeer; we jest. We express resentment. We detest these depthless pretenses—these present-tense verbs, expressed pell-mell. We prefer genteel speech, where sense redeems senselessness.

C.D. Wright
Personals

Some nights I sleep with my dress on. My teeth
are small and even. I don't get headaches.
Since 1971 or before, I have hunted a bench
where I could eat my pimento cheese in peace.
If this were Tennessee and across that river, Arkansas,
I'd meet you in West Memphis tonight. We could
have a big time. Danger, shoulder soft.
Do not lie or lean on me. I'm still trying to find a job
for which a simple machine isn't better suited.
I've seen people die of money. Look at Admiral Benbow. I wish
like certain fishes, we came equipped with light organs.
Which reminds me of a little known fact:
if we were going the speed of light, this dome
would be shrinking while we were gaining weight.
Isn't the road crooked and steep.
In this humidity, I make repairs by night. I'm not one
among millions who saw Monroe's face
in the moon. I go blank looking at that face.
If I could afford it I'd live in hotels. I won awards
in spelling and the Australian crawl. Long long ago.
Grandmother married a man named Ivan. The men called him
Eve. Stranger, to tell the truth, in dog years I am up there.

Evie Shockley
what's not to liken?

the 14-year-old girl was treated like:
    (a) a grown woman.
    (b) a grown man.

the bikini-clad girl was handled by the cop like:
    (a) a prostitute.
    (b) a prostitute by her pimp.

the girl was slung to the ground like:
    (a) a sack of garbage into a dumpster.
    (b) somebody had something to prove.

the girl's braids flew around her head like:
    (a) helicopter blades.
    (b) she'd been slapped.

the black girl was pinned to the ground like:
- (a) an amateur wrestler in a professional fight.
- (b) swimming in a private pool is a threat to national security.

the girl's cries sounded like:
- (a) the shrieks of children on a playground.
- (b) the shrieks of children being torn from their mothers.

the protesting girl was shackled like:
- (a) a criminal.
- (b) a runaway slave.

liken it or not

   —mckinney, texas, june 2015

SONNET

In Jen Bervin's "Working Note" in *Nets*, her treatment of Shakespeare's sonnets, she writes: "When we write poems, the history of poetry is with us, pre-inscribed in the white of the page; when we read or write poems, we do it with or against this palimpsest." Even if this is not entirely accurate—that we take on all of poetry's history—it still manages to get at a particular truth: we write ourselves into writing that has come before. Milton's sonnet, for instance, isn't only about the speaker's blindness; it's a commentary on the biblical "Parable of Talents." Its quotable last line, spoken by Patience as a reply to the speaker, upends the parable: "They also serve who only stand and wait." In fact, when you compare the endings of the following sonnets, the motif that perhaps connects them more than anything else is the idea of "sufficiency." How might the structure of the sonnet lend itself to such a stricture, such an acceptance?

Jen Bervin
from Nets

My mistress' eyes are nothing like the sun;
Coral is far more red than her lips' red;
If snow be white, why then her breasts are dun;
If hairs be wires, black wires grow on her head.
I have seen roses damasked, red and white,
But **no such roses** see I in her cheeks,
And in some perfumes is there more delight
Than in the breath that from my mistress reeks.
I love to hear her speak, yet well I know
That music hath a far more pleasing sound.
I grant I never saw a goddess go;
My mistress when she walks treads on the ground:
   And yet, by heaven, I think my love as rare
   As any she belied with false compare.

John Milton
Sonnet 19

When I consider how my light is spent,
  Ere half my days, in this dark world and wide,
  And that one talent which is death to hide
  Lodged with me useless, though my soul more bent
To serve therewith my Maker, and present
  My true account, lest He returning chide;
  "Doth God exact day-labour, light denied?"
  I fondly ask. But Patience, to prevent
That murmur, soon replies, "God doth not need
  Either man's work or His own gifts; who best
  Bear His mild yoke, they serve Him best. His state
Is kingly: thousands at His bidding speed
  And post o'er land and ocean without rest;
  They also serve who only stand and wait."

Gaspara Stampa (translated from the Italian by Laura Anna Stortoni and Mary Prentice Lillie)
Sonnet 132

When in my weeping I inquire of Love
  (Who so unwillingly gives ear to me)
A thousand times a day–never just once–
Why he will wound and pierce me all the time:
  "How can it be, since I gave heart and soul
To him, the day I took them both from me,
If everything enclosed within his breast
Is only joy and laughter, never sorrow,
  How can I feel cold jealousy and fear
And be deprived of all my joyfulness,
Living in him, and never in myself?"
  "I bid you die to joy and live in grief,"
Love answers me in his hard final sentence:
"Let this suffice you, that it makes you write."

Edna St. Vincent Millay
Love Is Not All (Sonnet XXX)

Love is not all: it is not meat nor drink
Nor slumber nor a roof against the rain;
Nor yet a floating spar to men that sink
And rise and sink and rise and sink again;

Love can not fill the thickened lung with breath,
Nor clean the blood, nor set the fractured bone;
Yet many a man is making friends with death
Even as I speak, for lack of love alone.
It well may be that in a difficult hour,
Pinned down by pain and moaning for release,
Or nagged by want past resolution's power,
I might be driven to sell your love for peace,
Or trade the memory of this night for food.
It well may be. I do not think I would.

Olena Kalytiak Davis
shattered sonnet #3

Love brought
              me a handful
of pussy willows to place
near my face. A sick head
and a sick heart ought be licked
back to health, said said Love,
all stealth. All stick and cue. Love,
didn't I tell you, not to foot
over threshold of mine? But
Love was over, Love was under.
Love was in. Love was wrought.
Love swept the house, then, Love was
done. Aye, There's the rub!
The phoenix and the turtle
dove? Ha! Love, Love is
              nought.

Terrance Hayes
American Sonnet for My Past and Future Assassin

I lock you in an American sonnet that is part prison,
Part panic closet, a little room in a house set aflame.
I lock you in a form that is part music box, part meat
Grinder to separate the song of the bird from the bone.
I lock your persona in a dream-inducing sleeper hold
While your better selves watch from the bleachers.
I make you both gym & crow here. As the crow
You undergo a beautiful catharsis trapped one night
In the shadows of the gym. As the gym, the feel of crow-
Shit dropping to your floors is not unlike the stars

Falling from the pep rally posters on your walls.
I make you a box of darkness with a bird in its heart.
Voltas of acoustics, instinct & metaphor. It is not enough
To love you. It is not enough to want you destroyed.

IDENTITY

As readers, many of us long to know: *Who is the person who made this poem? Who's responsible for this damn confusing or too beautiful thing!* We desire not just the poem, but the poet. Yet, if we go in search of the poet, we may not find what we thought or hoped we would. *My god, the woman killed herself … was this the last poem she penned? Did she use a pen? Did she stab herself in the neck with it?* Or we find a poet who appears to be nothing like the poem. *How could I have been so deceived, this made thing is a fake!* Yet again, we've forgotten that made things are always fakes. Would they be more or less authentic if another poet had made them? What is authentic, and what is authentic enough? These poems explore not only questions of identity and origin but also questions of existence—the processes and products of the self and the unknown.

Philip Larkin
This Be The Verse

They fuck you up, your mum and dad.
    They may not mean to, but they do.
They fill you with the faults they had
    And add some extra, just for you.

But they were fucked up in their turn
    By fools in old-style hats and coats,
Who half the time were soppy stern
    And half at one another's throats.

Man hands on misery to man.
    It deepens like a coastal shelf.
Get out as early as you can,
    And don't have any kids yourself.

Meena Alexander
Where Do You Come From?

I come from the nether regions

They serve me pomegranate seeds with morsels of flying fish

From time to time I wear a crown of blood streaked grass.

Mama beat me when I was a child for stealing honey from a honey pot

It swung from the rafters of the kitchen.

Why I stuffed my mouth with golden stuff, no one could tell.

King Midas wore a skin that killed him.

My nails are patterned ebony, Doxil will do that

They made a port under my collar bone with a plastic tube that runs into a blood vessel.

I set out with mama from Bombay harbor.

Our steamer was SS Jehangir, in honor of the World Conqueror—

They say he knelt on the battle field to stroke the Beloved's shadow.

The waves were dark in Bombay harbor, Gandhi wrote in his Autobiography

Writing too is an experiment with truth.

No one knows my name in Arabic means port.

On board white people would not come near us

Were they scared our brown skin would sully them?

Mama tried to teach me English in a sing song voice.

So you can swim into your life she said.

Wee child, my language tutor muttered ruler in hand, ready to strike,

Just pronounce the words right:

Pluck, pluck   *Suck, suck*

                   Duck, duck

                   Stuck, stuck.

May 12–July 4, 2018, NYC

Sylvia Plath
Poppies in October

Even the sun-clouds this morning cannot manage such skirts.
Nor the woman in the ambulance
Whose red heart blooms through her coat so astoundingly—

A gift, a love gift
Utterly unasked for
By a sky

Palely and flamily
Igniting its carbon monoxides, by eyes
Dulled to a halt under bowlers.

O my God, what am I
That these late mouths should cry open
In a forest of frost, in a dawn of cornflowers.

Louise Glück
The Red Poppy

The great thing
is not having
a mind. Feelings:
oh, I have those; they
govern me. I have
a lord in heaven
called the sun, and open
for him, showing him
the fire of my own heart, fire
like his presence.
What could such glory be
if not a heart? Oh my brothers and sisters,
were you like me once, long ago,
before you were human? Did you
permit yourselves
to open once, who would never
open again? Because in truth
I am speaking now
the way you do. I speak
because I am shattered.

SELF-EXPRESSION

There's no lack of self-expression in our world, much less in our literature and poetry. One version of religion says that God made us in his image, but this belies the obvious: humans made God in theirs. Self-expression is fine as far as it goes … but how far can it go? To paraphrase Ben Orki: instead of expressing yourself, try expressing the world.

It's not such an easy split. As Rachel Zucker writes in her essay-cum-poem: "The Self in Poetry ... What else is there? / Seriously. / Consider. / It is through the self that one organizes, makes sense of, tells the raw sense data of the world, which is everything that is not self."

Consider the ways in which each poem below grapples with expressing the self while also relating to the world of which the self is a part. Discern where and how these speakers embrace and merge, vent and rant, self-promote and self-deprecate, equivocate and isolate. Which are you most attracted to, repelled by, and bored with? And what does that underscore about your own self, your own desire to express?

Walt Whitman
from *Song of Myself* (1892 version)

1
I celebrate myself, and sing myself,
And what I assume you shall assume,
For every atom belonging to me as good belongs to you.

I loafe and invite my soul,
I lean and loafe at my ease observing a spear of summer grass.

My tongue, every atom of my blood, form'd from this soil, this air,
Born here of parents born here from parents the same, and their parents the same,
I, now thirty-seven years old in perfect health begin,
Hoping to cease not till death.

Creeds and schools in abeyance,
Retiring back a while sufficed at what they are, but never forgotten,
I harbor for good or bad, I permit to speak at every hazard,
Nature without check with original energy.

2
Houses and rooms are full of perfumes, the shelves are crowded with perfumes,
I breathe the fragrance myself and know it and like it,
The distillation would intoxicate me also, but I shall not let it.

The atmosphere is not a perfume, it has no taste of the distillation, it is odorless,
It is for my mouth forever, I am in love with it,
I will go to the bank by the wood and become undisguised and naked,
I am mad for it to be in contact with me.

The smoke of my own breath,
Echoes, ripples, buzz'd whispers, love-root, silk-thread, crotch and vine,
My respiration and inspiration, the beating of my heart, the passing of blood and air through my lungs,

The sniff of green leaves and dry leaves, and of the shore and dark-color'd sea-rocks, and of hay in the barn,
The sound of the belch'd words of my voice loos'd to the eddies of the wind,
A few light kisses, a few embraces, a reaching around of arms,
The play of shine and shade on the trees as the supple boughs wag,
The delight alone or in the rush of the streets, or along the fields and hill-sides,
The feeling of health, the full-noon trill, the song of me rising from bed and meeting the sun.

Have you reckon'd a thousand acres much? have you reckon'd the earth much?
Have you practis'd so long to learn to read?
Have you felt so proud to get at the meaning of poems?

Stop this day and night with me and you shall possess the origin of all poems,
You shall possess the good of the earth and sun, (there are millions of suns left,)
You shall no longer take things at second or third hand, nor look through the eyes of the dead, nor feed on the spectres in books,
You shall not look through my eyes either, nor take things from me,
You shall listen to all sides and filter them from your self.

3
I have heard what the talkers were talking, the talk of the beginning and the end,
But I do not talk of the beginning or the end.

There was never any more inception than there is now,
Nor any more youth or age than there is now,
And will never be any more perfection than there is now,
Nor any more heaven or hell than there is now.

Urge and urge and urge,
Always the procreant urge of the world.

Out of the dimness opposite equals advance, always substance and increase, always sex,
Always a knit of identity, always distinction, always a breed of life.

To elaborate is no avail, learn'd and unlearn'd feel that it is so.

Sure as the most certain sure, plumb in the uprights, well entretied, braced in the beams,
Stout as a horse, affectionate, haughty, electrical,
I and this mystery here we stand.

Clear and sweet is my soul, and clear and sweet is all that is not my soul.

Lack one lacks both, and the unseen is proved by the seen,
Till that becomes unseen and receives proof in its turn.

Showing the best and dividing it from the worst age vexes age,
Knowing the perfect fitness and equanimity of things, while they discuss I am silent, and go bathe and admire myself.

Welcome is every organ and attribute of me, and of any man hearty and clean,
Not an inch nor a particle of an inch is vile, and none shall be less familiar than the rest.

I am satisfied—I see, dance, laugh, sing;
As the hugging and loving bed-fellow sleeps at my side through the night, and
    withdraws at the peep of the day with stealthy tread,
Leaving me baskets cover'd with white towels swelling the house with their plenty,
Shall I postpone my acceptation and realization and scream at my eyes,
That they turn from gazing after and down the road,
And forthwith cipher and show me to a cent,
Exactly the value of one and exactly the value of two, and which is ahead?

4
Trippers and askers surround me,
People I meet, the effect upon me of my early life or the ward and city I live in, or the
    nation,
The latest dates, discoveries, inventions, societies, authors old and new,
My dinner, dress, associates, looks, compliments, dues,
The real or fancied indifference of some man or woman I love,
The sickness of one of my folks or of myself, or ill-doing or loss or lack of money, or
    depressions or exaltations,
Battles, the horrors of fratricidal war, the fever of doubtful news, the fitful events;
These come to me days and nights and go from me again,
But they are not the Me myself.

Apart from the pulling and hauling stands what I am,
Stands amused, complacent, compassionating, idle, unitary,
Looks down, is erect, or bends an arm on an impalpable certain rest,
Looking with side-curved head curious what will come next,
Both in and out of the game and watching and wondering at it.

Backward I see in my own days where I sweated through fog with linguists and
    contenders,
I have no mockings or arguments, I witness and wait.

5
I believe in you my soul, the other I am must not abase itself to you,
And you must not be abased to the other.

Loafe with me on the grass, loose the stop from your throat,
Not words, not music or rhyme I want, not custom or lecture, not even the best,
Only the lull I like, the hum of your valvèd voice.

I mind how once we lay such a transparent summer morning,
How you settled your head athwart my hips and gently turn'd over upon me,
And parted the shirt from my bosom-bone, and plunged your tongue to my bare-stript
    heart,

And reach'd till you felt my beard, and reach'd till you held my feet.

Swiftly arose and spread around me the peace and knowledge that pass all the argument of the earth,
And I know that the hand of God is the promise of my own,
And I know that the spirit of God is the brother of my own,
And that all the men ever born are also my brothers, and the women my sisters and lovers,
And that a kelson of the creation is love,
And limitless are leaves stiff or drooping in the fields,
And brown ants in the little wells beneath them,
And mossy scabs of the worm fence, heap'd stones, elder, mullein and poke-weed.

6
A child said *What is the grass?* fetching it to me with full hands;
How could I answer the child? I do not know what it is any more than he.

I guess it must be the flag of my disposition, out of hopeful green stuff woven.

Or I guess it is the handkerchief of the Lord,
A scented gift and remembrancer designedly dropt,
Bearing the owner's name someway in the corners, that we may see and remark, and say *Whose?*

Or I guess the grass is itself a child, the produced babe of the vegetation.

Or I guess it is a uniform hieroglyphic,
And it means, Sprouting alike in broad zones and narrow zones,
Growing among black folks as among white,
Kanuck, Tuckahoe, Congressman, Cuff, I give them the same, I receive them the same.

And now it seems to me the beautiful uncut hair of graves.

Tenderly will I use you curling grass,
It may be you transpire from the breasts of young men,
It may be if I had known them I would have loved them,
It may be you are from old people, or from offspring taken soon out of their mothers' laps,
And here you are the mothers' laps.

This grass is very dark to be from the white heads of old mothers,
Darker than the colorless beards of old men,
Dark to come from under the faint red roofs of mouths.

O I perceive after all so many uttering tongues,
And I perceive they do not come from the roofs of mouths for nothing.

I wish I could translate the hints about the dead young men and women,
And the hints about old men and mothers, and the offspring taken soon out of their laps.

What do you think has become of the young and old men?
And what do you think has become of the women and children?

They are alive and well somewhere,
The smallest sprout shows there is really no death,
And if ever there was it led forward life, and does not wait at the end to arrest it,
And ceas'd the moment life appear'd.

All goes onward and outward, nothing collapses,
And to die is different from what any one supposed, and luckier.

Maya Angelou
Still I Rise

You may write me down in history
With your bitter, twisted lies,
You may trod me in the very dirt
But still, like dust, I'll rise.

Does my sassiness upset you?
Why are you beset with gloom?
'Cause I walk like I've got oil wells
Pumping in my living room.

Just like moons and like suns,
With the certainty of tides,
Just like hopes springing high,
Still I'll rise.

Did you want to see me broken?
Bowed head and lowered eyes?
Shoulders falling down like teardrops,
Weakened by my soulful cries?

Does my haughtiness offend you?
Don't you take it awful hard
'Cause I laugh like I've got gold mines
Diggin' in my own backyard.

You may shoot me with your words,
You may cut me with your eyes,
You may kill me with your hatefulness,
But still, like air, I'll rise.

Does my sexiness upset you?
Does it come as a surprise
That I dance like I've got diamonds

At the meeting of my thighs?

Out of the huts of history's shame
I rise
Up from a past that's rooted in pain
I rise
I'm a black ocean, leaping and wide,
Welling and swelling I bear in the tide.

Leaving behind nights of terror and fear
I rise
Into a daybreak that's wondrously clear
I rise
Bringing the gifts that my ancestors gave,
I am the dream and the hope of the slave.
I rise
I rise
I rise.

Emilia Phillips
"You Should Write a Poem About That," They Say

No, I shouldn't   I'm ill-equipped to crack a Korbel bottle on the butt-end
    of every sinking ship   No, I don't need to

torture-n-rack that amoebic memory of the time I lost my virginity, which I don't
    remember too clearly anyway—or that day

I got caught picking my nose in first grade, the trailing flower girls
    petaling *shame, shame*   I don't want

to track how many steps it takes me to reach Chimney Rock, or bookmark every page
    in my Browser History   Believe me some secrets

want to leap from the Golden Gate and heave into the turbid bay, its anonymous
    blue cresting into angels' brief, shorn

wings   I don't keep a good record of all my losses, for casualties,
    remember, are the dead   *and* the injured

No, there's really no place   for my favorite word *landfill* or my old dog
    who used to roll on dead animals   A man

once told me I'm cold *for a woman*   Another said I *don't
    deserve*   No, I couldn't solve the paradox—

how many griefs would I have to remove from my heap of griefs
    until it no longer crushes me?   At a rainy spring

graduation the commencement speaker says *I can't wait to upload*
    my consciousness to the internet   I'm uneasy

with anything that stinks of the Singularity,   of my heartbeat
    becoming prosody   Sometimes I think my doing

is more like *don't*ing   moving always on the great American script
    of interchanges and exits   No, I don't wish to make

more of the mouthful of my mother's cigarettes I gulped from a Diet Rite
    can, the dog with no hair she kept in the spare

room   My poet's coat of arms is a cowbird on a skittish
    lamb   No thank you, I think I'll just lie

down and shut the blinds   Please bring me a sip of water   my mouth's dry
    and yet you'd ask me to magnify the sun to fire?

Rachel Zucker
The Self in Poetry: A GNAT (Grossly Non-Academic Talk) with a Weaving Metaphor

What else is there?

Seriously.

Consider.

It is through the self that one organizes, makes sense of, tells the raw sense data of the world, which is everything that is not self.

Objectivity is an idea, not even an ideal, like a unicorn—could but doesn't exist. Everything real is subjective: of, through self.

Consider:

This talk (without the first person pronoun) begins to sound like the big man on campus—professorial, author-ial, authoritative, authoritarian. Also ridiculous. A mockery. An exercise in excise. Awfully philosophical.

Do you believe that if one changes the relative distance between the self and the reader, or the self and the subject, that the result is a completely different story or poem?

Of course.

The lack of first person pronoun leads one to make assumptions about others' thoughts, feelings, intentions. Be declarative. Bossy. Rhetorical.

    1. resolved: the proximity of the self is a formal decision.
    2. resolved: form is the signature of the self.
    3. resolved: the subject matter is always the self.

You're right, of course. This is just an exercise. After all, the self has many names, the letter after "h" and before "j" is only the most common term of endearment.

One, you, she can get around it, can speak, so to speak, make speeches without it and the self is still there, for, as has been said before, what else is there? Who else is speaking?

The self is the one who speaks, sees, makes.

Rachel Zucker in preparation for the A.W.P. panel on the self in poetry wonders, "what else is there? Other than the self or self & other. Form? Language? The stuff of poetry? Are these ever separate?"

1. the relative propinquity and visibility of the self are formal decisions and all formal changes alter content.
2. Form (tight weave or basted stitch) is the signature of the self. They create each other.
3. What else is worth writing (about)?

The self is the basis for humanity and humility
for measure (the breath)
for sanity (to distinguish the self from others)
for love (to perceive the self in or wanting others)
for health (the immune system's ability to distinguish the self from others)

The basis for separate or same.

The self makes contact with all that is not self and compares and measures. What is separate? What is same? Poetry is this self-expression.

Self=through which everything.

The poet Rachel Zucker, in particular, has always been fascinated by the way her/the integrated self was undoing or undone—moments when this undoing is particularly extreme. The self endangered and vivified. Moments when the "what else is there" question terrifies.

She noticed: the woman is part girl and part daughter and part mother and of all the things she is not: male, dead, etc.

"What else is there?" Well, everything.

One sees color as it bounces off the physical world. One sees the world only ever through the self, bounced off the self. The measure. The basis.

Makes you sane, lonely, and objectified. Available. Love-able.

The literary tradition of great men thought the world a symbol of self as if self came first—a great blazing sun above the roiling sea and lusty wind and were always espousing which means mouthing off and marrying.

They make each other: self + wind + poem = poem + self (sound of wind) reader blown about, pulling the poem in close around her.

What else is there?

How obnoxious this is. Without the ___.

Disrespects you.

Without the self no other. Real other.

In her particular case something happens. To and in her and from and out of. The self inhabited and doubled and emptied and bursted forth from.

Inside/outside: obsessed with.

Unnatural. Natural. What a woman's body was made to do.

One and one make one inside one and out of one some new someone and what then of the "one"? The first one—woman—is she singular? Broken?

But this is not about babies, is about the self—fractured, liquid, seeping, having literally become multiple, its residue coating everything.

Death does this too, of course, not only birth, birthing. Not only women but that's the self she knows and the self is always, always particular.

By which Rachel Zucker means the white-hot self, the mother-self that burst forth unseen but felt and overtook her—irrevocable.

Without the self the poem lacks.

"Hello? Who's there?" No one? Then, who cares?

Sometimes poems try to go without.

The weather is.

The world is.

The roiling sea.

And people say "the speaker" and "the author," but if they aren't the self who the hell?

The poem is all self. All. The world as apprehended by the self and her senses. And the poem, for Rachel Zucker, at least, is made necessary when the self suddenly becomes visible and unavoidable. Not the reflection of self—narcissus in the still pool or the refracted self, self, self in the corner of the mind's dressing room mirror—but the self itself making and unmaking and being made.

It is the question, "what else is there?" that makes us human and have empathy for there is else: other, world. But never separable or perceptible from/without the self. Certainly not communicable.

(Woven into and from the world into and from the self.)

Do you understand? This is not to say the self is the frame around the poem, oh no. And not to say the self is the seminal seed or spark that makes it (us) all.

Because a poem is not an idea but has a body and this body is the self, let's call it "selvage."

The self in poetry, of poetry, is substance, subject and action. Content and action.

The self and the poem make each other real.

In a woven fabric, the selvage is the uncut edge that is on the right and left as it comes out of the loom. As such it will not fray because the weft threads double back on themselves, unfinished but structurally sound.

Exists.

The material world run through with the golden thread of self, the subject itself and witness itself doubled back is the made, finished/unfinished thing, everything else unravels or glistens like an emperor's new clothes: idea only.

MEMORY

In the scientific literature, it is unclear if both memory and imagination take place in the same parts of the brain. It is clear, however, that very many human brains see images when they are prompted about a memory. *Remember when you were in fourth grade…* and out flow pictures in the mind, for most of us.

Memory as related or as happens in a poem may or may not involve images. Sometimes words or phrases occur to us, for instance, that derive from our family or friends. We recall something that was spoken. *Godfrey! Mom would exclaim whenever Dad would do something she didn't approve of.* Sometimes we recall a past time and want to give it a memory—to give it a narrative or an explanation for why something happened as it did. Collectively, this can occur as myth or legend or oral history. William Wordsworth argued that memories are more valuable than the actual experience that produced the memory. (Did he argue this or is this a collective memory we have of what his poetry embodies?)

You can relive a memory any time you like, again and again. Freud would agree, though he found this mostly negative—your old, traumatic experiences can't be escaped easily, if at all. What underlies many poems that are about or involve memories is that you have *a choice* and power to make of them what you will.

Robert Frost's "The Road Not Taken" appears to illustrate the quintessence of choice. For more than a hundred years, millions of readers have believed that the poem is all about "taking the path less traveled" and how doing so—making *that* choice—is where one derives meaning. This falls neatly into another Americanism, "march to the beat of your own drum." But if you set aside pop culture's take-away and actually closely read the poem, you will come to very different, even opposing, conclusions. Is the road of the title "The Road Not Taken," the road that the speaker actually took? Does the idea of traveling down one road change the traveler who might go back and take the road not taken the first time? And what exactly is implied by the last line's "made all the difference"? Is the difference positive, negative, or ambiguous? It would appear that our past isn't just for memory's sake, or for nostalgia or regret, but exists so we might choose who we want to be today. So that in looking forward, even from the past (think about that "sigh" in the final stanza), we choose where we are now.

Robert Frost
The Road Not Taken

Two roads diverged in a yellow wood,
And sorry I could not travel both
And be one traveler, long I stood
And looked down one as far as I could
To where it bent in the undergrowth;

Then took the other, as just as fair,
And having perhaps the better claim,
Because it was grassy and wanted wear;
Though as for that the passing there
Had worn them really about the same,

And both that morning equally lay
In leaves no step had trodden black.
Oh, I kept the first for another day!
Yet knowing how way leads on to way,
I doubted if I should ever come back.

I shall be telling this with a sigh
Somewhere ages and ages hence:
Two roads diverged in a wood, and I—
I took the one less traveled by,
And that has made all the difference.

Brandon D. Johnson
Standing by a Shelf

for Reuben

When he looks at the edges,
The covers of books and records,
He remembers when and where
He got them, how it felt.
Everything's a testament

To life lived on the fringe
Of some sense of sanity.

All the vehicles for imbibing
These treasures are obsolete.
Even his eyes and ears, as their
Function fades under each year's
Mud and tussle to stay alive

The damned fine few who know
Try not to lose the memories,
Talk as if each was there
For the other, laughter supplants tears.
If he can, a story gets written
About each song, how a chord
A lyric, the last line of a book

Make more sense, the same as the
Warnings his mother threw
At fledgling feet like seeds in soil.
He wishes he could buy them all again,
Heed the messages, grow as if
Each signpost was a vitamin
Make what became a recollection
A catalyst for pathfinding and strength.

Natasha Trethewey
Theories of Time and Space

You can get there from here, though
there's no going home.

Everywhere you go will be somewhere
you've never been. Try this:

head south on Mississippi 49, one-
by-one mile markers ticking off

another minute of your life. Follow this
to its natural conclusion—dead end

at the coast, the pier at Gulfport where
riggings of shrimp boats are loose stitches

in a sky threatening rain. Cross over
the man-made beach, 26 miles of sand

dumped on a mangrove swamp—buried
terrain of the past. Bring only

what you must carry—tome of memory,
its random blank pages. On the dock

where you board the boat for Ship Island,
someone will take your picture:

the photograph—who you were—
will be waiting when you return.

John Z. Guzlowski
My Father's Mother Asks Him to Forget the War

My father sits at the table listening
to the photos spread before him.
The last one whispers, I am your mother,
hold me, I am dying, remember
that spring when your father died
before the war, before my death
became mixed with your dying.

I dressed in black, sold flowers
in the village, felt myself dying
in tongues and prayed for deliverance
for your birth, for you to hold me,
to remember me, nothing else mattered.

I knew it then and know it
still, just hold me, look at my face
make sense of the life I lived,
just hold me, hold me, anything.

Seamus Heaney
Digging

Between my finger and my thumb
The squat pen rests; snug as a gun.

Under my window, a clean rasping sound
When the spade sinks into gravelly ground:
My father, digging. I look down

Till his straining rump among the flowerbeds
Bends low, comes up twenty years away

Stooping in rhythm through potato drills
Where he was digging.

The coarse boot nestled on the lug, the shaft
Against the inside knee was levered firmly.
He rooted out tall tops, buried the bright edge deep
To scatter new potatoes that we picked
Loving their cool hardness in our hands.

By God, the old man could handle a spade.
Just like his old man.

My grandfather cut more turf in a day
Than any other man on Toner's bog.
Once I carried him milk in a bottle
Corked sloppily with paper. He straightened up
To drink it, then fell to right away

Nicking and slicing neatly, heaving sods
Over his shoulder, going down and down
For the good turf. Digging.

The cold smell of potato mould, the squelch and slap
Of soggy peat, the curt cuts of an edge
Through living roots awaken in my head.
But I've no spade to follow men like them.

Between my finger and my thumb
The squat pen rests.
I'll dig with it.

SUBLIMATION

Seamus Heaney's poem in the previous section "digs" into the past by writing about the past. Instead of taking a spade to the earth, as the speaker's forefathers did, the speaker takes to the page. Writing a poem can be a way of transforming and shaping memory and feeling, not just reliving it.

Sublimation rests on such transformation of interior life to exterior art, often motivated by catharsis, unrequited love, taboo, and yearning. About the value of sublimation, Gabriel Gudding cites his years of leading poetry workshops for incarcerated women: "Their writing frankly helps decrease the amount of pain in their world."

As a poet, you'll have to figure out your own pain levels. Do writing down and making poems out of intense emotions lessen and purge your pain, or do these activities propel and galvanize your pain, making closure or acceptance that much harder?

Lisel Mueller
When I Am Asked

When I am asked
how I began writing poems,
I talk about the indifference of nature.

It was soon after my mother died,
a brilliant June day,
everything blooming.

I sat on a gray stone bench
in a lovingly planted garden,
but the day lilies were as deaf
as the ears of drunken sleepers
and the roses curved inward.
Nothing was black or broken
and not a leaf fell
and the sun blared endless commercials
for summer holidays.

I sat on a gray stone bench
ringed with the ingenue faces
of pink and white impatiens
and placed my grief
in the mouth of language,
the only thing that would grieve with me.

Gwendolyn Brooks
the mother

Abortions will not let you forget.
You remember the children you got that you did not get,
The damp small pulps with a little or with no hair,
The singers and workers that never handled the air.
You will never neglect or beat
Them, or silence or buy with a sweet.
You will never wind up the sucking-thumb
Or scuttle off ghosts that come.
You will never leave them, controlling your luscious sigh,
Return for a snack of them, with gobbling mother-eye.
I have heard in the voices of the wind the voices of my dim killed children.
I have contracted. I have eased
My dim dears at the breasts they could never suck.
I have said, Sweets, if I sinned, if I seized

Your luck
And your lives from your unfinished reach,
If I stole your births and your names,
Your straight baby tears and your games,
Your stilted or lovely loves, your tumults, your marriages, aches, and your deaths,
If I poisoned the beginnings of your breaths,
Believe that even in my deliberateness I was not deliberate.
Though why should I whine,
Whine that the crime was other than mine?—
Since anyhow you are dead.
Or rather, or instead,
You were never made.
But that too, I am afraid,
Is faulty: oh, what shall I say, how is the truth to be said?
You were born, you had body, you died.
It is just that you never giggled or planned or cried.

Believe me, I loved you all.
Believe me, I knew you, though faintly, and I loved, I loved you
All.

Sherman Alexie
How to Write the Great American Indian Novel

All of the Indians must have tragic features: tragic noses, eyes, and arms.
Their hands and fingers must be tragic when they reach for tragic food.

The hero must be a half-breed, half white and half Indian, preferably
from a horse culture. He should often weep alone. That is mandatory.

If the hero is an Indian woman, she is beautiful. She must be slender
and in love with a white man. But if she loves an Indian man

then he must be a half-breed, preferably from a horse culture.
If the Indian woman loves a white man, then he has to be so white

that we can see the blue veins running through his skin like rivers.
When the Indian woman steps out of her dress, the white man gasps

at the endless beauty of her brown skin. She should be compared to nature:
brown hills, mountains, fertile valleys, dewy grass, wind, and clear water.

If she is compared to murky water, however, then she must have a secret.
Indians always have secrets, which are carefully and slowly revealed.

Yet Indian secrets can be disclosed suddenly, like a storm.
Indian men, of course, are storms. They should destroy the lives

of any white women who choose to love them. All white women love
Indian men. That is always the case. White women feign disgust

at the savage in blue jeans and T-shirt, but secretly lust after him.
White women dream about half-breed Indian men from horse cultures.

Indian men are horses, smelling wild and gamey. When the Indian man
unbuttons his pants, the white woman should think of topsoil.

There must be one murder, one suicide, one attempted rape.
Alcohol should be consumed. Cars must be driven at high speeds.

Indians must see visions. White people can have the same visions
if they are in love with Indians. If a white person loves an Indian

then the white person is Indian by proximity. White people must carry
an Indian deep inside themselves. Those interior Indians are half-breed

and obviously from horse cultures. If the interior Indian is male
then he must be a warrior, especially if he is inside a white man.

If the interior Indian is female, then she must be a healer, especially if she is inside
a white woman. Sometimes there are complications.

An Indian man can be hidden inside a white woman. An Indian woman
can be hidden inside a white man. In these rare instances,

everybody is a half-breed struggling to learn more about his or her horse culture.
There must be redemption, of course, and sins must be forgiven.

For this, we need children. A white child and an Indian child, gender
not important, should express deep affection in a childlike way.

In the Great American Indian novel, when it is finally written,
all of the white people will be Indians and all of the Indians will be ghosts.

Ashley Durant
Dreams

Tonight, I watch my husband sleep. He is dark
amid the grey dark, the terrorist. It helps me
to think that violent people also snore. It helps
me to think of a little seed of mercy here and there.
I sometimes practice seeing my infant son
as the terrorist's son. I think, *His son will also
amaze him by waving for the first time, by calling
his parents by name.* I'm not sure what I'm looking
for this exercise to do. It's a little like quizzing
yourself in a second language to see if you've still

got it. It even resembles another language, this process
of carrying away the rough sides of the imagination,
of delivering the mind's eye away from fear.
We remember too much; so we forget, gestures of faith
take practice. And peace takes peace. And we make
each other. And making each other takes seeing light
in the mind's eye, takes knowing: how dreams make real.

IMITATION

There are innumerable ways to imitate a poem. You can mimic its content in topic, theme, story, overall emotion, or mimic its structure in line, stanza, shape, punctuation, etc. You can attempt both at once, as Jeffrey Harrison does with Christopher Smart's poem below. Alternatively, you can imitate by responding directly to a poem or speaker in a poem, as Annie Finch does by embodying the voice of Andrew Marvell's "mistress." Sometimes imitation risks parody. So be it. One of the best ways to genuinely grasp a poem's inner-workings is by making serious fun of it, where you must follow each movement, turn, and subtlety, essentially reconstructing how the poem was originally made. There also exists a healthy tradition of writing a poem as a "variation" of another's poem; John Murillo employs Bishop's "One Art" as a muse worthy of any of the ancients. One key aspect of imitation is that one can never do it *precisely*—and in the imprecision something new is created, a by-product or a descendant, with a potential all its own.

Christopher Smart
from *Jubilate Agno*

For I will consider my Cat Jeoffry.
For he is the servant of the Living God duly and daily serving him.
For at the first glance of the glory of God in the East he worships in his way.
For this is done by wreathing his body seven times round with elegant quickness.
For then he leaps up to catch the musk, which is the blessing of God upon his prayer.
For he rolls upon prank to work it in.
For having done duty and received blessing he begins to consider himself.
For this he performs in ten degrees.
For first he looks upon his forepaws to see if they are clean.
For secondly he kicks up behind to clear away there.
For thirdly he works it upon stretch with the forepaws extended.
For fourthly he sharpens his paws by wood.
For fifthly he washes himself.
For sixthly he rolls upon wash.
For seventhly he fleas himself, that he may not be interrupted upon the beat.

For eighthly he rubs himself against a post.
For ninthly he looks up for his instructions.
For tenthly he goes in quest of food.
For having consider'd God and himself he will consider his neighbour.
For if he meets another cat he will kiss her in kindness.
For when he takes his prey he plays with it to give it a chance.
For one mouse in seven escapes by his dallying.
For when his day's work is done his business more properly begins.
For he keeps the Lord's watch in the night against the adversary.
For he counteracts the powers of darkness by his electrical skin and glaring eyes.
For he counteracts the Devil, who is death, by brisking about the life.
For in his morning orisons he loves the sun and the sun loves him.
For he is of the tribe of Tiger.
For the Cherub Cat is a term of the Angel Tiger.
For he has the subtlety and hissing of a serpent, which in goodness he suppresses.
For he will not do destruction, if he is well-fed, neither will he spit without provocation.
For he purrs in thankfulness, when God tells him he's a good Cat.
For he is an instrument for the children to learn benevolence upon.
For every house is incomplete without him and a blessing is lacking in the spirit.
For the Lord commanded Moses concerning the cats at the departure of the Children of Israel from Egypt.
For every family had one cat at least in the bag.
For the English Cats are the best in Europe.
For he is the cleanest in the use of his forepaws of any quadruped.
For the dexterity of his defence is an instance of the love of God to him exceedingly.
For he is the quickest to his mark of any creature.
For he is tenacious of his point.
For he is a mixture of gravity and waggery.
For he knows that God is his Saviour.
For there is nothing sweeter than his peace when at rest.
For there is nothing brisker than his life when in motion.
For he is of the Lord's poor and so indeed is he called by benevolence perpetually—
Poor Jeoffry! poor Jeoffry! the rat has bit thy throat.
For I bless the name of the Lord Jesus that Jeoffry is better.
For the divine spirit comes about his body to sustain it in complete cat.
For his tongue is exceeding pure so that it has in purity what it wants in music.
For he is docile and can learn certain things.
For he can set up with gravity which is patience upon approbation.
For he can fetch and carry, which is patience in employment.
For he can jump over a stick which is patience upon proof positive.
For he can spraggle upon waggle at the word of command.
For he can jump from an eminence into his master's bosom.
For he can catch the cork and toss it again.
For he is hated by the hypocrite and miser.
For the former is afraid of detection.

For the latter refuses the charge.
For he camels his back to bear the first notion of business.
For he is good to think on, if a man would express himself neatly.
For he made a great figure in Egypt for his signal services.
For he killed the Ichneumon-rat very pernicious by land.
For his ears are so acute that they sting again.
For from this proceeds the passing quickness of his attention.
For by stroking of him I have found out electricity.
For I perceived God's light about him both wax and fire.
For the Electrical fire is the spiritual substance, which God sends from heaven to sustain the bodies both of man and beast.
For God has blessed him in the variety of his movements.
For, tho he cannot fly, he is an excellent clamberer.
For his motions upon the face of the earth are more than any other quadruped.
For he can tread to all the measures upon the music.
For he can swim for life.
For he can creep.

Jeffrey Harrison
Arrival

after Christopher Smart

I will consider my son William,
who came into the world two weeks early, as if he couldn't wait;
who was carried on a river that gushed from his mother;
who was purple with matted black hair;
who announced his arrival not by crying but by peeing, with the umbilical cord still attached;
who looked all around with wide slate-blue eyes and smacked his lips as if to taste the world;
who took to his mother's breast right away;
who sucks my little finger with such vigor that it feels as if he's going to pull my fingernail right off;
who sometimes refuses my finger, screwing up his face in disgust as if I have stuck a pickled radish into his mouth;
whose face is beautiful and not like a shriveled prune;
whose hair, though black, is soft as milkweed;
who was born with long eyelashes that girls will someday envy;
whose fingernails are minuscule, thin and pliable;
whose toes are like caterpillars;
whose penis is a little acorn;
whose excrement is like the finest mustard;
who can squeak like a mouse and bleat like a lamb;
who hiccups and his whole body convulses;

who screams and turns red and kicks sometimes when we change his diaper;
who when he stops screaming is probably peeing;
whose deep sobs from the back of his throat bring tears to my own eyes;
who likes to be carried in a pouched sling;
who thinks he is a marsupial;
who has soft fur on his shoulders, back, and legs;
who is nocturnal and whose eyes are widest at night;
who will sleep sometimes if I lay him across my chest;
whose eyes flutter, whose nostrils dilate, and whose mouth twitches into strange
    grimaces and smiles as he dreams;
who is full of the living spirit which causes his body to wiggle and squirm;
who stretches his arms and arches his back and you can feel his great strength;
who lies with the soles of his feet together, as if praying with his feet;
who is a blessing upon our household and upon the world;
who doesn't know where the world ends and he begins;
who is himself the world;
who has a sweet smell.

Andrew Marvell
To His Coy Mistress

Had we but world enough and time,
This coyness, lady, were no crime.
We would sit down, and think which way
To walk, and pass our long love's day.
Thou by the Indian Ganges' side
Shouldst rubies find; I by the tide
Of Humber would complain. I would
Love you ten years before the flood,
And you should, if you please, refuse
Till the conversion of the Jews.
My vegetable love should grow
Vaster than empires and more slow;
An hundred years should go to praise
Thine eyes, and on thy forehead gaze;
Two hundred to adore each breast,
But thirty thousand to the rest;
An age at least to every part,
And the last age should show your heart.
For, lady, you deserve this state,
Nor would I love at lower rate.
    But at my back I always hear
Time's wingèd chariot hurrying near;
And yonder all before us lie

Deserts of vast eternity.
Thy beauty shall no more be found;
Nor, in thy marble vault, shall sound
My echoing song; then worms shall try
That long-preserved virginity,
And your quaint honour turn to dust,
And into ashes all my lust;
The grave's a fine and private place,
But none, I think, do there embrace.
   Now therefore, while the youthful hue
Sits on thy skin like morning dew,
And while thy willing soul transpires
At every pore with instant fires,
Now let us sport us while we may,
And now, like amorous birds of prey,
Rather at once our time devour
Than languish in his slow-chapped power.
Let us roll all our strength and all
Our sweetness up into one ball,
And tear our pleasures with rough strife
Through the iron gates of life:
Thus, though we cannot make our sun
Stand still, yet we will make him run.

Annie Finch
Coy Mistress

Sir, I am not a bird of prey:
a Lady does not seize the day.
I trust that brief Time will unfold
our youth, before he makes us old.
How could we two write lines of rhyme
were we not fond of numbered Time
and grateful to the vast and sweet
trials his days will make us meet?
The Grave's not just the body's curse;
no skeleton can pen a verse!
So while this numbered World we see,
let's sweeten Time with poetry,
and Time, in turn, may sweeten Love
and give us time our love to prove.
You've praised my eyes, forehead, breast:
you've all our lives to praise the rest.

John Murillo
Variations on a Theme by Elizabeth Bishop

Start with loss. Lose everything. Then lose it all again.
Lose a good woman on a bad day. Find a better woman,
then lose five friends chasing her. Learn to lose as if
your life depended on it. Learn that your life depends on it.
Learn it like karate, like riding a bike. *Learn it, master it.*
Lose money, lose time, lose your natural mind.
Get left behind, then learn to leave others. Lose and
lose again. Measure a father's coffin against a cousin's
crashing T-cells. Kiss your sister through prison glass.
Know why your woman's not answering her phone.
Lose sleep. Lose religion. Lose your wallet in El Segundo.
Open your window. Listen: the last slow notes
of a Donny Hathaway song. A child crying. Listen:
a drunk man is cussing out the moon. He sounds like
your dead uncle, who, before he left, lost a leg
to sugar. Shame. Learn what's given can be taken;
what can be taken, will. This you can bet on without
losing. Sure as nightfall and an empty bed. Lose
and lose again. Lose until it's second nature. *Losing
farther, losing faster.* Lean out your open window, listen:
the child is laughing now. No, it's the drunk man again
in the street, losing his voice, suffering each invisible star.

AVANT-GARDE

Who or what comprises the avant-garde? Tristan Tzara, a prominent member of Dadaism, seems to embed one answer in his guide to making a dadaist poem. The penultimate line reads "The poem will resemble you." Does that also mean you resemble the poem, a mere product of chance? The last line holds a special ambiguity: "And there you are—an infinitely original author of charming sensibility, though misunderstood by the vulgar herd." So on the one hand, you are original and charming; on the other, you are misunderstood by the masses. This sleight of hand implies that since seemingly anyone can follow a few simple instructions for making a poem, everyone—including each individual who makes up the "vulgar"—can be original. Tzara's little how-to may be a dare, but it is also a call to arms. If chance operations aren't your thing, however, create your own mini-manifesto. Old or young, it's never too late for a poet to pen a mission statement.

Tristan Tzara (translated from the French by Mark Yakich)
To make a dadaist poem

Get a newspaper.
Get a pair of scissors.
Choose an article from the paper the length you want to make your poem.
Cut out the article.
Then carefully cut out each of the words of the article and put them all in a bag.
Shake gently.
Then take out each clipping, one after the other.
Carefully copy them down in the order in which you took them out of the bag.
The poem will resemble you.
And voilà there you are—an infinitely original author of charming sensibility, though
 misunderstood by the masses.

REVISION

The art of revision is the art of re-seeing. Re-envisioning. How to do this? By making many, many, many new versions from your initial one. By making versions of versions. By making so many that even the "original" intent of the first version gets altered significantly or gets lost entirely. (Tweaks, while helpful and necessary at times, are not new versions.) The idea is to push and pull until you make poetic and perhaps personal discoveries. Sometimes you'll have to invent the discoveries.

Test your poem as you might a machine. Pushing its limitations until it's about to break. Sometimes you'll have to break it ... until it's no longer recognizable to itself—or to you.

Maya Abu Al-Hayyat (translated from the Arabic by Fady Joudah)
Revision

I must revise my work with the past,
take my time, without malice.
So far I have spread my past, quite well I'd say,
over men and aunties,
and was convinced that I would heal from it
once they were dead
and decomposed,
my ribs a broom
and my hands a canvas.
And especially after I give a lesson
on the imperishable land
and baby chicks that fall out of their nests
just before a crow eats them.

I must revise my work with the past,
my many loves
who died and still possess their corpses,
but also those who died
without declarable bodies.
I will inform them that I distributed the same poem
to each of them, though I didn't necessarily
love them, a point I have previously explained,
that I like to explain again
as I redistribute poems.
I will tell them about your corpse
sprayed with chlorine
in a plastic bag
and how we return.
It wasn't fair that you died
without a last scribble
in which you challenge something,
anything, so that we can say
"He finished his final painting,
didn't leave it suspended in our throats."
Whenever there's a going, there's no return.
They're distributing plastic bags to the masses,
spraying chlorine through massive pumps.
We're carrying our souls
right under our shoulders.

POET-TEACHERS

No matter how impartial, open, and available a poet-teacher tries to be, they will almost always teach you how to read and write like they do. This is no reason to cavil. Because you will inevitably mishear or otherwise miscomprehend something of what they are trying to impart. This is a kind of learning to profit from; let no one tell you differently. There will also come a time when you find that the best poet-teachers are the poems that other poets write. These poems are like the stories of Zen masters: they will teach you by illustrating a new feeling, idea, or a form. The difficulty will be learning how to become both your own teacher and student.

Marianne Boruch
Pencil

My drawing teacher said: Look, think, make a mark.
Look, I told myself.
And waited to be marked.

Clouds are white but they darken
with rain. Even a child blurs them back
to little woollies on a hillside, little
bundles without legs. Look, my teacher
would surely tell me, they're nothing

like that. *Like* that: the lie. *Like* that: the poem.
She said: Respond to the heaviest part
of the figure first. Density is
form. That I keep hearing *destiny*

is not a mark of character. Like *pilgrimage*
once morphed to *mirage* in a noisy room, someone
so earnest at my ear. Then *marriage* slid.
Mir-aage, Mir-aage, I heard the famous poet let loose
awry into her microphone, triumphant.
The figure to be drawn —
not even half my age. She's completely
emptied her face for this job of standing still an hour.
Look. Okay. But the little

dream in there, inside the *think*
that comes next. A pencil in my hand, its secret life
is charcoal, the wood already burnt,
a sacrifice.

Langston Hughes
Theme for English B

The instructor said,

> *Go home and write*
> *a page tonight.*
> *And let that page come out of you—*
> *Then, it will be true.*

I wonder if it's that simple?
I am twenty-two, colored, born in Winston-Salem.
I went to school there, then Durham, then here
to this college on the hill above Harlem.
I am the only colored student in my class.
The steps from the hill lead down into Harlem,
through a park, then I cross St. Nicholas,
Eighth Avenue, Seventh, and I come to the Y,
the Harlem Branch Y, where I take the elevator
up to my room, sit down, and write this page:

It's not easy to know what is true for you or me
at twenty-two, my age. But I guess I'm what
I feel and see and hear, Harlem, I hear you:
hear you, hear me—we two—you, me, talk on this page.
(I hear New York, too.) Me—who?
Well, I like to eat, sleep, drink, and be in love.
I like to work, read, learn, and understand life.
I like a pipe for a Christmas present,
or records—Bessie, bop, or Bach.
I guess being colored doesn't make me *not* like
the same things other folks like who are other races.
So will my page be colored that I write?

Being me, it will not be white.
But it will be
a part of you, instructor.
You are white—
yet a part of me, as I am a part of you.
That's American.
Sometimes perhaps you don't want to be a part of me.
Nor do I often want to be a part of you.
But we are, that's true!
As I learn from you,
I guess you learn from me—
although you're older—and white—
and somewhat more free.

This is my page for English B.

PROFESSIONALIZATION

David Lehman's "With Tenure" takes its cue from Ezra Pound's "Canto XLV," a poem that begins "*With Usura* / With usura hath no man a house of good stone …." Pound's poem is a dogmatic reaction against usury, the practice of loaning money at exorbitant interest rates. Lehman's poem, however, is a little more complicated in tone. The practice of tenure (which occurs less and less in higher education now) is railed against but to such amplification that its opposition seems sarcastic and comic. (This comes through even if we are unaware that the author of the poem is a tenured professor at a large East Coast university.)

Jehanne Dubrow's poem below appears at first to be pure parody. Is it? Or does it merely *verge* on parody? Why would the difference matter? Relatedly, how does professionalism deal with that which isn't solely *professional*?

David Lehman
With Tenure

If Ezra Pound were alive today
    (and he is)
he'd be teaching
at a small college in the Pacific Northwest
and attending the annual convention
of writing instructors in St. Louis
and railing against tenure,
saying tenure
is a ladder whose rungs slip out
from under the scholar as he climbs
upwards to empty heaven
by the angels abandoned
for tenure killeth the spirit
(with tenure no man becomes master)
Texts are unwritten with tenure,
under the microscope, *sous rature*
it turneth the scholar into a drone
decayeth the pipe in his jacket's breast pocket.
Hamlet was not written with tenure,
nor were written Schubert's lieder
nor Manet's *Olympia* painted with tenure.
No man of genius rises by tenure
Nor woman (I see you smile).
Picasso came not by tenure
nor Charlie Parker;
Came not by tenure Wallace Stevens
Not by tenure Marcel Proust
Nor Turner by tenure
With tenure hath only the mediocre
a sinecure unto death. Unto death, I say!
WITH TENURE
Nature is constipated the sap doesn't flow
With tenure the classroom is empty
    et in academia ego
the ketchup is stuck inside the bottle
the letter goes unanswered the bell doesn't ring.

Jehanne Dubrow
Portrait of an Administrator with Strategic Plan and Office Supplies

To sit on her couch was to be silenced
by upholstery, plush muffling of cushions
from which it was difficult to rise.
Arendt writes, *in politics obedience*
and support are the same, and for a time
I was obedient, my reports in ordered bullets:
collaborations, programs, opportunities.
The provost preferred speech contained—
a line of staples in a box. I remember
the fold between one week and the next.
She said to me, *these people are unreasonable.*
She said, *these people are quite reasonable.*
Inside her office everything was cream.
She told me what I heard I hadn't heard,
our last meeting like a memo full of typos
whited out, then shuffled through
the copier machine, language turned to shiny blurs.
Arendt writes, *most people will comply.*
For a time, it was easy to ignore the sharp
wedge of the provost's hair. I should have seen
she resembled more a letter opener on a desk,
how like a knife the piece of metal looks.
I told her what I heard I heard.
I told her that my expertise was words.
Arendt writes, *the holes of oblivion do not exist.*
A gifted bureaucrat, the provost taught me
truth was thin as paper—the little circles
she punched in it remain, and still
I hold this punctured story to the light.

LITERARY MAGAZINES

Literary magazines are the testing ground for your work as a poet. They exist for your trial and error. When you receive a rejection, you will on some level take it personally. Allow that feeling to come. It will pass, though perhaps not as quickly as you would like it to. Or, hold onto that hurt and possibly furious feeling and let it be the thorn in your side—the thorn that motivates you to work harder on your poems, to make new versions of them, and then to send poems out again.

Etheridge Knight
Rejections

We reject these poems because of the space taken
in sorrow,
that they do not speak of the promised horse of healing.

We reject these bone dark words
because they are joyless in shape
and silent of a rising wind.

Poetry should be easier, forgiven like,
not drug from innards,
too much of old men in dying light,
those moon sorrowed people
living in sexless rooms.

Put this darkness back into your pen.
Don't mail this scorpion again.

Submit something of a turn lifting,
the beginning of the sun about all froze,
written fully in a day of light.

PUBLICATION

They will tell you not to evaluate your self-worth based on your publications. This is true. Then, they will evaluate you based on your publications. This is also true. Hold these two truths, one in each hand, then clap. This is not a Zen koan.

Franz Wright
Publication Date

One of the few pleasures of writing
is the thought of one's book in the hands of a kindhearted
intelligent person somewhere. I can't remember what the others are right now.
I just noticed that it is my own private

National I Hate Myself and Want to Die Day
(which means the next day I will love my life
and want to live forever). The forecast calls
for a cold night in Boston all morning

and all afternoon. They say
tomorrow will be just like today,
only different. I'm in the cemetery now
at the edge of town, how did I get here?

A sparrow limps past on its little bone crutch saying
I am Federico García Lorca
risen from the dead—
literature will lose, sunlight will win, don't worry.

SERIES, SEQUENCE

What is the difference between a poem written in series and one written in sequence? Split hairs, as poets do. Once again, pattern and variation will be key to approaching these poems. Now, however, the patterns and variations can occur within sections and across sections.

Lyn Heijinian's poems here, only three of the dozens that comprise the various editions of her collection *My Life*, may at first seem baffling. Even after many readings, you may comprehend the intent only intuitively. Consider how her poems deal with the action of memory itself. How might one talk about the space-time continuum in her poems?

Mary Leader's "Series as Opposed to Sequence" will likely strike you very differently than the others here. It is not a narrative, there are few characters, as such, and no plot to speak of. So, is it a set of lyric poems, or is it actually a narrative of a different kind, one we're not familiar with? What bearing do the section titles No. 1, No. 2, No. 3, etc., have on the poem's intent? What other arts does the poem invoke? And where, perhaps most importantly, is the poem itself telling you *how* to read it?

Nâzim Hikmet (translated from the Turkish by Randy Blasing and Mutlu Konuk)
On Living

I
Living is no laughing matter:
    you must live with great seriousness
        like a squirrel, for example—
I mean without looking for something beyond and above living,
        I mean living must be your whole occupation.
Living is no laughing matter:
    you must take it seriously,
        so much so and to such a degree

that, for example, your hands tied behind your back,
                          your back to the wall,
or else in a laboratory
    in your white coat and safety glasses,
        you can die for people—
even for people whose faces you've never seen,
even though you know living
        is the most real, the most beautiful thing.
I mean, you must take living so seriously
  that even at seventy, for example, you'll plant olive trees—
  and not for your children, either,
  but because although you fear death you don't believe it,
  because living, I mean, weighs heavier.

II
Let's say we're seriously ill, need surgery—
which is to say we might not get up
                      from the white table.
Even though it's impossible not to feel sad
                      about going a little too soon,
we'll still laugh at the jokes being told,
we'll look out the window to see if it's raining,
or still wait anxiously
                for the latest newscast …
Let's say we're at the front—
      for something worth fighting for, say.
There, in the first offensive, on that very day,
    we might fall on our face, dead.
We'll know this with a curious anger,
    but we'll still worry ourselves to death
      about the outcome of the war, which could last years.
Let's say we're in prison
and close to fifty,
and we have eighteen more years, say,
                before the iron doors will open.
We'll still live with the outside,
with its people and animals, struggle and wind—
                      I mean with the outside beyond the walls.
I mean, however and wherever we are,
    we must live as if we will never die.

III
This earth will grow cold,
a star among stars

             and one of the smallest,
a gilded mote on blue velvet—
             I mean *this*, our great earth.
This earth will grow cold one day,
not like a block of ice
or a dead cloud even
but like an empty walnut it will roll along
             in pitch-black space …
You must grieve for this right now
—you have to feel this sorrow now—
for the world must be loved this much
                    if you're going to say "I lived" ….

Charles Reznikoff
Children (from *Holocaust*)

1

Once, among the transports, was one with children—two freight cars full.
The young men sorting out the belongings of those taken to the gas chambers
had to undress the children—they were orphans—
and then take them to the "lazarette."
There the S.S. men shot them.

2

A large eight-wheeled car arrived at the hospital
where there were children;
in the two trailers—open trucks—were sick women and men
lying on the floor.
The Germans threw the children into the trucks
from the second floor and the balconies—
children from one year old to ten;
threw them upon the sick in the trucks.
Some of the children tried to hold on to the walls,
scratched at the walls with their nails;
but the shouting Germans
beat and pushed the children towards the windows.

3

The children arrived at the camp in buses,
guarded by gendarmes of the French Vichy government.
The buses stopped in the middle of the courtyard

and the children were quickly taken off
to make room for the buses following.
Frightened but quiet,
the children came down in groups of fifty or sixty to eighty;
the younger children holding on to older ones.
They were taken upstairs to empty halls—
without any furniture
and only dirty straw bags on the floor, full of bugs:
children as young as two, three, or four years of age,
all in torn clothes and dirty,
for they had already spent two or three weeks in other camps,
uncared for;
and were now on their way to a death camp in Poland.
Some had only one shoe.
Many had diarrhea
but they were not allowed in the courtyard
where the water closets were;
and, although there were chamber pots in the corridor of each story,
these were too large for the small children.

The women in the camp who were also deportees
and about to be taken to other camps
were in tears:
they would get up before sunrise
and go into the halls where the children were—
in each a hundred to a hundred and twenty—
to mend the children's clothing;
but the women had no soap to clean the children,
no clean underwear to give them,
and only cold water with which to wash them.
When soup came for the children,
there were no spoons;
and it would be served in tins
but the tins were sometimes too hot for the children to hold.

After nine at night no one—except for three or four who had a permit—
was allowed to stay with the children.
Each room was then in darkness,
except for one bulb painted blue by blackout instructions.
The children would wake at night
calling for their mothers
and would then wake each other,
and sometimes all in the room would start crying out
and even wake the children in other rooms.

A visitor once stopped one of the children:
a boy of seven or eight, handsome, alert and gay.
He had only one shoe and the other foot was bare,
and his coat of good quality had no buttons.
The visitor asked him for his name
and then what his parents were doing;
and he said, "Father is working in the office
and Mother is playing the piano."
Then he asked the visitor if he would be joining his parents soon—
they always told the children they would be leaving soon to rejoin their parents—
and the visitor answered, "Certainly. In a day or two."
At that the child took out of his pocket
half an army biscuit he had been given in camp
and said, "I am keeping this half for Mother";
and then the child who had been so gay
burst into tears.

4

Other children, also separated from their parents,
arrived in buses,
and were put down in the courtyard of the camp—
a courtyard surrounded by barbed wire
and guarded by gendarmes.
On the day of leaving for the death camp
they were awakened at five in the morning.
Irritable, half asleep, most of them refused to get up and go down to the courtyard.
Women—French volunteers, for they were still in France—
urged the children gently
to obey—they must!—and vacate the halls.
But many still would not leave the straw bags on which they slept
and then the gendarmes entered,
and took up the children in their arms;
the children screamed with fear,
struggled and tried to grasp each other.

5

Women guards at the women's section of the concentration camp
were putting little children into trucks
to be taken away to the gas chambers
and the children were screaming and crying, "Mama, Mama,"
even though the guards were trying to give them pieces of candy to quiet them.

Lyn Hejinian
from *My Life*

A pause, a rose, something on paper

A moment yellow, just as four years later, when my father returned home from the war, the moment of greeting him, as he stood at the bottom of the stairs, younger, thinner than when he had left, was purple—though moments are no longer so colored. Somewhere, in the background, rooms share a pattern of small roses. Pretty is as pretty does. In certain families, the meaning of necessity is at one with the sentiment of pre-necessity. The better things were gathered in a pen. The windows were narrowed by white gauze curtains which were never loosened. Here I refer to irrelevance, that rigidity which never intrudes. Hence, repetitions, free from all ambition. The shadow of the redwood trees, she said, was oppressive. The plush must be worn away. On her walks she stepped into people's gardens to pinch off cuttings from their geraniums and succulents. An occasional sunset is reflected on the windows. A little puddle is overcast. If only you could touch, or, even, catch those gray great creatures. I was afraid of my uncle with the wart on his nose, or of his jokes at our expense which were beyond me, and I was shy of my aunt's deafness who was his sister-in-law and who had years earlier fallen into the habit of nodding, agreeably. Wool station. See lightning, wait for thunder. Quite mistakenly, as it happened. Long time lines trail behind every idea, object, person, pet, vehicle, and event. The afternoon happens, crowded and therefore endless. Thicker, she agreed. It was a tic, she had the habit, and now she bobbed like my toy plastic bird on the edge of its glass, dipping into and recoiling from the water. But a word is a bottomless pit. It became magically pregnant and one day split open, giving birth to a stone egg, about as big as a football. In May when the lizards emerge from the stones, the stones turn gray, from green. When daylight moves, we delight in distance. The waves rolled over our stomachs, like spring rain over an orchard slope. Rubber bumpers on rubber cars. The resistance on sleeping to being asleep. In every country is a word which attempts the sound of cats, to match an insolable portrait in the clouds to a din in the air. But the constant noise is not an omen of music to come. "Everything is a question of sleep," says Cocteau, but he forgets the shark, which does not. Anxiety is vigilant. Perhaps initially, even before one can talk, restlessness is already conventional, establishing the incoherent border which will later separate events from experience. Find a drawer that's not filled up. That we sleep plunges our work into the dark. The ball was lost in a bank of myrtle. I was in a room with the particulars of which a later nostalgia might be formed, an indulged childhood. They are sitting in wicker chairs, the legs of which have sunk unevenly into the ground, so that each is sitting slightly tilted and their postures make adjustment for that. The cows warm their own barn. I look at them fast and it gives the illusion that they're moving. An "oral history" on paper. *That* morning this morning. I say it about the psyche because it is not optional. The overtones are a denser shadow in the room characterized by its habitual readiness, a form of charged waiting, a perpetual attendance, of which I was thinking when I began the paragraph, "So much of childhood is spent in a manner of waiting."

As for we who "love to be astonished"

You spill the sugar when you lift the spoon. My father had filled an old apothecary jar with what he called "sea glass," bits of old bottles rounded and textured by the sea, so abundant on beaches. There is no solitude. It buries itself in veracity. It is as if one splashed in the water lost by one's tears. My mother had climbed into the garbage can in order to stamp down the accumulated trash, but the can was knocked off balance, and when she fell she broke her arm. She could only give a little shrug. The family had little money but plenty of food. At the circus only the elephants were greater than anything I could have imagined. The egg of Columbus, landscape and grammar. She wanted one where the playground was dirt, with grass, shaded by a tree, from which would hang a rubber tire as a swing, and when she found it she sent me. These creatures are compound and nothing they do should surprise us. I don't mind, or I won't mind, where the verb "to care" might multiply. The pilot of the little airplane had forgotten to notify the airport of his approach, so that when the lights of the plane in the night were first spotted, the air raid sirens went off, and the entire city on that coast went dark. He was taking a drink of water and the light was growing dim. My mother stood at the window watching the only lights that were visible, circling over the darkened city in search of the hidden airport. Unhappily, time seems more normative than place. Whether breathing or holding the breath, it was the same thing, driving through the tunnel from one sun to the next under a hot brown hill. She sunned the baby for sixty seconds, leaving him naked except for a blue cotton sunbonnet. At night, to close off the windows from view of the street, my grandmother pulled down the window shades, never loosening the curtains, a gauze starched too stiff to hang properly down. I sat on the windowsill singing sunny lunny teena, ding-dang-dong. Out there is an aging magician who needs a tray of ice in order to turn his bristling breath into steam. He broke the radio silence. Why would anyone find astrology interesting when it is possible to learn about astronomy. What one passes in the Plymouth. It is the wind slamming the doors. All that is nearly incommunicable to my friends. Velocity and throat verisimilitude. Were we seeing a pattern or merely an appearance of small white sailboats on the bay, floating at such a distance from the hill that they appeared to be making no progress. And for once to a country that did not speak another language. To follow the progress of ideas, or that particular line of reasoning, so full of surprises and unexpected correlations, was somehow to take a vacation. Still, you had to wonder where they had gone, since you could speak of reappearance. A blue room is always dark. Everything on the boardwalk was shooting toward the sky. It was not specific to any year, but very early. A German goldsmith covered a bit of metal with cloth in the 14th century and gave mankind its first button. It was hard to know this as politics, because it plays like the work of one person, but nothing is isolated in history—certain humans are situations. Are your fingers in the margin. Their random procedures make monuments to fate. There is something still surprising when the green emerges. The blue fox has ducked its head. The front rhyme of harmless with harmony. Where is my honey running. You cannot linger "on the lamb." You cannot determine the nature of progress until you assemble all of the relatives.

It seemed that we had hardly begun and we were already there

We see only the leaves and branches of the trees close in around the house. Those submissive games were sensual. I was no more than three or four years old, but when crossed I would hold my breath, not from rage but from stubbornness, until I lost consciousness. The shadows one day deeper. Every family has its own collection of stories, but not every family has someone to tell them. In a small studio in an old farmhouse, it is the musical expression of a glowing optimism. A bird would reach but be secret. Absence of allusion: once, and ring alone. The downstairs telephone was in a little room as dark as a closet. It made a difference between the immediate and the sudden in a theater filled with transitions. Without what can a person function as the sea functions without me. A typical set of errands. My mother stood between us and held our hands as we waded into the gray-blue water, lecturing us on the undertow, more to add to the thrill of the approaching water than to warn us of any real danger, since she would continue to grip us by the hand when the wave came in and we tried to jump over it. The curve of the rain, more, comes over more often. Four seasons circle a square year. A mirror set in the crotch of the tree was like a hole in the out-of-doors. I could have ridden in the car forever, or so it seemed, watching the scenery go by, alert as to the circumstances of a dream, and that peaceful. Roller coast. The fog lifts a late sunrise. There are floral twigs in position on it. The roots of the locust tree were lifting the corner of the little cabin. Our unease grows before the newly restless. There you are, and you know it's good, and all you have to do is make it better. He sailed to the war. A life no more free than the life of a lost puppy. It became popular and then we were inundated with imitations. My old aunt entertained us with her lie, a story about an event in her girlhood, a catastrophe in a sailboat that never occurred, but she was blameless, unaccountable, since, in the course of the telling, she had come to believe the lie herself. A kind of burbling in the waters of inspiration. Because of their recurrence, what had originally seemed merely details of atmosphere became, in time, thematic. As if sky plus sun *must* make leaves. A snapdragon volunteering in the garden among the cineraria gapes its maw between the fingers, and we pinched the buds of the fuchsia to make them pop. Is that willful. Inclines. They have big calves because of those hills. Flip over small stones, dried mud. We thought that the mica might be gold. A pause, a rose, something on paper, in a nature scrapbook. What follows a strict chronology has no memory. For me, they must exist, the contents of that absent reality, the objects and occasions which now I reconsidered. The smells of the house were thus a peculiar mix of heavy interior air and the air from outdoors lingering over the rose bushes, the camellias, the hydrangeas, the rhododendron and azalea bushes. Hard to distinguish hunger from wanting to eat. My grandmother was in the kitchen, her hands on her hips, wearing what she called a "washdress," watching a line of ants cross behind the faucets of the sink, and she said to us, "Now *I* am waging war." There are strings in the terrible distance. They are against the blue. The trees are continually receiving their own shadows.

Mary Leader
Series as Opposed to Sequence

No. 1

The overall rhythmic profile
Of hills
Washes and alluvial fans
Would rise and fall over the entirety
Ledges of cliffs and steep canyon walls
Would rise and fall over the entirety
While chattering in their midst is a thriving anthill
There are these very large clouds that seem to tilt
He is looking up at the sky and thinks *there's an intelligence behind all of this*

No. 2

The desert is associated with
Preserving itself as long as it can
Dependent upon
Sustaining instruments
Hallucinations and insanity
A lightness and constant ambiguity
That basic ambiguity
Gray-green or blue-green
The possibility of not necessarily listening just to one thing or the other
Where there are no words at all

No. 3

When the structures begin
Sustained from the very beginning with very small slow changes
Usually comprising paired mallet instruments and sometimes two pianos
Each group is lightly doubled
When the structures begin
Where the A sections are slow and the B section moves up
Just after dusk
Each group is lightly doubled
And when listening in particular to two pieces
Primarily on one or two nights
Each group is lightly doubled
Fascinated by the symmetry

No. 4

Usually a single plant produces only a few flowers each season
This
Of course is
An old technique
It threatens one's normal thinking
The percussion is omnipresent
Clicking sticks
Just after dusk
They're pulsed
The realm of pulsation
To supply the ongoing pulse
The pulse which begins and ends
After about forty minutes
After more than a thousand years
A series of spasmodic jerks
He sort of reaches out
A wordless response to
Purely
Rapid eighth notes
This is an extremely emotional moment

No. 5

A vision
At 2000 to 4000 feet elevation
That you'd never get if the notes were sustained
Begins with this pulsation
Of available vibrations
Fruit red
Of the most intense and sophisticated sort
Ripening
In the desert or in grassland
Like strings or the electric organ
Repeating over and over again
"Fruit Red"
Gravel or coarse sandy soil
Sets up a kind of rhythmic energy
It's as if you're in the desert and you're running as fast as you can

No. 6

Gray-green or blue-green
Birds open the fleshy fruit from the side

Going into a text and then out of it again
That constant flickering of attention
All sequences
Simultaneously
Continued
Between what the text says and its pure sensual sound
A light radiating out of the dark infinitude
Out of this complete continuity
A-B-A
A-B-C-B-A
From beginning to end

No. 7

Reading his work to the present
With regard to where the stresses and where the beginnings and endings are
Dependent upon
The recipient
With the apical cup not prominent
But more chromatic and darker in harmony
Its own harmonic cycle
He then goes on to more complex pieces
With a few scales
Slowly
In the desert in a land belonging to no one
It is to this possibility that the words refer
And no more and no less

No. 8

Produced thirty-one flowers
Produced thirty-one flowers
Repetitive in any literal sense
In order to set up the feeling
Structure and harmony
The surrounding woody vegetation for protection from animals
Different things are happening at the same time
Or later if the weather is cool
Often move at a very slow rate of change
Are fast and use the same harmonic cycle
So the voices continue without words
With twenty-four open blossoms
Another plant on the desert at Sacaton was photographed
Normally over by seven o'clock the following morning
Another plant on the desert at Sacaton was photographed

For the lower part of it is brittle and easily broken
Another plant on the desert at Sacaton was photographed
And a single flower may scent the air for 100 feet

No. 9

But one unusually large plant in Tucson
Just after dusk
A kind of barge of light
Just after dusk
A large arch
Just after dusk
His death at age 80
Just after dusk
At which point the chorus sings "dee-dee-dee-dee-dee-"
And is itself an arch form
Without anything else added or subtracted

No. 10

Of hills
Of washes
Of alluvial fans
Ledges of cliffs and steep canyon walls
Late in May or in June
With a few scales
Floating down a river in very dark surroundings in complete darkness
Glissandos which with contact microphones attached
Resolved to put a plant of light in the last part
Between fascinated by the symmetry
Different from
The recipient
He sort of reaches out
A series of spasmodic jerks
The perfume is liberated in profusion

No. 11

COLLECTIONS

Among the many books Czesław Miłosz wrote and edited, there is an anthology of poetry titled *A Book of Luminous Things*. For each of the 300 hundred poems included, he wrote a brief header note. I sometimes wonder whether he ever looked back over the book and had regrets about the poems he didn't include or the ones he no longer admired as he once did, or whether he wanted to edit some of his notes. Once you finish writing or editing a poetry collection and it goes out into the world, it's no longer entirely yours. You have little power over how readers receive the book and whether or not they do as you intended. That is one of the hidden costs of publication. After publication you may view your book as a headstone, memorializing a life, real or literary, that no longer is. Don't take it so hard. Let Miłosz's "Dedication" remind you that regret holds the possibility of acceptance.

Czesław Miłosz
Dedication

You whom I could not save
Listen to me.
Try to understand this simple speech as I would be ashamed of another.
I swear, there is in me no wizardry of words.
I speak to you with silence like a cloud or a tree.

What strengthened me, for you was lethal.
You mixed up farewell to an epoch with the beginning of a new one,
Inspiration of hatred with lyrical beauty,
Blind force with accomplished shape.

Here is the valley of shallow Polish rivers. And an immense bridge
Going into white fog. Here is a broken city,
And the wind throws the screams of gulls on your grave
When I am talking with you.

What is poetry which does not save
Nations or people?
A connivance with official lies,
A song of drunkards whose throats will be cut in a moment,
Readings for sophomore girls.
That I wanted good poetry without knowing it,
That I discovered, late, its salutary aim,
In this and only this I find salvation.

They used to pour millet on graves or poppy seeds
To feed the dead who would come disguised as birds.

I put this book here for you, who once lived
So that you should visit us no more.

Warsaw, 1945

POETIC PRACTICES

You will discover some poetic practices on your own; others you will be taught. One that nearly all poets come to use is the list. This ordinary habit of writing things down allows you not to forget them, or to see them to make sure they are real, or to work them out visually in order to have control over them. The trick, if we can call it that, with shaping a list in a poem is that *it should appear random but not be random*. Take advantage of each relationship—juxtaposition and lacuna—between items on the list. The most challenging and compelling part of the list will be how it ends—that last thing your reader takes away.

Zeina Hashem Beck's poem about "fixing," a practice in itself, begins with "And" and concludes on a note that transforms everything that's come before on the list. In reading the poem for a second and third time, appreciate how it unfolds and embodies sublimation, ars poetica, and the form of a love letter. Michael Torres' poem, another list, begins with an ostensible writing prompt and unfurls with a series of questions. In a poem, try answering these questions. Then try writing your own version of the prompt.

Zeina Hashem Beck
You Fixed It

And if the compass broke you fixed it, fastened
the pencil to it with a rubber band,
and if there was no hot water you fixed it, learnt
to sit on that plastic stool in the bathroom
and count, and if it was too cold outside
you fixed it, and there was the smell of burnt
lemon on the brazier, or the *click*
click click of the gas heater.
And if you were bored you fixed it, learnt to cut
paper and color the scraps, learnt to write
on the walls, and if you wrote on the walls you
fixed it, scrubbed them with your mom who yelled
at your big brother who what on earth
was he doing just watching? And if the TV blurred
you fixed it, adjusted the antenna to catch
those Japanese cartoons translated into Arabic
on the Syrian channel, and if the cartoons

hadn't begun you fixed it, danced
to those nationalistic Syrian songs about Hafiz, repeated
ya hala ya hala ya hala heh. And if you didn't have enough
books you fixed it, read that French-Arabic dictionary the size
of your torso, stared at the words *crépuscule* and الغسق.
And if you tripped on the missing tile you fixed it,
learnt to count your steps in the dark
afternoon without electricity, and if there was no
electricity you fixed it, gauged
how dark it was by whether or not you could see
your thumb, and if you couldn't see your thumb
you fixed it, got the candle from under the sink,
and if the sink was leaking you fixed it, tied
a cloth to the pipe, and if the pipe burst
you fixed it, pressed your palms
against the hole in the wall until
Mom called the grocer to call the butcher to call
the plumber next to him, and if there was a hole
in your sock you fixed it, learnt to fold it
under your big toe. And if your window shattered
you fixed it, taped cardboard to the frame,
and if someone died you fixed it by telling stories
about how crusty their *lahm bi 'ajeen* was,
and if the *lahm bi 'ajeen* was too crusty
you fixed it by dipping it in the tahini,
and if your sorrow hardened you fixed it
by dipping it in seawater, and if your country
hardened, if your country hardened you fixed it
by dipping it in song.

Michael Torres
Writing Prompt

Imagine you're an astronaut stuck in outer space. And it's just you. Only you. What would you write about? What

do you see outside your spaceship windshield? What do you miss? Who is your brother now, all those miles down? Where's west? What would you have brought, had you known you would be out here, maybe forever, all by yourself?

What about regret? What if

there are whole days where you don't think of your hands? How closely related is loneliness to remembrance?—when you let yourself think about it?

Do the stars feel heavier now?

Is there, truly, anything you would do over?—knowing everything you know now? If regret was a type of animal, any animal, what song would it sing in you?

Outside are all these tiny windows you can't look through.

Do you miss having a sky to throw wishes against? What did it look like last?—describe the blue.

What phrases do you miss people saying? By "people" I mean:

write about something small—but with great detail—about everyone you love.

What blurs then builds a forest inside you? Is that too specific? Pretend

it's summer again and that you're the fire for it—would it even be worth writing about?

Would you, by now, meaning in outer space, and very much alone, want to replay the moments of your life you wished had gone differently?—Or have you gotten over it all already? What stage are we in? Is being stuck in space like dying and not getting to ghost-visit your own funeral? Which is the first moment you'd go back to in order to change it? By *it* I mean where the regret sprang from. Would you feel bad about the rippling? Is worry just a wider room? There is always a box in which regret will fit. After you tape it shut, describe the sound. Describe the blue.

MOODS

Catullus in the last century BCE: "I hate and I love. Maybe you have to know why. / I don't know, but as it happens I am crucified."

Thoreau in his *Journal*, August 28, 1951: "The poet is a man [sic] who lives at last by watching his moods."

Mary Ruefle in a 2014 interview: "[P]oetry is a matter of mood. What I respond to in January, I may not respond to in July. The greatest literature of all, however, is that which has the power to take you out of your present mood and put you into the mood of what you're reading. That's the really great stuff: literature that can override the mood match."

Poets are up and then they are down. This can also be true of poetry readers. Before you read the following poems—about sorrow, anger, happiness—notice what kind of mood you are bringing to your reading. What do you expect to get out of reading *right now*? An epiphany? A commiseration? A surprise? Later, when you find yourself in a wholly different mood, re-read the poems. What has changed, what has remained or stayed with you? How does your mood modulate while reading a poem?

Frank Bidart
Catullus: Odi et Amo

I hate *and* love. Ignorant fish, who even
wants the fly while writhing.

Catullus: Excrucior

I hate and—love. The sleepless body hammering a nail nails
itself, hanging crucified.

Catullus: Id faciam

What I hate I love. Ask the crucified hand that holds
the nail that now is driven into itself, why.

Allison Benis White
from *Please Bury Me in This*

Looking up in the dark I thought, Tell me something you've never told anyone.

I tried in the closet but the rope broke.

Maybe the relief of conversation, of something almost happening.

The way in the morning, lying on the floor, the light through the blinds cuts my face.

Less than hope: wishing.

How sugar became snow, poured over wet glue on a cardboard roof.

I remember the paper house, hung from a cage hook in my room, swaying.

Not fonder, not fonder—the heart grows stranger.

Safia Elhillo
Self-Portrait with Profanity

ninety-nine names for my god
though i know none for my [   ]

a failing not of my deity but of
my arabic   not the language

itself rather the overeager mosaic
i hoard   i steal   i borrow

from pop songs   & mine
from childhood fluency   i guard

my few swearwords like tinkling
silver anklets   spare & precious

& never nearly enough to muster
a proper arabic anger   proper arabic

vulgarity   only a passing spar
always using the names of animals

i am not polite   i am only inarticulate
overproud   of my little arsenal

a stranger blows a wet tobacco kiss
through the window   of my taxi

& i deploy   my meager weapons
[dog]   [pig]   [donkey]

& finally   my crown jewel
i pass my tongue across my teeth

crane my neck about the window
& call   [your mother's   ]

Jack Gilbert
A Brief for the Defense

Sorrow everywhere. Slaughter everywhere. If babies
are not starving someplace, they are starving
somewhere else. With flies in their nostrils.
But we enjoy our lives because that's what God wants.
Otherwise the mornings before summer dawn would not
be made so fine. The Bengal tiger would not
be fashioned so miraculously well. The poor women
at the fountain are laughing together between
the suffering they have known and the awfulness
in their future, smiling and laughing while somebody
in the village is very sick. There is laughter
every day in the terrible streets of Calcutta,
and the women laugh in the cages of Bombay.
If we deny our happiness, resist our satisfaction,
we lessen the importance of their deprivation.
We must risk delight. We can do without pleasure,
but not delight. Not enjoyment. We must have

the stubbornness to accept our gladness in the ruthless
furnace of this world. To make injustice the only
measure of our attention is to praise the Devil.
If the locomotive of the Lord runs us down,
we should give thanks that the end had magnitude.
We must admit there will be music despite everything.
We stand at the prow again of a small ship
anchored late at night in the tiny port
looking over to the sleeping island: the waterfront
is three shuttered cafés and one naked light burning.
To hear the faint sound of oars in the silence as a rowboat
comes slowly out and then goes back is truly worth
all the years of sorrow that are to come.

Jane Kenyon
Happiness

There's just no accounting for happiness,
or the way it turns up like a prodigal
who comes back to the dust at your feet
having squandered a fortune far away.

And how can you not forgive?
You make a feast in honor of what
was lost, and take from its place the finest
garment, which you saved for an occasion
you could not imagine, and you weep night and day
to know that you were not abandoned,
that happiness saved its most extreme form
for you alone.

No, happiness is the uncle you never
knew about, who flies a single-engine plane
onto the grassy landing strip, hitchhikes
into town, and inquires at every door
until he finds you asleep midafternoon
as you so often are during the unmerciful
hours of your despair.

It comes to the monk in his cell.
It comes to the woman sweeping the street
with a birch broom, to the child
whose mother has passed out from drink.
It comes to the lover, to the dog chewing
a sock, to the pusher, to the basket maker,

and to the clerk stacking cans of carrots
in the night.
       It even comes to the boulder
in the perpetual shade of pine barrens,
to rain falling on the open sea,
to the wineglass, weary of holding wine.

DEPRESSION

Any psychiatrist will tell you that depression goes hand-in-hand with anxiety. The following poems speak to this linkage, sometimes spiced up with a bit of mania. For that is what coping with depression amounts to: attempting to find the right recipe or concoction—of talk therapy, medication, meditation, exercise, alcohol, drugs, herbal remedies, etc.—just to make it through another day. Eating in particular often becomes existential: T. S. Eliot's Prufrock famously asks "Do I dare to eat a peach?"; and, the first line of Chelsea Martin's poem declares "Eating food from McDonald's is mathematically impossible." Getting into a state where not every third thought involves death, or a state in which one doesn't pine for death's cousin sleep … is not very easy. So what can a poem about depression do for you? Empathize? Philosophize? Extemporize? Yes and yes and yes. Any of these can do the necessary work of distraction.

T. S. Eliot
The Love Song of J. Alfred Prufrock

    S'io credesse che mia risposta fosse
    A persona che mai tornasse al mondo,
    Questa fiamma staria senza piu scosse.
    Ma percioche giammai di questo fondo
    Non torno vivo alcun, s'i'odo il vero,
    Senza tema d'infamia ti rispondo.

Let us go then, you and I,
When the evening is spread out against the sky
Like a patient etherized upon a table;
Let us go, through certain half-deserted streets,
The muttering retreats
Of restless nights in one-night cheap hotels
And sawdust restaurants with oyster-shells:
Streets that follow like a tedious argument
Of insidious intent
To lead you to an overwhelming question …

Oh, do not ask, "What is it?"
Let us go and make our visit.

In the room the women come and go
Talking of Michelangelo.

The yellow fog that rubs its back upon the window-panes,
The yellow smoke that rubs its muzzle on the window-panes,
Licked its tongue into the corners of the evening,
Lingered upon the pools that stand in drains,
Let fall upon its back the soot that falls from chimneys,
Slipped by the terrace, made a sudden leap,
And seeing that it was a soft October night,
Curled once about the house, and fell asleep.

And indeed there will be time
For the yellow smoke that slides along the street,
Rubbing its back upon the window-panes;
There will be time, there will be time
To prepare a face to meet the faces that you meet;
There will be time to murder and create,
And time for all the works and days of hands
That lift and drop a question on your plate;
Time for you and time for me,
And time yet for a hundred indecisions,
And for a hundred visions and revisions,
Before the taking of a toast and tea.

In the room the women come and go
Talking of Michelangelo.

And indeed there will be time
To wonder, "Do I dare?" and, "Do I dare?"
Time to turn back and descend the stair,
With a bald spot in the middle of my hair —
(They will say: "How his hair is growing thin!")
My morning coat, my collar mounting firmly to the chin,
My necktie rich and modest, but asserted by a simple pin—
(They will say: "But how his arms and legs are thin!")
Do I dare
Disturb the universe?
In a minute there is time
For decisions and revisions which a minute will reverse.

For I have known them all already, known them all:
Have known the evenings, mornings, afternoons,
I have measured out my life with coffee spoons;

I know the voices dying with a dying fall
Beneath the music from a farther room.
      So how should I presume?

And I have known the eyes already, known them all—
The eyes that fix you in a formulated phrase,
And when I am formulated, sprawling on a pin,
When I am pinned and wriggling on the wall,
Then how should I begin
To spit out all the butt-ends of my days and ways?
      And how should I presume?

And I have known the arms already, known them all—
Arms that are braceleted and white and bare
(But in the lamplight, downed with light brown hair!)
Is it perfume from a dress
That makes me so digress?
Arms that lie along a table, or wrap about a shawl.
      And should I then presume?
      And how should I begin?

Shall I say, I have gone at dusk through narrow streets
And watched the smoke that rises from the pipes
Of lonely men in shirt-sleeves, leaning out of windows? …

I should have been a pair of ragged claws
Scuttling across the floors of silent seas.

And the afternoon, the evening, sleeps so peacefully!
Smoothed by long fingers,
Asleep … tired … or it malingers,
Stretched on the floor, here beside you and me.
Should I, after tea and cakes and ices,
Have the strength to force the moment to its crisis?
But though I have wept and fasted, wept and prayed,
Though I have seen my head (grown slightly bald) brought in upon a platter,
I am no prophet—and here's no great matter;
I have seen the moment of my greatness flicker,
And I have seen the eternal Footman hold my coat, and snicker,
And in short, I was afraid.

And would it have been worth it, after all,
After the cups, the marmalade, the tea,
Among the porcelain, among some talk of you and me,
Would it have been worth while,
To have bitten off the matter with a smile,
To have squeezed the universe into a ball

To roll it towards some overwhelming question,
To say: "I am Lazarus, come from the dead,
Come back to tell you all, I shall tell you all"—
If one, settling a pillow by her head
      Should say: "That is not what I meant at all;
      That is not it, at all."

And would it have been worth it, after all,
Would it have been worth while,
After the sunsets and the dooryards and the sprinkled streets,
After the novels, after the teacups, after the skirts that trail along the floor—
And this, and so much more?—
It is impossible to say just what I mean!
But as if a magic lantern threw the nerves in patterns on a screen:
Would it have been worth while
If one, settling a pillow or throwing off a shawl,
And turning toward the window, should say:
      "That is not it at all,
      That is not what I meant, at all."

No! I am not Prince Hamlet, nor was meant to be;
Am an attendant lord, one that will do
To swell a progress, start a scene or two,
Advise the prince; no doubt, an easy tool,
Deferential, glad to be of use,
Politic, cautious, and meticulous;
Full of high sentence, but a bit obtuse;
At times, indeed, almost ridiculous—
Almost, at times, the Fool.

I grow old … I grow old …
I shall wear the bottoms of my trousers rolled.

Shall I part my hair behind? Do I dare to eat a peach?
I shall wear white flannel trousers, and walk upon the beach.
I have heard the mermaids singing, each to each.

I do not think that they will sing to me.

I have seen them riding seaward on the waves
Combing the white hair of the waves blown back
When the wind blows the water white and black.
We have lingered in the chambers of the sea
By sea-girls wreathed with seaweed red and brown
Till human voices wake us, and we drown.

Chelsea Martin
McDonalds Is Impossible

Eating food from McDonald's is mathematically impossible.
Because before you can eat it, you have to order it.
And before you can order it, you have to decide what you want.
And before you can decide what you want, you have to read the menu.
And before you can read the menu, you have to be in front of the menu.
And before you can be in front of the menu, you have to wait in line.
And before you can wait in line, you have to drive to the restaurant.
And before you can drive to the restaurant, you have to get in your car.
And before you can get in your car, you have to put clothes on.
And before you can put clothes on, you have to get out of bed.
And before you can get out of bed, you have to stop being so depressed.
And before you can stop being so depressed, you have to understand what depression is.
And before you can understand what depression is, you have to think clearly.
And before you can think clearly, you have to turn off the TV.
And before you can turn off the TV, you have to free your hands.
And before you can free your hands, you have to stop masturbating.
And before you can stop masturbating, you have to get off.
And before you can get off, you have to imagine someone you really like with his pants off, encouraging you to explore his enlarged genitalia.
And before you can imagine someone you really like with his pants off encouraging you to explore his enlarged genitalia, you have to imagine that person stroking your neck.
And before you can imagine that person stroking your neck, you have to imagine that person walking up to you looking determined.
And before you can imagine that person walking up to you looking determined, you have to choose who that person is.
And before you can choose who that person is, you have to like someone.
And before you can like someone, you have to interact with someone.
And before you can interact with someone, you have to introduce yourself.
And before you can introduce yourself, you have to be in a social situation.
And before you can be in a social situation, you have to be invited to something somehow.
And before you can be invited to something somehow, you have to receive a telephone call from a friend.
And before you can receive a telephone call from a friend, you have to make a reputation for yourself as being sort of fun.
And before you can make a reputation for yourself as being sort of fun, you have to be noticeably fun on several different occasions.
And before you can be noticeably fun on several different occasions, you have to be fun once in the presence of two or more people.

And before you can be fun once in the presence of two or more people, you have to be drunk.
And before you can be drunk, you have to buy alcohol.
And before you can buy alcohol, you have to want your psychological state to be altered.
And before you can want your psychological state to be altered, you have to recognize that your current psychological state is unsatisfactory.
And before you can recognize that your current psychological state is unsatisfactory, you have to grow tired of your lifestyle.
And before you can grow tired of your lifestyle, you have to repeat the same patterns over and over endlessly.
And before you can repeat the same patterns over and over endlessly, you have to lose a lot of your creativity.
And before you can lose a lot of your creativity, you have to stop reading books.
And before you can stop reading books, you have to think that you would benefit from reading less frequently.
And before you can think that you would benefit from reading less frequently, you have to be discouraged by the written word.
And before you can be discouraged by the written word, you have to read something that reinforces your insecurities.
And before you can read something that reinforces your insecurities, you have to have insecurities.
And before you can have insecurities, you have to be awake for part of the day.
And before you can be awake for part of the day, you have to feel motivation to wake up.
And before you can feel motivation to wake up, you have to dream of perfectly synchronized conversations with people you desire to talk to.
And before you can dream of perfectly synchronized conversations with people you desire to talk to, you have to have a general idea of what a perfectly synchronized conversation is.
And before you can have a general idea of what a perfectly synchronized conversation is, you have to watch a lot of movies in which people successfully talk to each other.
And before you can watch a lot of movies in which people successfully talk to each other, you have to have an interest in other people.
And before you can have an interest in other people, you have to have some way of benefiting from other people.
And before you can have some way of benefiting from other people, you have to have goals.
And before you can have goals, you have to want power.
And before you can want power, you have to feel greed.
And before you can feel greed, you have to feel more deserving than others.
And before you can feel more deserving than others, you have to feel a general disgust with the human population.
And before you can feel a general disgust with the human population, you have to be emotionally wounded.

And before you can be emotionally wounded, you have to be treated badly by someone you think you care about while in a naive, vulnerable state.

And before you can be treated badly by someone you think you care about while in a naive, vulnerable state, you have to feel inferior to that person.

And before you can feel inferior to that person, you have to watch him laughing and walking towards his drum kit with his shirt off and the sun all over him.

And before you can watch him laughing and walking towards his drum kit with his shirt off and the sun all over him, you have to go to one of his outdoor shows.

And before you can go to one of his outdoor shows, you have to pretend to know something about music.

And before you can pretend to know something about music, you have to feel embarrassed about your real interests.

And before you can feel embarrassed about your real interests, you have to realize that your interests are different from other people's interests.

And before you can realize that your interests are different from other people's interests, you have to be regularly misunderstood.

And before you can be regularly misunderstood, you have to be almost completely socially debilitated.

And before you can be almost completely socially debilitated, you have to be an outcast.

And before you can be an outcast, you have to be rejected by your entire group of friends.

And before you can be rejected by your entire group of friends, you have to be suffocatingly loyal to your friends.

And before you can be suffocatingly loyal to your friends, you have to be afraid of loss.

And before you can be afraid of loss, you have to lose something of value.

And before you can lose something of value, you have to realize that that thing will never change.

And before you can realize that that thing will never change, you have to have the same conversation with your grandmother forty or fifty times.

And before you can have the same conversation with your grandmother forty or fifty times, you have to have a desire to talk to her and form a meaningful relationship.

And before you can have a desire to talk to her and form a meaningful relationship, you have to love her.

And before you can love her, you have to notice the great tolerance she has for you.

And before you can notice the great tolerance she has for you, you have to break one of her favorite china teacups that her mother gave her and forget to apologize.

And before you can break one of her favorite china teacups that her mother gave her and forget to apologize, you have to insist on using the teacups for your imaginary tea party. And before you can insist on using the teacups for your imaginary tea party, you have to cultivate your imagination.

And before you can cultivate your imagination, you have to spend a lot of time alone.

And before you can spend a lot of time alone, you have to find ways to sneak away from your siblings.

And before you can find ways to sneak away from your siblings, you have to have siblings.

And before you can have siblings, you have to underwhelm your parents.
And before you can underwhelm your parents, you have to be quiet, polite and unnoticeable.
And before you can be quiet, polite and unnoticeable, you have to understand that it is possible to disappoint your parents.
And before you can understand that it is possible to disappoint your parents, you have to be harshly reprimanded.
And before you can be harshly reprimanded, you have to sing loudly at an inappropriate moment.
And before you can sing loudly at an inappropriate moment, you have to be happy.
And before you can be happy, you have to be able to recognize happiness.
And before you can be able to recognize happiness, you have to know distress.
And before you can know distress, you have to be watched by an insufficient babysitter for one week.
And before you can be watched by an insufficient babysitter for one week, you have to vomit on the other, more pleasant babysitter.
And before you can vomit on the other, more pleasant babysitter, you have to be sick.
And before you can be sick, you have to eat something you're allergic to.
And before you can eat something you're allergic to, you have to have allergies.
And before you can have allergies, you have to be born.
And before you can be born, you have to be conceived.
And before you can be conceived, your parents have to copulate.
And before your parents can copulate, they have to be attracted to one another.
And before they can be attracted to one another, they have to have common interests.
And before they can have common interests, they have to talk to each other.
And before they can talk to each other, they have to meet.
And before they can meet, they have to have in-school suspension on the same day.
And before they can have in-school suspension on the same day, they have to get caught sneaking off campus separately.
And before they can get caught sneaking off campus separately, they have to think of somewhere to go.
And before they can think of somewhere to go, they have to be familiar with McDonald's.
And before they can be familiar with McDonald's, they have to eat food from McDonald's.

And eating food from McDonald's is mathematically impossible.

Jack Spicer
Psychoanalysis: An Elegy

What are you thinking about?

I am thinking of an early summer.
I am thinking of wet hills in the rain

Pouring water. Shedding it
Down empty acres of oak and manzanita
Down to the old green brush tangled in the sun,
Greasewood, sage, and spring mustard.
Or the hot wind coming down from Santa Ana
Driving the hills crazy,
A fast wind with a bit of dust in it
Bruising everything and making the seed sweet.
Or down in the city where the peach trees
Are awkward as young horses,
And there are kites caught on the wires
Up above the street lamps,
And the storm drains are all choked with dead branches.

What are you thinking?

I think that I would like to write a poem that is slow as a summer
As slow getting started
As 4th of July somewhere around the middle of the second stanza
After a lot of unusual rain
California seems long in the summer.
I would like to write a poem as long as California
And as slow as a summer.
Do you get me, Doctor? It would have to be as slow
As the very tip of summer.
As slow as the summer seems
On a hot day drinking beer outside Riverside
Or standing in the middle of a white-hot road
Between Bakersfield and Hell
Waiting for Santa Claus.

What are you thinking now?

I'm thinking that she is very much like California.
When she is still her dress is like a roadmap. Highways
Traveling up and down her skin
Long empty highways
With the moon chasing jackrabbits across them
On hot summer nights.
I am thinking that her body could be California
And I a rich Eastern tourist
Lost somewhere between Hell and Texas
Looking at a map of a long, wet, dancing California
That I have never seen.
Send me some penny picture-postcards, lady,
Send them.

One of each breast photographed looking
Like curious national monuments,
One of your body sweeping like a three-lane highway
Twenty-seven miles from a night's lodging
In the world's oldest hotel.

What are you thinking?

I am thinking of how many times this poem
Will be repeated. How many summers
Will torture California
Until the damned maps burn
Until the mad cartographer
Falls to the ground and possesses
The sweet thick earth from which he has been hiding.

What are you thinking now?

I am thinking that a poem could go on forever.

Dean Young
Cotton in a Pill Bottle

I love the fog. It's not 100 degrees.
It's not Mary sobbing on the phone or powder-
white mildew killing the rose. My father
lost inside it keeps pretending he's dead
just so he can get a little peace.
It's not made of fire or afraid of fire
like me, it has nothing to do with smoke.
There's never any ash, anything to sift through.
You just put your hand on the yellow rail
and the steps seem to move themselves.
It doesn't have a job to do.
It's morning all afternoon.
It loves the music but would be
just as happy listening to the game.
Still, I don't know what frightens me.
It doesn't blame anyone.
You'll never see tears on its cheeks.
It'll never put up a fight.
I love how the fog lies down in the air,
how it can only get so far from the sea.

John Keats
To Sleep

O soft embalmer of the still midnight,
    Shutting, with careful fingers and benign,
Our gloom-pleas'd eyes, embower'd from the light,
    Enshaded in forgetfulness divine:
O soothest Sleep! if so it please thee, close
    In midst of this thine hymn my willing eyes,
Or wait the "Amen," ere thy poppy throws
    Around my bed its lulling charities.
Then save me, or the passed day will shine
Upon my pillow, breeding many woes,—
    Save me from curious Conscience, that still lords
Its strength for darkness, burrowing like a mole;
    Turn the key deftly in the oiled wards,
And seal the hushed Casket of my Soul.

Louise Bogan
Solitary Observation Brought Back from a Sojourn in Hell

At midnight tears
Run into your ears.

MEDITATION

Abandon all hope, says the Buddhist master Atisha. This seems, at first, to be a declaration that humanity's plight in the universe is hopeless—and one may or may not agree, depending on personal disposition or the time of day. But there is an alternative idea here, too: When you give up hope for something, which involves a future whether soon or far off, you can focus on the present. You are allowed to think what you want and to inhabit the moment. You could call this mindfulness, or you could call it simply slowing down and paying close attention. Above all else meditation seems dependent on this ability.

    Can slowing down and observing everything become, in fact, terrifying and induce an anxiety all its own? Absolutely. But perhaps no more so than the patterns you've likely been treading for a long time, full of anxiety and quiet terror. If there is something beyond these alternatives, it might be a mindfulness that skirts the edge of mindlessness.

    Abandoning hope may also propel something else: ridding yourself of fear. Fear that your hopes won't come to fruition, or at least become more than mere hopes.

Li Bai (translated from the Chinese by Sam Hamill)
Zazen on Ching-t'ing Mountain

The birds have vanished down the sky.
Now the last cloud drains away.

We sit together, the mountain and me,
until only the mountain remains.

Jenny Xie
To Be a Good Buddhist Is Ensnarement

The Zen priest says I am everything I am not.

In order to stop resisting, I must not attempt to stop resisting.

I must believe there is no need to believe in thoughts.

Oblivious to appetites that appear to be exits, and also entrances.

What is there to hoard when the worldly realm has no permanent vacancies?

Ten years I've taken to this mind fasting.

My shadow these days is bare.

It drives a stranger, a good fool.

Nothing can surprise.

Clarity is just questioning having eaten its fill.

Robert Hass
Meditation at Lagunitas

All the new thinking is about loss.
In this it resembles all the old thinking.
The idea, for example, that each particular erases
the luminous clarity of a general idea. That the clown-
faced woodpecker probing the dead sculpted trunk
of that black birch is, by his presence,
some tragic falling off from a first world
of undivided light. Or the other notion that,
because there is in this world no one thing
to which the bramble of *blackberry* corresponds,
a word is elegy to what it signifies.
We talked about it late last night and in the voice
of my friend, there was a thin wire of grief, a tone

almost querulous. After a while I understood that,
talking this way, everything dissolves: *justice,
pine, hair, woman, you* and *I*. There was a woman
I made love to and I remembered how, holding
her small shoulders in my hands sometimes,
I felt a violent wonder at her presence
like a thirst for salt, for my childhood river
with its island willows, silly music from the pleasure boat,
muddy places where we caught the little orange-silver fish
called *pumpkinseed*. It hardly had to do with her.
Longing, we say, because desire is full
of endless distances. I must have been the same to her.
But I remember so much, the way her hands dismantled bread,
the thing her father said that hurt her, what
she dreamed. There are moments when the body is as numinous
as words, days that are the good flesh continuing.
Such tenderness, those afternoons and evenings,
saying *blackberry, blackberry, blackberry*.

Katie Peterson
Meditation Denying Everything

Because it is a pearly evening
I am sitting in the window reading
a book I have read before.
Branches emphasize
their heft and sway over their shadows.
Some kind of extra firmament,
an ear over the earth's ear,
extra, as language is to prayer.
Narratives of elsewhere: in the eye
inside my eye that vision makes when you tell it to
when you shut your eyes so hard they hurt
you get more vista and less twist
of road, and then you're looking
at a valley you named yourself
and irrigated yourself,
full of bitterroot, magnolia in the clefts
of rock, sage, at last a harvest,
a desert that belongs to you—

The trick to renunciation is starting now.
The secret of detachment
is having already given up,

a transcript of speech whose cadences are lost,
the human need for a body to fill in
all your body's deficiencies, those clefts and dents
already given up, the narrative of a life
completely altered in the retrospect
that knowledge brings and so discredited
the point of memory utterly lost.
That piece of land has always been
suitable for a house. That nest has never
been ready for eight baby birds
who, top-heavy, frightened their own branch
and home and scared themselves
completely and remarkably away.

Do you hear that? It's the wind
negotiating the spine of one leaf
it cannot decide whether to raise
a fragment of an inch.

Duncan writes *as a reader*
struggles with a strong sentence, I struggle
at certain unmistakable times
with what's furtive and most right.
When people marry they finish their names.
I am still listening for mine
to begin. My spine
wants a bicycle to order its work, a red
bicycle, a hill into a heart
of a city that holds something I want.

The pattern of the air around that leaf
is like someone tracing my ribcage
with his index finger
and then walking away.
Who can blame us for wanting other worlds,
but shall we take them,
or let them come to us? Is the spirit just an ear
more like a mouth
that bites the air and turns it into blood?

A voice in the next room goes to sleep.
Sleep moves in the branches of the oak
become a rootless mass
unsung by skeleton or name or height.
My friend who says
she does not believe in Paradise
believes in rest: I believe that,

or more likely I like to think of her,
the way she held my name in her small mouth,
as she held her own name. I like to think of anyone
who on a night like this
would reach towards my ribcage
and trace it delicately and walk away.

PROCRASTINATION

It always seems to come down to opportunity cost vis-à-vis the cost of living. *If I am going to run these errands—to the grocery store, the post office, the pet store, and on and on—what will I be unable to do? Get that heap of laundry done? Pick up the house? Clean out the trunk of the car? Put dinner on the table?*

What you really need to do, if you are going to call yourself a poet, is go into the room and sit down and imagine you are that ape in James Tate's "Teaching the Ape to Write Poems"; pretend Dr. Bluespire (no one knows who he is, don't worry) is whispering in your ear *You look like a god sitting there. / Why don't you try writing something?*

But you are not a god, are you?

Not yet. Set down this book and make something that didn't exist before. It might be the last anyone hears of you.

W.S. Merwin
The Unwritten

Inside this pencil
crouch words that have never been written
never been spoken
never been taught

they're hiding

they're awake in there
dark in the dark
hearing us
but they won't come out
not for love not for time not for fire

even when the dark has worn away
they'll still be there
hiding in the air
multitudes in days to come may walk through them
breathe them
be none the wiser

what script can it be
that they won't unroll
in what language
would I recognize it
would I be able to follow it
to make out the real names
of everything

maybe there aren't
many
it could be that there's only one word
and it's all we need
it's here in this pencil

every pencil in the world
is like this

END NOTES

Life is a subspecies of death ... and a very rare one at that, so alleged Nietzsche. The idea of legacy—not just a poet's but anybody's—propels many of us to do good deeds, to attempt lasting works, to raise thoughtful children who will go on to raise thoughtful children who do good deeds and lasting works. At any point in the lineage, however, there will be endings. Slow closures, clipped ones, messy or neat or indifferent. Is life so valuable because it ends? Is it more valuable when it's vibrant or fragile? We seem to be at once compelled to live and compelled to think about what not living will be like. Poems may not be able to answer all our questions, but so often they probe and explore where we are unwilling or afraid to go.

Ron Koertge
Ornithology

Walking toward the library, I pass three children
staring down at a dead crow and daring each other
to poke it with a stick.

I stop, too, because I know a little about crows—
how, for instance, they are different from ravens.
I could tell these well-dressed children a lot.

Ravens are black with a purple tint while crows
are denied that royal hue. A crow's tale is squared-off
like the crew-cut on the boy at Menchie's who hands
them the expensive frozen yogurt

while a raven's tale is triangular, a shape discovered
by the Persians and beloved by the 17th century
mathematician Blaise Pascal. Furthermore, ravens
love solitude and prefer remote hills and woods
while a crow will perch on a stop sign and brag
about it endlessly.

But that isn't what they are concerned about.
They want to know about Death. And for that
I would have to fetch the skull from my desktop
and ask the sun to hide its face behind a dark,
galleon-shaped cloud and then—

Oh, wait. They're offering me the stick. All
they really want to know is will I poke the corpse.

Of course. And when I do and it moves, they
run away shrieking and delighted. More alive,
if possible, than before.

Yehuda Amichai (translated from the Hebrew by Benjamin and Barbara Harshav)
All the Generations Before Me

All the generations before me contributed me
Little by little so I will emerge here in Jerusalem
All at once, like a prayer house or a philanthropy.
That compels. My name is the name of my contributors.
That compels.

I approach the age of my father's death.
My will has many patches,
I have to change my life and my death
Day by day, to fulfill all the prophecies
That prophesied me. So they won't be a lie.
That compels.

I passed my fortieth year. There are jobs
I cannot get. If I were in Auschwitz
They wouldn't have sent me to work,
They would have burned me right away.
That compels.

Wanda Coleman
Things No One Knows

overcome by the stink of mildewed wash, i have
been three months behind in my rent for thirty years. my
countrymen do not love me. even my lines have
lines. we are getting old in a city where the old are
invisible. i have nothing new to eat and barely five minutes
to use the jane. and less time than that to revisit my
father's grave. i've worn the same underwear for fifteen
of those thirty years and some pieces longer than that

writing friends is a luxury, enemies a necessity. my car
was stripped and stolen months ago and i have no
money with which to repair or replace it. my mentors have
exiled me to the outskirts of nappy literacy. my wallet is
dying of militant brain cancer. my lust for my country
is frigid. the light excludes me and there is
no degree for what is learned in the dark

i am too clumsy to steal big. there is a boogieman in
New York City who conspires against and spreads
rumors about my lost lip. i am so economically crippled
even my begging cup has mold sprouting in its well. my
son has mistaken me for a dragon and his history teachers keep
trying to hose out these flames in my mouth. i do not
attend my high school class reunions because too many of
my classmates died in Vietnam or in the liquor lockers
of America or in those classrooms long ago. there is
a boogiewoman in Oberlin who conspires against me, her
jealousy inspired by my imaginary imaginings

i am trapped in the hold of my greedy grief
and expect to keep circling. i expect my son to escape
and my husband to die during exquisite crisis. the federal
bureau of pajamas is after my hot cross buns. i expect to
awaken from sleep soon. i expect my banana nut bread to
go stale and uneaten. i expect to die poemless and to be
cremated in state ovens. i expect my ashes
to be scattered like pollen, to take wing on the wind

like buddhaflies

Victoria Chang
from OBIT

Caretakers—died in 2009, 2010, 2011, 2012, 2013, 2014, 2015, 2016, 2017, one after another. One didn't show up because her husband was arrested. Most others watched the clock. Time breaks for the living eventually and we can walk out of doors. The handle of time's door is hot for the dying. What use is a door if you can't exit? A door that can't be opened is called a wall. On the other side, glass can bloom. My father is on the other side of the wall. Tomatoes are ripening on the other side. I can see them through the window that also can't be opened. A window that can't be opened is just a see-through wall. Sometimes we're on the inside as on a plane. Most of the time, we're on the outside looking in such as doggie day care. I don't know if the tomatoes are the new form of his language or if they're simply for eating. I can't ask him because on the other side, there are no words. All I can do is stare at the nameless bursting tomatoes and know they have to be enough.

*

The Blue Dress—died on August 6, 2015, along with the little blue flowers, all silent. Once the petals looked up. Now small pieces of dust. I wonder whether they burned the dress or just the body? I wonder who lifted her up into the fire? I wonder if her hair brushed his cheek before it grew into a bonfire? I wonder what sound the body made as it burned? They dyed her hair for the funeral, too black. She looked like a comic character. I waited for the next comic panel, to see the speech bubble and what she might say. But her words never came and we were left with the stillness of blown glass. The irreversibility of rain. And millions of little blue flowers. Imagination is having to live in a dead person's future. Grief is wearing a dead person's dress forever.

Carolyn Forché
Mourning

A peacock on an olive branch looks beyond
the grove to the road, beyond the road to the sea,
blank-lit, where a sailboat anchors to a cove.
As it is morning, below deck a man is pouring water into a cup,
listening to the radio-talk of the ships: barges dead
in the calms awaiting port call, pleasure boats whose lights
hours ago went out, fishermen setting their nets for mullet,
as summer tavernas hang octopus to dry on their lines,
whisper smoke into wood ovens, sweep the terraces
clear of night, putting the music out with morning
light, and for the breadth of an hour it is possible
to consider the waters of this sea *wine-dark*, to remember
that there was no word for blue among the ancients,

but there was the whirring sound before the oars
of the great triremes sang out of the seam of world,
through pine-sieved winds silvered by salt flats until
they were light enough to pass for breath from the heavens,
troubled enough to fell ships and darken thought—
then as now the clouds pass, roosters sleep in their huts,
the sea flattens under glass air, but there is nothing to hold us there:
not the quiet of marble nor the luff of sail, fields of thyme,
a vineyard at harvest, and the sea filled with the bones of those
in flight from wars east and south, our wars, their remains
scavenged on the seafloor and in its caves, belongings now
a flotsam washed to the rocks. Stand here and look
into the distant haze, there where the holy mountain
with its thousand monks wraps itself in shawls of rain,
then look to the west, where the rubber boats tipped
into the tough waves. Rest your eyes there, remembering the words
of Anacreon, himself a refugee of war, who appears
in the writings of Herodotus:
How the waves of the sea kiss the shore!
For if the earth is a camp and the sea
an ossuary of souls, light your signal fires
wherever you find yourselves.
Come the morning, launch your boats.

Wisława Szymborska (translated from the Polish by Joanne Trzeciak)
Under a Certain Little Star

My apologies to chance for calling it necessity.
My apologies to necessity in case I'm mistaken.
Don't be angry, happiness, that I take you for my own.
May the dead forgive me that their memory's but a flicker.
My apologies to time for the quantity of world overlooked per second.
My apologies to an old love for treating a new one as the first.
Forgive me, far-off wars, for carrying my flowers home.
Forgive me, open wounds, for pricking my finger.
My apologies for the minuet record, to those calling out from the abyss.
My apologies to those in train stations for sleeping soundly at five in the morning.
Pardon me, hounded hope, for laughing sometimes.
Pardon me, deserts, for not rushing in with a spoonful of water.
And you, O hawk, the same bird for years in the same cage,
staring, motionless, always at the same spot,
absolve me even if you happen to be stuffed.
My apologies to the tree felled for four table legs.

My apologies to large questions for small answers.
Truth, do not pay me too much attention.
Solemnity, be magnanimous toward me.
Bear with me, O mystery of being, for pulling threads from your veil.

Soul, don't blame me that I've got you so seldom.
My apologies to everything that I can't be everywhere.
My apologies to all for not knowing how to be every man and woman.
I know that as long as I live nothing can excuse me,
since I am my own obstacle.
Do not hold it against me, O speech, that I borrow weighty words,
and then labor to make them light.

Notes

In "Metaphor," the answer to the riddle poem "85" is: fish and river. According to Crossely-Holland, the likely source of the poem is Symphosius' Riddle 12, *Flumen et Piscis*.

Acknowledgments

A special thanks to my editor, Amy Martin, who shepherded this project with great care and patience. Thank you to Bloomsbury's production team: Hali Han, Zeba Talkhani, and Karthiga Sithanandam.

Thank you to my students Emma Jackson, Ayana Cormier, Mia Bordelon, and Myranda Cook for their keen edits in preparing this book for publication. A huge thank you to Marigny Beter whose double- and triple-checks of the poems were invaluable.

Thank you to my great friend Chris Schaberg.

Thank you to the following for permission to reprint certain poems.

Maya Abu al-Hayyat, "Revision" from *You Can Be the Last Leaf*. Translation copyright © 2022 by Fady Joudah. Reprinted with permission of The Permissions Company, LLC, on behalf of Milkweed Editions.

Virginia Hamilton Adair, "Now You Need Me" from *Ants on the Melon*. Copyright © 1996 by Virginia Hamilton Adair. Used with permission of Random House, an imprint and division of Penguin Random House LLC.

Elizabeth Alexander, "Ars Poetica #100: I Believe" from *American Sublime*. Copyright © 2005 by Elizabeth Alexander. Reprinted with permission of The Permissions Company, LLC, on behalf of Graywolf Press.

Meena Alexander, "Where Do You Come From?" Copyright © 2005 by Meena Alexander. Used with permission of the Estate of Meena Alexander.

Sherman Alexie, "How to Write the Great American Indian Novel" from *The Summer of Black Widows*. Copyright © 1996 by Sherman Alexie. Reprinted with permission of Hanging Loose Press.

Yehuda Amichai, "All the Generations Before Me" from *Yehuda Amichai, A Life of Poetry, 1948–1994*, selected and translated by Benjamin and Barbara Harshav. Reprinted with permission of the Estate of Yehuda Amichai with Cooperation of the Deborah Harris Agency.

Curt Anderson, "Platonic Love" from *The Occasionist*. Reprinted with permission of the author.

Maya Angelou, "Still I Rise" from *And Still I Rise*. Copyright © 1978 by Maya Angelou. Used with permission of Random House, an imprint and division of Penguin Random House LLC.

Anonymous, Old English riddle from the Exeter Book: 85 ("My home's not silent") from *The Exeter Book Riddles*, edited by Kevin Crossley-Holland. Reprinted with permission of Enitharmon Press.

Craig Arnold, "Bird-Understander" from *Poetry Magazine*. Copyright © 2009 by Craig Arnold. Reprinted with permission of The Permissions Company, LLC on behalf of the Estate of Craig Arnold.

John Ashbery, "Paradoxes and Oxymorons" from *Shadow Train*. Copyright © 1980, 1981 by John Ashbery. Used with permission of Georges Borchardt, Inc., on behalf of the estate of the author.

W.H. Auden, "Musée des Beaux Arts" from *W.H. Auden: Collected Poems*, edited by Edward Mendelson. Copyright © 1940, 1968 by W.H. Auden. Used with permission of Random House, an imprint and division of Penguin Random House LLC.

Li Bai, "Zazen on Ching-t'ing Mountain" from *Crossing the Yellow River: Three Hundred Poems from the Chinese*, translated by Sam Hamill. Copyright © 2000 by Sam Hamill. Reprinted with permission of The Permissions Company, LLC on behalf of Tiger Bark Press.

Amiri Baraka, "Preface to a Twenty-Volume Suicide Note" from *Transbluesency: The Selected Poems of Amiri Baraka/LeRoi Jones, 1961–1995*. Copyright © 2014 by the Estate of Amiri Baraka. Used with permission of Grove/Atlantic, Inc.

Zeina Hashem Beck, "You Fixed It" from *Louder Than Hearts*. Reprinted with permission of Bauhan Publishing, LLC.

Jen Bervin, excerpt from *Nets*. Copyright © 2003 by Jen Berbin. Reprinted with permission of the author and Ugly Duckling Presse.

Frank Bidart, "Catullus: Odi et Amo" from *Half-Light*. Copyright © 2017 by Frank Bidart. Reprinted with permissions Farrar, Straus & Giroux, LLC.

Elizabeth Bishop, "One Art" from *Poems*. Copyright © 2011 by The Alice H. Methfessel Trust. Publisher's Note and compilation copyright © 2011 by Farrar, Straus and Giroux. Reprinted with permission of Farrar, Straus and Giroux.

Louise Bogan, "Solitary Observation Brought Back from a Sojourn in Hell" from *Poems and New Poems*. Copyright © 1968 by Louise Bogan. Reprinted with permission of Farrar, Straus & Giroux, LLC.

Christian Bök, excerpt from Chapter E of *Eunoia*. Copyright © 2001 Coach House Books. Reprinted with permission of the author.

Jorge Luis Borges, "Borges and I." Copyright © 1998 by Maria Kodama, translation copyright © 1998 by Penguin Random House LLC; from *Collected Fictions: Volume 3* by Jorge Luis Borges, translated by Andrew Hurley. Used with permission of Viking Books, an imprint of Penguin Publishing Group, a division of Penguin Random House LLC.

Marianne Boruch, "Pencil" from *Cadaver, Speak: Poems*. Copyright © 2014 by Marianna Boruch. Reprinted with permission of The Permissions Company, LLC on behalf of Copper Canyon Press.

Gwendolyn Brooks, "the mother" from *Blacks*. Copyright © 1991 by Gwendolyn Brooks Blakely. Reprinted with permission of the Estate of Gwendolyn Brooks.

Jericho Brown, "Ganymede" from *The Tradition*. Copyright © 2019 by Jericho Brown. Reprinted with permission of The Permissions Company, LLC, on behalf of Copper Canyon Press.

Suzanne Buffam, "A Great Book can be read again and again" from *A Pillow Book*. Copyright © 2016 by Suzanne Buffam. Reprinted with permission of the author.

Charles Bukowski, "so you want to be a writer?" from *sifting through the madness for the Word, the line, the way*. Copyright © 2003 by the Estate of Charles Bukowski. Reprinted with permission of HarperCollins Publishers.

Victoria Chang, excerpt from *OBIT*. Copyright © 2020 by Victoria Chang. Reprinted with permission of The Permissions Company, LLC, on behalf of Copper Canyon Press.

Leila Chatti, "Confession" from *Deluge*. Copyright © 2020 Leila Chatti. Reprinted with permission of The Permissions Company, LLC, on behalf of Copper Canyon Press.

T'ao Ch'ien, "Substance, Shadow, and Spirit," translated by Stephen Owen. Reprinted with permission of the translator.

Michael Chitwood, "Here I Am, Lord" from *Poor-Mouth Jubilee*. Copyright © 2010 by Michael Chitwood. Reprinted with permission of The Permissions Company, LLC on behalf of Tupelo Press.
Wanda Coleman, "Things No One Knows" from *Wicked Enchantment: Selected Poems*. Copyright © 1998 by Wanda Coleman. Reprinted with permission of The Permissions Company, LLC on behalf of Black Sparrow / David R. Godine, Publisher, Inc.
Billy Collins, "Introduction to Poetry" from *The Apple That Astonished Paris*. Copyright © 1988 by Billy Collins. Reprinted with permission of The Permissions Company, LLC on behalf of the University of Arkansas Press.
E.E. Cummings, "somewhere i have never travelled, gladly beyond" from *Complete Poems: 1904–1962*, edited by George J. Firmage. Copyright © 1931, 1959, 1991 by the Trustees for the E.E. Cummings Trust. Copyright © 1979 by George James Firmage. Used with permission of Liveright Publishing Corporation.
Mahmoud Darwish, "Viewpoint," translated by Fady Joudah, from *The New York Review of Books*. Reprinted with permission of the translator.
Olena Kalytiak Davis, "shattered sonnet #3" from *Shattered Sonnets, Love Cards, and Other Off and Back Handed Importunities*. Copyright © 2015 by Olena Kalytiak Davis. Reprinted with permission of The Permissions Company, LLC, on behalf of Copper Canyon Press.
Emily Dickinson, "Tell all the Truth but tell it slant–," "After great pain, a formal feeling comes–," "Because I could not stop for Death," and "I cannot live with You" from *The Poetry of Emily Dickinson*, edited by Thomas H. Johnson. Copyright © 1951, 1955 by the President and Fellows of Harvard College. Copyright © renewed 1979, 1983 by the President and Fellows of Harvard College. Copyright © 1914, 1918, 1919, 1924, 1929, 1930, 1932, 1935, 1937, 1942 by Martha Dickinson Bianchi. Copyright © 1952, 1957, 1958, 1963, 1965 by Mary L. Hampson. Used with permission.
Jehanne Dubrow, "Portrait of an Administrator with Strategic Plan and Office Supplies" from *Wild Kingdom*. Copyright © 2021 by Jehanne Dubrow. Reprinted with permission of Louisiana State University Press.
Ashley Durant, "Dreams." Used with permission of the author.
Carolina Ebeid, "Punctum/Metaphor" from *You Ask Me to Talk about the Interior*. Copyright © 2016 by Carolina Ebeid. Used with permission of the author.
Russell Edson, "The Adventures of a Turtle" from *Little Mr. Prose Poem: Selected Poems of Russell Edson*, edited by Craig Morgan Teicher. Copyright © 1977 by Russell Edson. Reprinted with permission of The Permissions Company, LLC on behalf of BOA Editions, Ltd.
Safia Elhillo, "Profanity" (first section only, which was published as "Self-Portrait with Profanity") from *Poetry* (September 2018) from *Girls That Never Die*. Copyright © 2023 by Safia Elhillo. Used with permission of One World, an imprint of Random House, a division of Penguin Random House LLC.
Lynn Emanuel, "The Politics of Narrative: Why I Am a Poet" from *Then, Suddenly*. Copyright © 1999. Reprinted with permission of the University of Pittsburgh Press.
Annie Finch, "Coy Mistress" from *Eve*, later in *Spells: New and Selected Poems*. Copyright © 2013 by Annie Finch. Published by Wesleyan University Press and reprinted with permission.
Jameson Fitzpatrick, "The Last Analysis; or, I Woke Up" from *Pricks in the Tapestry*. Originally in *Poetry* (January 2017) as "I Woke Up." Copyright © 2017, 2020 by Jameson Fitzpatrick. Reprinted with permission of the author.

Carolyn Forché, "Mourning" from *In the Lateness of the World*. Copyright © 2021 by Carolyn Forché. Used with permission of Penguin Press, an imprint of Penguin Publishing Group, a division of Penguin Random House LLC.

Ross Gay, "ode to the flute" from *Catalogue of Unabashed Gratitude*. Copyright © 2015 by Ross Gay. Reprinted with permission of the University of Pittsburgh Press.

Jack Gilbert, "A Brief for the Defense" from *Refusing Heaven: Poems*. Copyright © 2005 by Jack Gilbert. Used with permission of Alfred A. Knopf, an imprint of the Knopf Doubleday Publishing Group, a division of Penguin Random House LLC

Allen Ginsberg, "A Supermarket in California" from *Collected Poems 1947–1980*. Copyright © 1955 by Allen Ginsberg. Reprinted with permission of HarperCollins Publishers.

Louise Glück, "The Red Poppy" from *The Wild Iris*. Copyright © 1992 by Louise Gluck. Reprinted with permission of HarperCollins Publishers.

Benjamin Gucciardi, "Advice to Pallbearers" from *West Portal*. Reprinted courtesy of the University of Utah Press.

John Z. Guzlowski, "My Father's Mother Asks Him to Forget the War" from *Echoes of Tattered Tongues: Memory Unfolded*. Copyright © 2016 by John Z. Guzlowski. Reprinted with permission of Aquila Polonica Ltd.

Kimiko Hahn, "Ode to the Whitman Line 'When lilacs last in the dooryard bloom'd.'" Originally published in Poem-a-Day on December 12, 2019, by the Academy of American Poets. Reprinted with permission of the author.

Haiku by Jyoin, "A hazy moonlit night" translated by Ikuho Amano and James Shea, from *Poetry Magazine*. Reprinted with permission of the translators.

francine j. harris, "katherine with the lazy eye. short. and not a good poet" from *allegiance*. Copyright © 2012 by francine j. harris. Reprinted with permission of Wayne State University Press.

Jeffrey Harrison, "Arrival" from *Signs of Arrival*. Copyright © 1996 by Jeffrey Harrison. Reprinted with permission of the author.

Matthea Harvey, "Pity the Bathtub Its Forced Embrace of the Human Form" from *Pity the Bathtub Its Forced Embrace of the Human Form*. Copyright © 2000 by Matthea Harvey. Reprinted with permission of The Permissions Company, LLC on behalf of Alice James Books.

Robert Hass, "Meditation at Lagunitas" from *Praise*. Copyright © 1979 by Robert Hass. Reprinted with permission of HarperCollins Publishers, Inc.

Terrance Hayes, "American Sonnet for My Past and Future Assassin" from *American Sonnets for My Past and Future Assassin*. Copyright © 2018 by Terrance Hayes. Used with permission of Penguin, an imprint of the Knopf Doubleday Publishing Group, a division of Penguin Random House LLC.

Seamus Heaney, "Digging" from *Death of a Naturalist*. Copyright © 1966 by Seamus Heaney. Used with permission of Farrar, Straus & Giroux, LLC.

Lyn Hejinian, excerpt from *My Life*. Copyright © 1987, 2013 by Lyn Hejinian. Published by Wesleyan University Press and reprinted with permission.

Nâzim Hikmet, "On Living" from *Poems of Nâzim Hikmet*, translated by Randy Blasing and Mutlu Konuk. Copyright © 1994, 2002 by Randy Blasing and Mutlu Konuk. Reprinted with permission of Persea Books, Inc.

Tony Hoagland, "Reading *Moby-Dick* at 30,000 Feet" from *Donkey Gospel*. Copyright © 1998 by Tony Hoagland. Reprinted with permission of The Permissions Company, LLC.

Miroslav Holub, "Napoleon" from *Poems Before and After*. Copyright © 2006 by Miroslav Holub. Reprinted with permission of Bloodaxe Books Ltd.

Cathy Park Hong, "Ontology of Chang and Eng, the Original Siamese Twins" from *Translating Mo'um*. Copyright © 2002 by Cathy Park Hong. Reprinted with permission of Hanging Loose Press.

Marie Howe, "Part of Eve's Discussion" from *The Good Thief*. Copyright © 1988 by Marie Howe. Reprinted with permission of Persea Books, Inc.

Amorak Huey, "We Were All Odysseus in Those Days." Copyright © 2019 by Amorak Huey. Reprinted with permission of the author.

Langston Hughes, "Theme for English B" from *The Collected Works of Langston Hughes*. Copyright © 2002 by Langston Hughes. Used with permission of Alfred A. Knopf, an imprint of the Knopf Doubleday Publishing Group, a division of Penguin Random House LLC.

Kim Hyesoon, "Horizon," translated by Vanessa Falso. Reprinted with permission of the translator.

David Ignatow, "No Theory" from *Figures of the Human*. Copyright © 1948 by David Ignatow. Published by Wesleyan University Press and used with permission.

Lucy Ives, "Early Poem" from *Orange Roses*. Copyright © 2013 by Lucy Ives. Reprinted with permission of the author.

Edmond Jabès, excerpt from *The Little Book of Unsuspected Subversion*, translated from the French by Rosmarie Waldrop. Copyright © 1982 by Éditions Gallimard. Translation copyright © 1996 by the Board and Trustees of the Leland Stanford Junior University.

Brandon D. Johnson, "Standing by a Shelf." Copyright © 2022 by Brandon D. Johnson.

Mitsuharu Kaneko, "Opposition," translated by Loren Goodman. Copyright © 2025. Reprinted with permission of the translator and the Japan Writers' Association.

Jane Kenyon, "Happiness" from *Collected Poems*. Copyright © 2005 by the Estate of Jane Kenyon. Reprinted with permission of The Permissions Company, LLC on behalf of Graywolf Press.

Etheridge Knight, "Rejections" from *The Lost Etheridge: Uncollected Poems of Etheridge Knight*. Reprinted with permission of Kinchafoonee Creek Press.

Jennifer L. Knox, "Hive Minds" from *Days of Shame and Failure*. Copyright © 2015 by Jennifer L. Knox. Reprinted with permission of the author.

Ron Koertge, "Ornithology" from *The Ogre's Wife*. Copyright © 2013 by Ron Koertge. Reprinted with permission of The Permissions Company, LLC on behalf of Red Hen Press.

Yusef Komunyakaa, "Facing It" from *Pleasure Dome: New and Collected Poems*. Copyright © 2001 by Yusef Komunyakaa. Published by Wesleyan University Press and used with permission.

Philip Larkin, "This Be The Verse" from *Collected Poems*. Copyright © Estate of Philip Larkin. Reprinted with permission of Farrar, Straus & Giroux, LLC.

Mary Leader, "Series as Opposed to Sequence" from *The Penultimate Suitor*. Copyright © 2001 by Mary Leader. Reprinted with permission of the University of Iowa Press.

Li-Young Lee, "This Room and Everything in It" from *The City in Which I Love You*. Copyright © 1990 by Li-Young Lee. Reprinted with permission of The Permissions Company, LLC on behalf of BOA Editions, Ltd.

David Lehman, "With Tenure" from *Operation Memory*. Copyright © 1990, 2023 by David Lehman. Reprinted with permission of the author.

Denise Levertov, "The Secret" from *O Taste and See: New Poems*. Copyright © 1964 by Denise Levertov. Reprinted with permission of New Directions Publishing Corp.

Timothy Liu, "The Silence" from *Don't Go Back to Sleep*. Copyright © 2014 by Timothy Liu. Reprinted with permission of Saturnalia Books.

Cecilia Llompart, "Eight Buffalo" from *The Wingless*. Copyright © 2014 by Cecilia Llompart. Reprinted with permission of The Permissions Company, LLC on behalf of Carnegie Mellon University Press.

Layli Long Soldier, "38" from *Whereas*. Copyright © 2017 by Layli Long Soldier. Reprinted with permission of The Permissions Company, LLC on behalf of Graywolf Press.

Archibald MacLeish, "Ars Poetica" from *Collected Poems 1917–1982*. Copyright © 1985 by The Estate of Archibald MacLeish. Reprinted with permission of HarperCollins Publishers.

Chelsea Martin, "McDonalds Is Impossible" from *No Posit Volume 1*. Copyright © 2008 by Chelsea Martin. Reprinted with permission of the author.

Khaled Mattawa, "Ecclesiastes" from *Tocqueville*. Copyright © 2010 by Khaled Mattawa. Reprinted with permission of New Issues Poetry & Prose.

Bernadette Mayer, "The Tragic Condition of the Statue of Liberty." Reprinted with permission of the Estate of Bernadette Mayer.

Shane McCrae, "The Boy Calls Twilight" from *Mule*. Copyright © 2010 by Shane McCrae. Reprinted with permission of The Permissions Company, LLC on behalf of the Cleveland State University Poetry Center.

Raymond McDaniel, "Hothouse" from *The Cataracts*. Copyright © 2016, 2018 by Raymond McDaniel. Reprinted with permission of The Permissions Company, LLC on behalf of Coffee House Press.

Heather McHugh, "Language Lesson 1976" from *Hinge & Sign: Poems 1968–1993*. Copyright © 1994 by Heather McHugh. Published by Wesleyan University Press and used with permission.

W.S. Merwin, "The Unwritten" from *The Second Four Books of Poems*. Copyright © 1973 by W.S. Merwin. Reprinted with permission of Bloodaxe Books Ltd. and The Permissions Company LLC on behalf of Copper Canyon Press.

Dunya Mikhail, "The War Works Hard" from *The War Works Hard*. Copyright © 2005 by Dunya Mikhail and Elizabeth Winslow. Reprinted with permission of New Directions Publishing Corp.

Edna St. Vincent Millay, "Love Is Not All (Sonnet XXX)" from *Collected Poems*. Copyright © 1931, 1958 by Edna St. Vincent Millay and Norma Millay Ellis. Reprinted with permission of The Permissions Company, LLC on behalf of Holly Peppe, Literary Executor, The Millay Society.

Czesław Miłosz, "Dedication" from *The Collected Poems: 1931–1987*. Copyright © 1988 by Czesław Miłosz Royalties, Inc. Reprinted with permission of HarperCollins Publishers.

Ye Mimi, "His Days Go By the Way Her Years" from *His Days Go By the Way Her Years*, translated by Steve Bradbury. Reprinted with permission of the translator.

Lenelle Moïse, "the children of immigrants" from *Haiti Glass*. Copyright © 2014 by Lenelle Moïse. Reprinted with permission of The Permissions Company, LLC on behalf of City Lights Books.

Lisel Mueller, "When I Am Asked" from *Alive Together: New and Selected Poems*. Copyright © 1996 by Lisel Mueller. Reprinted with permission of Louisiana State University Press.

Edward Mullany, "A Rugged Coast" from *Figures for an Apocalypse*. Reprinted with permission of Publishing Genius.

Harryette Mullen, "Any Lit" from *Sleeping with the Dictionary*. Copyright © 2002 by Harryette Mullen. Reprinted with permission of the University of California Press.

John Murillo, "Variations on a Theme by Elizabeth Bishop" from *Kontemporary Amerikan Poetry*. Copyright © 2020 by John Murillo. Reprinted with permission of The Permissions Company, LLC on behalf of Four Way Books.

Pablo Neruda, "VI, VII, XXXIII, XXXVIII XLIV" from *The Book of Questions*, translated by William O'Daly. Copyright © 1974 by Pablo Neruda and the Heirs of Pablo Neruda. English translation copyright © 1991, 2001 by William O'Daly. Reprinted with permission of The Permissions Company, LLC on behalf of Copper Canyon Press.

Mũkoma wa Ngũgĩ, "Hunting Words with My Father [Preface]" from *Logotherapy*. Copyright © 2016 by Mukoma Wa Ngugi. Reprinted with permission of University of Nebraska Press.

Naomi Shihab Nye, "Gate A-4" from *Honeybee*. Copyright © 2008 by Naomi Shihab Nye. Used with permission of Greenwillow Books/HarperCollins Children's Books.

Frank O'Hara, "Having a Coke with You" from *The Collected Poems of Frank O'Hara*. Copyright © 1971 by Maureen Granville-Smith, Administratrix of the Estate of Frank O'Hara, copyright renewed 1999 by Maureen O'Hara Granville-Smith and Donald Allen. Used with permission of Alfred A. Knopf, an imprint of the Knopf Doubleday Publishing Group, a division of Penguin Random House LLC.

Sharon Olds, "Not Once" from *Balladz*. Copyright © 2022 by Sharon Olds. Used with permission of Alfred A. Knopf, an imprint of the Knopf Doubleday Publishing Group, a division of Penguin Random House LLC.

José Olivarez, "Ars Poetica" from *Promises of Gold*, translated by David Ruano González. Translation copyright © 2023 by David Ruano González. Reprinted with permission of Henry Holt and Company.

Mary Oliver, "Wild Geese" from *Dream Work*. Copyright © 1992 by Mary Oliver. Used with permission of Grove/Atlantic, Inc.

Zaki Ovais, "Someone I'm Afraid Of" from *I Am a Rohingya: Poetry from the Camps and Beyond*, edited by James Byrne and Shehzar Doja. Copyright © 2019. Reprinted with permission of Arc Publications.

Molly Peacock, "Altruism" from *Cornucopia: New and Selected Poems 1975–2002*. Copyright © 2002 by Molly Peacock. Used with permission of W.W. Norton & Company, Inc.

Fernando Pessoa, "Autopsychography," "The Tobacco Shop," and "Others Narrate with Lyres or Harps" from *Fernando Pessoa & Co.: Selected Poems*, edited and translated by Richard Zenith. Translation copyright © 1998 by Richard Zenith. Used with permission of Grove/Atlantic, Inc.

Katie Peterson, "Meditation Denying Everything" from *Permission*. Copyright © 2013 by Katie Peterson. Reprinted with permission of the author.

Emilia Philips, "'You Should Write a Poem About That,' They Say" from *Embouchure*. Copyright © 2021 by Emilia Philips. Reprinted with permission of the University of Akron Press.

Irma Pineda, "'My Voice Will Weigh on You,'" translated by Wendy Call from bilingual Isthmus Zapotec and Spanish originals by Irma Pineda, from *Guie' ni zinebe / La flor que se llevó* (Pluralia, Mexico City, 2013).

Wang Ping, "The Price of a Finger" from *Ten Thousand Waves: Poems*. Copyright © 2014 by Wang Ping. Reprinted with permission of the author.

Sylvia Plath, "Poppies in October" from *The Collected Poems*. Copyright © 1962 by Sylvia Plath. Reprinted with permission of HarperCollins Publishers.

Francis Ponge, "Crate," translated by Joshua Corey and Jean-Luc Garneau from *Partisan of Things*. Reprinted with permission of Joshua Corey.

N.H. Pritchard, "Gyre's Galax" from *The Matrix: Poems 1960–1970*. Copyright © The Estate of Norman H. Pritchard. Reprinted with permission of Ugly Duckling Press.

Charles Reznikoff, "Children" from *Holocaust*. Copyright © 1975 by Charles Reznikoff. Reprinted with permission of The Permissions Company, LLC on behalf of Black Sparrow / David R. Godine, Publisher, Inc.

Adrienne Rich, "Diving into the Wreck" from *Diving into the Wreck: Poems 1971–1972*. Copyright © 1973 by Adrienne Rich. Used with permission of W.W. Norton & Company, Inc.

Mary Ruefle, "One Book" from *The Most of It*. Copyright © 2008 by Mary Ruefle. Reprinted with permission of The Permissions Company, LLC on behalf of Wave Books.

Muriel Rukeyser, "Waiting for Icarus" from *The Collected Poems of Muriel Rukeyser*. Copyright © 1973 by Muriel Rukeyser. Reprinted with permission of Creative Artists Agency.

Kay Ryan, "All Your Horses" from *Erratic Facts*. Copyright © 2015 by Kay Ryan. Used with permission of Grove/Atlantic, Inc.

Sonia Sanchez, "Blues Haiku" from *Like the Singing Coming Off the Drums*. Copyright © 1998 by Sonia Sanchez. Used with permission of Beacon Press.

Sappho, "Fragment 22" from *If Not, Winter: Fragments of Sappho*, translated by Anne Carson. Copyright © 2002 by Anne Carson. Used with permission of Alfred A. Knopf, an imprint of the Knopf Doubleday Publishing Group, a division of Penguin Random House.

Jason Schneidermann, "Dramaturgy" from Virginia Quarterly Review; forthcoming in *Self Portrait of Icarus as a Country on Fire*. Copyright © 2024, 2021 by Jason Schneiderman. Reprinted with permission of The Permissions Company, LLC on behalf of Red Hen Press.

Frederick Seidel, "Widening Income Inequality" from *Widening Income Inequality*. Copyright © 2016 by Frederick Seidel. Reprinted with permission of Farrar, Straus and Giroux, LLC.

Vijay Seshadri, "Memoir" from *3 Sections*. Copyright © 2013 by Vijay Seshadri. Reprinted with permission of The Permissions Company, LLC on behalf of Graywolf Press.

Diane Seuss, "Romantic Poetry" from *Modern Poetry*. Copyright © 2024 by Diane Seuss. Reprinted with permission of The Permissions Company, LLC on behalf of Graywolf Press.

Evie Shockley, "what's not to liken?" from *semiautomatic*. Copyright © 2017 by Evie Shockley. Published by Wesleyan University Press and used with permission.

Kedarnath Singh, "An Argument about Horses," translated by Vinay Dharwadker from *Banaras and Other Poems*. Used with permission of the translator.

Gary Snyder, "Waiting for a Ride" from *Danger on Peaks*. Copyright © 2004 by Gary Snyder. Reprinted with permission of The Permissions Company, LLC on behalf of Counterpoint Press.

Jack Spicer, "Psychoanalysis: An Elegy" from *My Vocabulary Did This to Me: The Collected Poetry of Jack Spicer*. Copyright © 2008 by the Estate of Jack Spicer. Published by Wesleyan University Press and reprinted with permission.

Kim Stafford, "At the Student Poetry Reading" from *Poetry*. Copyright © 2021 by Kim Stafford. Used with permission of The Permissions Company, LLC on behalf of the author.

Gaspara Stampa, "Sonnet 132," translated by Laura Anna Stortoni and Mary Prentice Lillie from *Women Poets of the Italian Renaissance*. Copyright © 1997 by Laura Anna Stortoni. Used with permission of Italica Press.

Gerald Stern, "Your Animal" from *This Time: New and Selected Poems*. Copyright © 1998 by Gerald Stern. Reprinted with permission of W.W. Norton & Company, Inc.

Anne Stevenson, "Vertigo" from *Poems 1955–2005*. Reproduced with permission of Bloodaxe Books, Ltd.

Bianca Stone, "Making Applesauce with My Dead Grandmother" from *The Mobius Strip Club of Grief*. Copyright © 2018 by Bianca Stone. Reprinted with permission of Tin House Books.

Mathias Svalina, "Creation Myth" from *Destruction Myth*. Copyright © 2009 by Mathias Svalina. Reprinted with permission of The Permissions Company, LLC on behalf of the Cleveland State University Poetry Center.

Anna Swir, "Poetry Reading" from *Talking to My Body*, translated by Czesław Miłosz and Leonard Nathan. Copyright © 1996 Czeslaw Milosz and Leonard Nathan. Reprinted with permission of The Permissions Company, LLC, on behalf of Copper Canyon Press.

Mary Szybist, "How (Not) to Speak of God" from *Incarnadine*. Copyright © 2013 by Mary Szybist. Reprinted with permission of The Permissions Company, LLC on behalf of Graywolf Press.

Wisława Szymborska, "Under a Certain Little Star" from *Miracle Fair*, translated by Joanne Trzeciak. Copyright © 2001 by Joanna Trzeciak. Used with permission of W.W. Norton & Company, Inc.

James Tate, "Goodtime Jesus" from *Selected Poems*. Copyright © 1991 by James Tate. Published by Wesleyan University Press and reprinted with permission.

Michael Torres, "Writing Prompt." Copyright © 2023 by Michael Torres. Reprinted with permission of the author.

Truong Tran, "what remains two" from *Placing the Accents*. Copyright © 1999 by Truong Tran. Reprinted with permission of Apogee Press.

Natasha Trethewey, "Theories of Time and Space" from *Native Guard: Poems*. Copyright © 2006 by Natasha Trethewey. Reprinted with permission of HarperCollins Publishers.

Julia Vinograd, "Ginsberg" from *A Symphony for Broken Instruments: Selected & Unpublished Poems of Julia Vinograd*. Reprinted with permission of Zeitgeist Press.

G.C. Waldrep, "Apocatastasis" from *Goldbeater's Skin*. Copyright © 2003 by G.C. Waldrep. Reprinted with permission of The Permissions Company, LLC on behalf of The Center for Literary Publishing, Colorado State University.

Bryan Walpert, "No Metaphor" from *Etymology*. Reprinted with permission of the author.

Jillian Weise, "Nondisabled Demands" from *Cyborg Detective*. Copyright © 2018, 2019 by Jillian Weise. Reprinted with permission of The Permissions Company, LLC on behalf of BOA Editions, Ltd.

Joe Wenderoth, "Writer" from *It Is If I Speak*. Copyright © 2000 by Joe Wenderoth. Published by Wesleyan University Press and reprinted with permission.

Allison Benis White, "Looking up in the dark I thought" from *Please Bury Me in This*. Copyright © 2017 by Allison Benis White. Both reprinted with permission of The Permissions Company, LLC on behalf of Four Way Books.

Elizabeth Willis, "In Strength Sweetness" from *Address*. Copyright © 2011 by Elizabeth Willis. Reprinted with permission of Wesleyan University Press.

Yolanda Wisher, "no more grandma poems." Copyright © 2021 by Yolanda Wisher. Reprinted with permission of the author.

C.D. Wright, "Personals" from *Steal Away: Selected and New Poems*. Copyright © 2002 by C.D. Wright. Reprinted with permission of The Permissions Company, LLC, on behalf of Copper Canyon Press.

Franz Wright, "Publication Date" from *God's Silence*. Copyright © 2006 by Franz Wright. Used with permission of Alfred A. Knopf, an imprint of the Knopf Doubleday Publishing Group, a division of Penguin Random House, LLC.

James Wright, "Lying in a Hammock at William Duffy's Farm in Pine Island, Minnesota" from *Above the River: The Complete Poems and Selected Prose*. Copyright © 1990 by James Wright. Published by Wesleyan University Press and used with permission.

Jenny Xie, "To Be a Good Buddhist Is Ensnarement" from *Eye Level*. Copyright © 2018 by Jenny Xie. Reprinted with permission of The Permissions Company, LLC on behalf of Graywolf Press.

Dean Young, "Cotton in a Pill Bottle" from *Bender: New and Selected Poems*. Copyright © 2012 by Dean Young. Reprinted with permission of The Permissions Company, LLC, on behalf of Copper Canyon Press.

Moon Bo Young, "Down Jacket God" from *Pillar of Books*, translated by Hedgie Choi. Copyright © 2021 by Moon Bo Young. Reprinted with permission of Black Ocean.

Rachel Zucker, "The Self in Poetry: A GNAT (Grossly Non-Academic Talk) with a Weaving Metaphor" from poets.org. Reprinted with permission of the author.

Index of Titles & First Lines

(Titles are shown in italics. If the title and first line are identical, only the title is listed.)

] 43
1. Because pockets are not a natural right 97
38 81
85 48

A black cat among roses 70
A BOX 76
A Brief for the Defense 183
A child said *What is the grass?* fetching it to me with full hands 139
A Great Book can be read again and again 66
A hazy moonlit night—a bird has left its shit on the fence post 69
A large box is handily made of what is necessary to replace any substance 76
A man sings 36
A man trades his son for horses 63
A pause, a rose, something on paper 171
A peacock on an olive branch looks beyond 203
A person, for you, is a book 27
A poem should be palpable and mute 7
A rose, rose. A violet, violet. A jade, jade 74
A Rugged Coast 101
A single flow'r he sent me, since we met 73
A Supermarket in California 68
A tuba and a man stroll through 50
A young man learns to shoot 61
Abortions will not let you forget 150
About suffering they were never wrong 29
Advice to Pallbearers 36
After great pain, a formal feeling comes 55
All of the Indians must have tragic features: tragic noses, eyes, and arms 151
All the Generations Before Me 201

All the generations before me contributed me 201
All the new thinking is about loss 196
All Your Horses 52
Altruism 29
American Sonnet for My Past and Future Assassin 132
An Argument about Horses 52
An obstinacy of buffalo 71
And if the compass broke you fixed it, fastened 179
and it was political 93
And why is the sun such a bad companion 26
Any Lit 32
Apocatastasis 51
Arrival 155
Ars Poetica 7
Ars Poetica 8
Ars Poetica #100: I Believe 8
As for we who "love to be astonished" 172
At midnight tears 195
At the Student Poetry Reading 112
At this height, Kansas 120
Autopsychography 86

Because I could not stop for Death 56
Because it is a pearly evening 197
Bent double, like old beggars under sacks 32
Between my finger and my thumb 148
Bird-Understander 19
Blues Haiku [let me be yo wil] 18
Borges and I 77

Cantico del Sole 58
Caretakers—died in 2009, 2010, 2011, 2012, 2013, 2014, 2015, 2016, 2017 203
Catullus: Excrucior 182

Catullus: Id faciam 182
Catullus: Odi et Amo 182
Chang spoke / Eng paused 14
Children (from Holocaust*)* 168
Children, when was 101
Confession 63
Cotton in a Pill Bottle 194
Coy Mistress 157
Crate 75
Creation Myth 64

Dedication 178
Digging 148
Diving into the Wreck 10
Do you not believe that death lives 26
Down Jacket God 116
Dramaturgy 99
Dreams 152
Dulce et decorum est 32

Early Poem 109
Eating food from McDonald's is mathematically impossible 189
Ecclesiastes 22
Eight Buffalo 71
Enfettered, these sentences repress free speech. The 128
Even the sun-clouds this morning cannot manage such skirts 134

Facing It 39
First having read the book of myths 10
For I will consider my Cat Jeoffry 153
For the instruments are by their rhymes 51
Fragment 22 43
from A Pillow Book: "A Great Book can be read again and again ... " 66
from Chapter E of Eunoia 128
from Jubilate Agno 153
from Macbeth (Act V, Scene V) 21
from My Life 171
from Nets 130
from OBITS 203
from Please Bury Me in This 182
from Song of Myself 136
from The Book of Questions 25
from The Little Book of Unsuspected Subversion 95

Ganymede 63
Gate A-4 119
Get a newspaper 159
Ginsberg 92
Give me your tired, your poor 92
God wears a massive down jacket 116
Goodtime Jesus 115
Gyre's Galax 33

Had we but world enough and time 156
Haiku 69
Halfway between *crib* and *cage* the French language places *crate* 75
Happiness 184
Having a Coke with You 45
He said he would be back and we'd drink wine together 62
he smells like bottled root beer 17
Here I Am, Lord 49
Here, the sentence will be respected 81
His Days Go by the Way Her Years 17
Hive Minds 76
Horizon 46
Hothouse 74
Houses and rooms are full of perfumes, the shelves are crowded with perfumes 136
How magnificent the war is! 94
How many books have I read? 67
How (Not) to Speak of God 47
How to Write the Great American Indian Novel 151
Hunting Words with My Father [Preface] 79

I ask them to take a poem 16
I believe in you my soul, the other I am must not abase itself to you 138
I can never remake the thing I have destroyed 31
I cannot consider scent without you, I cannot 68
I cannot live with You 56
I celebrate myself, and sing myself 136
I come from the nether regions 133
I dig her up and plop her down in a wicker chair 116
I hate *and* love. Ignorant fish, who even 182

I hate and—love. The sleepless body hammering a nail nails 182
I have heard what the talkers were talking, the talk of the beginning and the end 137
I guess you could call me broken 112
I live a life of appetite and, yes, that's right 30
I lock you in an American sonnet that is part prison 132
I love the fog. It's not 100 degrees 194
I must revise my work with the past 159
I Saw in Louisiana A Live-Oak Growing 67
I will consider my son William 155
I, too, dislike it 9
I'm a hungry star in the sky 17
I'm curled into a ball 113
I'm nothing 87
I'm writing a play about a Kommandant at Auschwitz 99
If Ezra Pound were alive today 163
if it doesn't come bursting out of you 124
Imagine you're an astronaut stuck in outer space. And it's just you. Only you. What 180
In Strength Sweetness 41
In the beginning there were only streets 64
in the wind / an inky air 41
Inside this pencil 199
Introduction to Poetry 16
is even more fun than going to San Sebastian, Irún, Hendaye, Biarritz, Bayonne 45
Is peace the peace of the dove 26
it has long been forgotten this practice of the mother 37
It isn't fair to us. You owe it to the reader 112
It seemed that we had hardly begun and we were already there 173
It was like the moment when a bird decides not to eat from your hand 75
It's Borges, the other one, that things happen to 77

Jesus got up one day a little later than usual 115
Jill's a good kid who's had some tough luck 102

katherine with the lazy eye. short. and not a good poet 23

Language Lesson 1976 54
Lately, I've become accustomed to the way 114
let me be yo wil 18
Let us go then, you and I 185
Lie still now 44
Limitations 25
Living is no laughing matter 166
Looking up in the dark I thought, Tell me something you've never told anyone 182
Love (III) 28
Love bade me welcome. Yet my soul drew me back 28
Love brought 132
Love is Not All (Sonnet XXX) 131
Love is not all: it is not meat nor drink 131
Love remains a kind of present tense 51
Love Songs (section III) 44
Lying in a Hammock at William Duffy's Farm in Pine Island, Minnesota 70

Making Applesauce with My Dead Grandmother 116
McDonalds Is Impossible 189
Meditation at Lagunitas 196
Meditation Denying Everything 197
Memoir 9
Migration is derived from the word "migrate," 8
Mind led body 16
Mourning 203
Musée des Beaux Arts 29
My apologies to chance for calling it necessity 204
My black face fades 39
My drawing teacher said: Look, think, make a mark 160
My father sits at the table listening 148
My Father's Mother Asks Him to Forget the War 148
My home's not silent, but I am not 48
My mistress' eyes are nothing like the sun 130
My voice will weigh on you 71

Napoleon 101
ninety-nine names for my god 182
No. 1 174
No blame. Anyone who wrote *Howl* and *Kaddish* 92
No Metaphor 50
no more grandma poems 125
No Theory 85
No theory will stand up to a chicken's guts 85
No, I shouldn't I'm ill-equipped to crack a Korbel bottle on the butt-end 141
Nondisabled Demands 112
Not Once 18
Not once—not when I toppled, rigid, a 18
Now that the TV is gone and the music 59
Now You Need Me 49

O soft embalmer of the still midnight 195
O Western wind when wilt thou blow 18
ode to the flute 36
Ode to the Whitman Line "When lilacs last in the dooryard bloom'd" 68
Of many reasons I love you here is one 19
Oh, I wish I had died before this and was in oblivion, forgotten 63
On Living 166
Once, among the transports, was one with children—two freight cars full 168
One Art 22
One Book 67
One morning I burst into my father's study and said 79
One must have a mind of winter 27
One of the few pleasures of writing 165
One Perfect Rose 73
Ontology of Chang and Eng, the Original Siamese Twins 14
Opposition 98
Ornithology 200
Orwell says somewhere that no one ever writes the real story of their life 9
Others Narrate with Lyres or Harps 87
Over my head, I see the bronze butterfly 70
overcome by the stink of mildewed wash, i have 202

Paradoxes and Oxymorons 54
Part of Eve's Discussion 75
Pencil 160
Personals 129
Pity the Bathtub Its Forced Embrace of the Human Form 37
Pity the bathtub that belongs to the queen its feet 37
Platonic Love 86
Poetry 9
Poetry Reading 113
Poetry, I tell my students 8
Poppies in October 134
Portrait of an Administrator with Strategic Plan and Office Supplies 164
Preface to a Twenty-Volume Suicide Note 114
Psalm 23 48
Psychoanalysis: An Elegy 192
Publication Date 165
Punctum / Metaphor 51

Reading Moby-Dick *at 30,000 Feet* 120
Rejections 165
Revision 159
Riding in the car with my mother 76
Romantic Poetry 59

Say when rain 52
Self-Portrait with Profanity 182
Series as Opposed to Sequence 174
Shards 31
shattered sonnet #3 132
She took the spareribs out of the oven 78
Sir, I am not a bird of prey 157
so you want to be a writer? 124
Solitary Observation Brought Back from a Sojourn in Hell 195
Some nights I sleep with my dress on. My teeth 129
Someone I'm Afraid Of 17
[somewhere i have never travelled,gladly beyond] 73
Sonnet 19 131
Sonnet 132 131
Sorrow everywhere. Slaughter everywhere. If babies 183

Sound variegated through beneath lit 33
Standing at the baggage passing time: 118
Standing by a Shelf 146
Start with loss. Lose everything. Then lose it all again 158
Still I Rise 140
Substance, Shadow, and Spirit 117
Substance to Shadow 117
Subversion is the very movement of writing: the very moment of death 95

Tell all the truth but tell it slant 55
the 14-year-old girl was treated like 129
The Adventures of a Turtle 75
The art of losing isn't hard to master 22
The birds have vanished down the sky 196
The Boy Calls Twilight 42
The boy calls twilight *little dark* the night 42
the children of immigrants 12
The difference between narcissus 16
The final end of all but purified souls 114
The first sentence is a sentence about writing 109
The Fish 127
The Garden by Moonlight 70
The great thing 135
The instructor said 161
The Last Analysis; or, I Woke Up 93
The Lord is my shepherd; I shall not want 48
The Love Song of J. Alfred Prufrock 185
the mother 150
The poet is a faker 86
The Politics of Narrative: Why I Am a Poet 102
The Price of a Finger 103
The Red Poppy 135
The ribbed black of the umbrella 49
The Road Not Taken 146
The Secret 40
The Self in Poetry: A GNAT (Grossly Non-Academic Talk) with a Weaving Metaphor 142
The Silence 78
The Snow Man 27
The subtlest strain a great musician weaves 25

The thought of what America would be like 58
The three of them were sitting in the sun 52
The Tobacco Shop 87
The Tragic Condition of the Statue of Liberty 92
The trick is that you're willing to help them 22
The turtle carries his house on his back 75
The Tyger 21
The Unwritten 199
The War Works Hard 94
The Zen priest says I am everything I am not 196
Theme for English B 161
Theories of Time and Space 147
There's just no accounting for happiness 184
They fuck you up, your mum and dad 133
they said 126
Things No One Knows 202
This Be The Verse 133
This morning, I heard you were found in your McDonald's uniform 23
This poem is concerned with language on a very plain level 54
This Room and Everything in It 44
To Be a Good Buddhist Is Ensnarement 196
To His Coy Mistress 156
To make a dadaist poem 159
To make the sound of your footsteps 36
To sit on her couch was to be silenced 164
To Sleep 195
Tomorrow, and tomorrow, and tomorrow 21
Tonight, I watch my husband sleep. He is dark 152
Trippers and askers surround me 138
Two girls discover 40
Two roads diverged in a yellow wood 146
Tyger Tyger, burning bright 21

Under a Certain Little Star 204

Variations on a Theme by Elizabeth Bishop 158
Vertigo 16
Viewpoint 16

wade 127
Waiting for a Ride 118
Waiting for Icarus 62
Walking toward the library, I pass three children 200
Wandering around the Albuquerque Airport Terminal 119
We dine at Adorno and return to my Beauvoir 86
We might have coupled 44
We reject these poems because of the space taken 165
We Were All Odysseus in Those Days 61
Western Wind 18
What are you thinking about? 192
What else is there? 142
What I hate I love. Ask the crucified hand that holds 182
What if we got outside ourselves and there 29
what remains two 37
What thoughts I have of you tonight, Walt Whitman 68
what's not to liken? 129
When Americans say a man 54
When he looks at the edges 146
When I am a toddler, a child, a tween, a teen, and a young adult 12
When I Am Asked 150
When I consider how my light is spent 131
When I was a boy 98
When in my weeping I inquire of Love 131
When the rains come 49
Where Do You Come From? 133
Where is the child I was 26
Who drew it 46
"Why do you hate nature?" asked the boy's stepmother 101
Why does the hat of night 25
Why We Oppose Pockets for Women 97
Widening Income Inequality 30
Wild Geese 71
With Tenure 163
With your right hand, you slip 103
Writer 27
Writing Prompt 180

You are a ukulele beyond my microphone 32
You can get there from here, though 147
You do not have to be good 71
You Fixed It 179
You may write me down in history 140
"You Should Write a Poem About That," They Say 141
You whom I could not save 178
Your Animal 114

Zazen on Ching-t'ing Mountain 196